Management for Professionals

The Springer series "Management for Professionals" comprises high-level business and management books for executives, MBA students, and practice-oriented business researchers. The topics cover all themes relevant to businesses and the business ecosystem. The authors are experienced business professionals and renowned professors who combine scientific backgrounds, best practices, and entrepreneurial vision to provide powerful insights into achieving business excellence.

The Series is SCOPUS-indexed.

Klaus Solberg Söilen

Intelligence Studies in Business

A Guide to Navigating the Competitive Landscape

Springer

Klaus Solberg Söilen
Department of Business Studies
Halmstad University
Halmstad, Sweden

ISSN 2192-8096 ISSN 2192-810X (electronic)
Management for Professionals

ISBN 978-3-031-76490-5 ISBN 978-3-031-76491-2 (eBook)
https://doi.org/10.1007/978-3-031-76491-2

This Springer imprint is published by the registered company Springer Nature Switzerland AG
The registered company address is: Gewerbestrasse 11, 6330 Cham, Switzerland

Leonardo Loredan (1501), Doge of Venice, *portrait* by Giovanni Bellini, wearing the *corno ducale*.

Dedicated to Marcus “Husky” Wallenberg

Preface

This book is designed as a comprehensive guide for anyone who considers themselves a knowledge worker. The ultimate question we aim to answer is how to make the Intelligence Ecosystem function effectively.

My students, who are my primary audience, asked me to keep it short and concise and not to use more math than necessary. The predecessor to this book is titled "Introduction to Private and Public Intelligence – The Swedish School of Competitive Intelligence" (2005). It has been used as a textbook for my courses in Intelligence Studies in Business for over 20 years, predominantly at Blekinge Institute of Technology and Halmstad University in Sweden. It was published a year after I completed my dissertation on industrial espionage at the University of Leipzig in 2004 and had initially existed as a compendium.

However, much has happened in intelligence research over the last two decades. Over time, most of the course material consisted of additional compendiums. For the normative part of the course, I have been using another book I wrote, titled "Geoeconomics," in part also to theoretically formulate my understanding of why China was succeeding as an economic superpower. At the same time, there was a pressing need to update the non-normative, or instrumental, part of the subject. I wanted to keep all politics out of this book. That said, there are numerous ways of teaching intelligence, and I do not claim to know the best way, only the one that makes the most sense for me.

It soon became apparent that simply updating the old book was insufficient. The field has evolved significantly over the past two decades, necessitating the creation of an entirely new book rather than a mere update. It's enough to think about the introduction of Open AI and Big Data Analytics (BDA).

I apologize for all the different terms imposed on the reader in this book. However, terms and their definitions matter, and there's also an evolution of terms that is natural and part of the development of this field of study. The aim is to make this subject matter as scientific as possible, even though I do not claim it can be considered a science in all its parts yet. For anyone wanting to get started quickly, you can go straight to Chap. 3. The book, from there on, reads much like a manual.

The book primarily focuses on Intelligence Analysis. Still, since the theory—the science—is much the same for State Intelligence, I believe that it can be of interest to a broader group of Intelligence Professionals. Thus, when applicable, I have tried to use examples from both the state or military side and the private side, aware that most of my students are business students. In many cases, it is also difficult to keep them apart, even if you want to. So, I truly believe there is a study of "Intelligence studies" that encompasses both the private and the state and public side, even though this is not the way the term is usually understood. To avoid any confusion, the book is therefore called "International Studies in Business," which is also the name of the journal.

From my perspective, all Intelligence functions work for the benefit of the nation, whether in private companies, state, or public institutions. While this may even sound a bit too romantic to some, and we know that most businesses simply work for the profit of their owners, a nation consisting of companies that only work for individual short-term profits will never contribute to building a strong nation, far less develop a culture that attracts outsiders' curiosity. For that, our companies need to take on responsibility for society at large. Hence, the subtitle of the book: "A guide to Navigating the Competitive Landscape." It is this long-term thinking that the Chinese are so good at, which we largely lack or have lost in the West.

As an academic, in this book, I follow the tradition from Stevan Dedijer in Sweden and, from a larger perspective, that of Michael Porter, Kent Sherman, Claude Shannon, and Frank H. Knight in the United States. Intellectually, I am more influenced by European continental thinking, but this shines less true in this book.

I have used AI tools not only to check grammar and syntax but also facts and to help with some examples. However, at large, the content is based on my research, teaching, and experience and, of course, the contributions of numerous researchers and colleagues.

The opportunity to update this material arose when I handed over the editorship of the *Journal of Intelligence Studies in Business* (JISIB) to Andrejs Cekuls at the University of Latvia after 12 years. Therefore, Andrejs is the first person I would like to thank. I would also like to thank my close and long-time colleague, Jonathan Calof, who provided detailed feedback on an earlier version of this manuscript. We have studied and taught the same subjects for more than two decades, though we teach them quite differently. Per Jenster, who was somewhat of a mentor to me when I started teaching at Copenhagen Business School 25 years ago, has also been a significant influence. He was a student of John E. Prescott and brought the Competitive Intelligence perspective to Europe, merging it with a European focus and his extensive business acumen. I followed Jenster to China twice to work on research and business school projects, first at China Europe International Business School (CEIBS) in Shanghai and later in Chengdu. Over the years, I have realized that our views on International Business and competitiveness have become quite similar.

I must also thank Joseph Le Bihan, my teacher in Geopolitics at École des hautes études commerciales de Paris (HEC) Paris and a living legend who has shaped two generations of intelligence professionals in France, even though I am not sure what he would make of this instrumental, non-normative book. My long-time brother-in-arms, Rainer Michaeli, and his staff at the Institute for Competitive Intelligence (ICI) in Germany have been instrumental in organizing conferences and sharing their close ties in the industry. I would also like to thank the companies I have worked with during the past 25 years, some of which are listed in this book as examples or on my LinkedIn profile. Others have been deliberately omitted due to strict Non-disclosure agreement (NDAs). Thanks also to Anders Carlsson at Blekinge Institute of Technology (BTH), an expert in forensics with whom I have cooperated for many years, giving courses to various branches of Swedish police, military, customs, and security. I have had the chance to work with many members of Strategic and Competitive Intelligence Professionals (SCIP) over the years and welcome the new leadership of Paul Santilli.

Thanks to Lamiae Benhayoun at Rabat Business School for constructive input on numerous research projects during the past years. To Henri Dou for a long-term friendship and your conferences on Corica, organized with the University of Corsica. Other valuable and regularly occurring conferences include the Veille Stratégique, Scientifique et Technologique (VSST), led for many years by the brilliant Bernard Dousset at the University of Toulouse, the always friendly Sahbi Sidhom and Kamel Smaili from the Information Systems and Economic Intelligence (SIIE), the International Conference on Technology Management, Operations, and Decisions (IEEE ICTMOD), led by the capable Mourad Oubrich, the International Conference on Computational Collective Intelligence (ICCCI), and the European Conference on Information Systems (ECIS), among others.

Thanks also to Philip Alipour, Philippe Clerc, Nisha Sewdass, Magnus Hoppe, Richard Klavans, Gabriel Anderbjörk, Ingemar Svensson, Ben Gilad, Brian Fuller, Ralf Wagner, Knut Norrman Egeland, Sven Hamrefors, Hand Hedin, Rom Gayoso, Petter Larsson, Dirk Vriens, Alexander Maune, Avner Barnea, Scott Erickson, Christophe Bisson, Per Frankelius, Brigitte Gay, Alfredo Passos, John E. Prescott, Frank Mathot, Pascal Frion, Pierre Larat, Udo Hohlfeld, Pierre Memheld, Tetiana Momot, Anass El Haddadi, Patrik Olsson, Suki Fuller, Lilit Axner, Arthur Weiss, Michael Neugarten, Nils Morris, Luis Madureira, Way Chen, Adis Sabanovic, Douglas Bernhardt, Arik Johnson, Erik Glitman, Mauricio Kovacevic, Mats Björe, Jesper Martell, Eduardo Bermudez, Sheila Wright, Johan Hammarlund, Mike Teodorescu, Thorsten Bill, Craig S. Fleisher, Thierry Warin, Nathalie de Marcellis-Warrin, Wilma Viviers, and Alessandro Comai who have all contributed to research, courses, seminars, publications, or conferences in the field. At the end, I would like to thank all of my students in intelligence studies for their valuable input and good discussions over the past quarter century.

This book is dedicated to Marcus Wallenberg, whose family strives not only to achieve competitive advantages for their companies but also to contribute to the development and well-being of all citizens in Swedish society:

> "*Labor responsibilis nationem aedificat.*" ("Responsible work builds the nation.")

My academic career has largely revolved around digitalization in business. For my master's thesis at HEC and later as an exchange student to Scuola di Direzione Aziendale (SDA) Bocconi, I was interested in quantitative trading and the mathematization of finance, especially derivatives. Some years later, I had the opportunity to pursue a Ph.D. under the statistician Klaus Lange in Leipzig, focusing mainly on

Information Sciences and Economics, paid for by my former employer Known as KMPG always (KPMG).

Later, and throughout my career as a business teacher, I became interested in Digital Marketing and how computers have radically changed the entire profession. Over the past decade, the distinction between Marketing and Intelligence Studies has diminished to the point where they are often just two sides of the same technology. Most of my teaching continues to focus on these two areas: Marketing and Intelligence, with the occasional course in Scientific Method.

Growing up, my late father always showed a strong interest in global events, which we discussed with avid curiosity around the dinner table. At his work, as head of the Norwegian Public Roads Administration in Oppland, he would continuously circulate piles of articles to all managers via the internal post service, marking passages he especially wanted them to read, to stay on top of their game as engineers. Thus, I can say that my interest in Intelligence would never have developed without his influence.

The aim of this book is to be scientific, but also practical. It has been written for my students, past and future, with the practitioner in mind. If it attracted interest beyond this group, I would be most honored.

Halmstad, Sweden Klaus Solberg Söilen

Contents

List of Figures

List of Tables

1 Introduction to Intelligence Studies in Business

In this introductory chapter, we present the reasons for Intelligence Studies in Business and provide a brief outline and scope of the content. While this book emphasizes what many know simply as Business Intelligence (BI), which is intelligence in private companies, the fundamental principles apply to state and Military Intelligence as well. Effective intelligence functions help organizations stay competitive by continuously scanning the environment for relevant information and providing actionable insights to managers and top leaders regardless of the types of organizations they work in.

1.1 Why Study Intelligence?

Today, as many as half of the global workforce could be classified as knowledge workers. A Knowledge Worker is someone who primarily deals with information or develops and uses knowledge in the workplace, rather than engaging in manual or mechanical labor. Intelligence Experts, a specialized subset of knowledge workers, focus primarily on the collection, analysis, interpretation, and dissemination of information to support decision-making processes. Reading a book on Intelligence is relevant for all Knowledge Workers, but it is particularly pertinent for Intelligence Analysts, Data Scientists, Policymakers, Market Researchers, and Business Leaders, as it offers numerous benefits to enhance their professional capabilities and broaden their understanding of the field.

As the title implies, the focus here is on Intelligence Studies in business, which means there is less emphasis on State and Military Intelligence. However, all intelligence professionals will recognize that the fundamental science of Intelligence is the same, benefiting both camps.

The essence of Intelligence is to scan the surrounding world for relevant information, to ascertain what is happening that affects the competitiveness of our

K. Solberg Söilen, *Intelligence Studies in Business*, Management for Professionals,
https://doi.org/10.1007/978-3-031-76491-2_1

organization (need-to-know, strong signals, trends, etc.). We use this information to produce reports or advice to enable managers to make better decisions.[1]

Our industries and markets are becoming increasingly competitive. It is no longer sufficient to merely know how to produce something in demand. We must continuously improve our offerings; our customers have numerous alternatives, and as the business has become truly global, we face a multitude of potential competitors. As I try to illustrate, the fear of being outcompeted is particularly acute for countries that rely more on services than on production. Consequently, the strategic shift to services seen in much of the West since the turn of the millennium poses greater risks for both companies and nation-states.[2]

Some see the Intelligence function as just war by other means,[3] others see it as more instrumental and technical, as an extension of IT systems.[4] Some see it as peripheral, others as the spider in the web surrounding government and business infiltrating organizational life like a superstructure.[5] I think all of this is correct and in this book we shall try to catch the essence of all these dimensions.

In one sense, everyone in an organization is responsible for gathering competitive information. However, in reality, not everyone has the time or inclination to do this systematically. Managers, too, have lives outside of work. As will come as no surprise to the reader, different organizations structure their intelligence functions in various ways.[6] Companies lacking an effective intelligence function are falling behind many without knowing why. Research also suggests that having had a robust intelligence system in the past is no guarantee of maintaining one in the future. Companies often do not have a good memory for these practices, and the know-how often leaves an organization simply when key personnel change jobs. Even companies from the same country, with the same owners, can adopt very different approaches to the intelligence function. The case of Ericsson and the Swedish Cellulose Company (SCA) serves as an example.[7]

Today, all competitive organizations primarily work with information. Their success hinges on how they handle this information. The technology applied, mostly software, is primarily there to facilitate the process; it never explains why things happen, and it seldom aids in the actual understanding of the data... Wait a minute, that is no longer true, with AI.

Now, research suggests that AI technology functions almost as a capable intelligence analyst by itself.[8] However, we still need the knowledge to verify what the AI produces, and we must now develop skills in prompt engineering to know not only what to ask but also how to ask it. If we simply rely on what the AI generates, we

[1] Söilen (2018).

[2] Söilen (2012).

[3] Fialka (1997).

[4] Ward and Peppard (1996/2009).

[5] Herman (1996).

[6] Söilen (2010a).

[7] Söilen (2017a).

[8] Söilen (2024).

are left with perfectly analyzed data, professionally presented in an impeccable format, that may turn out to be completely false. The strategy also carries a risk so that it can take a long time before someone spots an error, just because everything else looks so convincing. In other words, we are living in dangerous times. AI has become an indispensable second brain, but at the same time, it is also a force for massive manipulation. This will be discussed in much detail in the book.

We have been tricked before, and we continue to be deceived in other ways too. For example, using statistics and mathematics in text poses similar challenges. At best, statistical analysis provides a snapshot of reality, showing the correlation between two variables, but it does not reveal any intermediary variables or the original causes of a specific event. We must determine these ourselves through a method of logical reduction, eliminating less plausible causes by using our knowledge and a good portion of critical thinking. Statistics do not tell us why something happens. For that, we need broad reading, and even this will only give us a fraction of the reality, as we are humans with all the cognitive limitations and biases that imply. Therefore, we must use the language of mathematics with care, strive to identify and reduce our biases, and we must encourage people to read and gain experience to enhance our knowledge relevant to whatever industry we are in. AI and Big Data Analytics are helping provide solutions to these problems, but we must still understand the subject matter to know if what we are presented with is true.

At the end of the day, the beautiful tables with data that we examine will only make sense if we have a deeper knowledge of the subject matter presented and are able to ask critical questions. Merely passing on wonderfully designed PowerPoints to others in the organization does not constitute good Intelligence work. Instead, we must strive to understand the industry we are in, the markets, and the disciplines and theories we use to interpret our environment, whether it be engineering in production or international marketing in sales. Our understanding should not be confined to a number of theories and 2 × 2 matrices, as made famous by consulting companies even though some are useful too. We must grasp the laws, the history, and the geography of whatever place we are studying to make sense of it all. For example, we need to go out and examine the actual infrastructure in specific countries to answer questions about supply lines. This is an ambitious scope for any discipline, including the social sciences which is already somewhat familiar with how to try to understand complex macro factors.

But do we really need a separate course in Intelligence to understand all this? Isn't it sufficient to take more common courses like Marketing, Finance, and Economics, perhaps incorporating aspects of decision-making or Game Theory to grasp these concepts? While these courses can be valuable in the context of the knowledge economy, I believe that Intelligence Studies is potentially one of the most useful courses a student can take to prepare for a business career. To my knowledge, no other subject tries to teach students and practitioners how to gain an overview of all external events that affect an organization's competitive advantage and to analyze them in a structured manner.

The field of Decision Support Systems (DSS) focuses on computer-based systems that support decision-making. Information Systems (IS) focus on aspects like data management, information flow, and the integration of technologies.[9] Intelligence Studies, on the other hand, is more practical, more strategic, and provides a better bird's-eye view of the information activities and what the firm needs to do. It is an interdisciplinary field focused on the collection, analysis, and use of information for strategic purposes that is quick to adjust to new technologies.[10] It is commonly associated with national security and defense but also encompasses Competitive and Business Intelligence. These are all different but overlapping aspects of information processing, analysis, and application within organizations.

Today, mainstream economics is often overly theoretical, fragmented, and distanced from knowledge about specific industries and markets. In this sense, a keen interest in intelligence as an activity, I would argue, is a more productive way to learn about business than reading Economics, especially as it has developed after the Second World War.[11] Within Business Studies, Strategy courses tend to be presented as 'best-of' topics and have their favorite tools. In general, most subjects taught in business schools today are too far removed from the realities they aim to describe. As such, they have largely lost sight of what lies at the heart of economics: the concept of competitive advantage.[12] Since there are no broadly accepted theories in this subject, at least not yet, we shall not call it an applied science in the way we think of the study of economics or political science, but rather an applied field of study or discipline. We also note that the science bit in this field is shared by the scientific method and by formal logic.

We shall soon examine the historical context in some detail, but the importance of building a formal intelligence organization was realized more than 200 years ago by the Prussian and Russian armies. In the realm of business, this was first understood with the paradigm shift that occurred with the Information Age and the development of computers after the Second World War. It became clear that competitive advantage is more about what you know than what machinery you own or how much money you have on corporate accounts.

The challenge for the new knowledge worker who emerged from the information age is that it was not obvious how to measure productivity. It still isn't. A farmer is measured by the amount of produce he delivers, a factory worker by the quantity of goods produced, but how do you measure the productivity of a knowledge worker like an intelligence analyst? The intelligence analyst, like many managers, produces reports, as written documents but more often as advice. To determine their effectiveness, the analyst must not only retain these reports but also demonstrate how they have been used to make decisions. Furthermore, they must be able to assess if the decisions made were sound and if there were any shortcomings in the report that negatively affected the decision. Today, this is very difficult to do, but with increased levels of computerization we now see how this process promises to improve in the future with the integration of business intelligence software and AI, into what is

[9] For overview of research see Trieu (2017).

[10] Söilen (2016b).

[11] Söilen (2021c).

[12] A recent exception is Zekos (2023).

called AI factories. It is already happening as we write this, and it is still very early. Open AI started in 2023. It is like asking how performant the PC is after 1973 with the introduction of the Altair 8800. Who will lead this technology we do not know yet.

At the state or macro level, we are witnessing a period of significant transformation, characterized by a shift of power from the Western hemisphere to the Eastern, a process that has been underway since the end of the Cold War but is now gradually solidifying. The failure of many Western practices has become apparent, such as the massive joint ventures that followed globalization merely enabled Asian countries to catch up faster with Western technologies, the excessive focus on services before production, the move away from mercantilism, and a shift away from productive fields like engineering and science in favour of softer subjects and the expansion of a large public sector that has become ever more inefficient. These were all major strategic errors from the perspective of the competitive advantage of nations. We in the West have not been confronted with a direct economic competitor since the heights of the Ottomans, in the sixteenth and seventeenth centuries, so we are pretty new to this scenario.[13]

Today, the nation-states achieving economic success include countries like China, Singapore, South Korea, but also Norway. These represent models of state capitalism rather than free-market liberalism. The individualist, liberal model supported by neoclassical economics, based on the writings of figures like Adam Smith (I prefer to refer to them as the marginalist school), Walras, Marshall, and Samuelson, faces greater challenges in convincing contemporary practitioners, not to mention the voters. As Piketty has shown in his extensive empirical study on capital, such societies have led to an extreme concentration of wealth at the very top with very little trickle-down effect. After a period of prosperity, which lasted for about four generations (and was only prolonged during the past two generations through massive debt, on all levels), populations in the Western world are experiencing a decline in their standard of living, which is likely to stir more social unrest, just as it did about a century ago. I write this as a general background to the challenges ahead. This book is purely instrumental and does not delve into any political, social, or ideological issues.

1.2 Outline of the Book

This book deals with the processes and techniques of Intelligence. It begins by guiding you, the reader, through important concepts and definitions pertinent to this field of study. We explore the methods used for gathering information and the ways of classifying them. We discuss the reasons for the existence of an intelligence function in both public and private organizations and demonstrate how this function has evolved since the end of the Second World War. We not only examine the analysis of information gathering and how organizations establish intelligence systems, but

[13] The Soviets were, first of all, a military threat, not an economic one.

we also elucidate the logic behind the classification of data. Towards the end of the book, we present and discuss the technological side of intelligence and its ethical aspects, even though the focus of this book is not on technical solutions. For those topics, there are other courses and books on Business Intelligence (software), Cybersecurity, and IT Forensics.

This book has ten chapters. The introductory chapter gives an overview of the study itself. Chapter 2 lays out the history of the study and introduces the reader to the most important terminology used throughout the book. Chapter 3 sets the scene for how we are to understand the study, starting with a few broad models for understanding the surrounding world. Now we are in a flow, and the proceeding chapters follow pretty closely the way I have ordered my lectures. With no time to waste, we go into the science of intelligence in Chap. 4. This corresponds to the first part of the constructive content. It is followed by Chap. 5 which is the second part introducing the reader to intelligence analysis. We start with how we are to understand analysis, or, as I like to call it, the language of analysis. We then go on to present a long row of different analyses with examples. Chapter 6 is about how the report could look like, even though there are no standard rules here. Chapter 7 discusses how to set up the intelligence function in an organization. Even though this is not a book on intelligence technology we must get a minimum of grip on the topic even if we are just on the user's side. Then towards the end follows an extensive chapter on the ethics of intelligence, which is important not only for private organizations but also for state and military organizations. We wrap it up by showing how to make it all work under the label the Intelligence Ecosystem.

1.3 The Scope of the Book

This book adopts a very broad scope from the outset, encompassing all factors that affect an organization. The focus will be less on people and more on human behaviour-specific actions and events. For those interested in the normative aspects, I have written a book titled 'Geoeconomics.'[14] We will also concentrate on products, markets, and industries, aiming to provide a comprehensive general overview, unlike my previous books on Market Intelligence and Trade Show Intelligence, which are more specific topics.[15]

For reasons that will soon become clear, it is practical to divide Intelligence Studies into two distinct parts, tailored for two different types of organizations: (1) private companies and (2) public or state organizations, such as the military. However, the core methodologies remain largely the same. Hundreds of thousands of professionals work with these frameworks, from market researchers and military intelligence experts to data scientists, contributing to a diverse network of roles and technologies that support their professions.

[14] Söilen (2012).

[15] On Market Intelligence see Jenster and Söilen (2009). On trade show intelligence, see Söilen (2010a, 2013).

This is how I often begin my lectures, setting the stage for what is to come:

When we step outside on a cold evening and look around, we get a sense of all the elements that influence us as human beings, and all the possibilities of what might occur. It's the stars above, the cars driving by, the weather, but most importantly, all the potential outcomes of our encounters with other humans. For a company or an organization, the approach is similar, but we are guided to take a more systematic approach to the opportunities and threats imposed by our environment. We identify these factors, analyze them, and make decisions based on what is best for the survival and prosperity of the organization. This is the essence of Intelligence.

Human existence finds itself suspended between the infinity of the cosmos above, with hundreds of billions of stars in our galaxy and more than a trillion galaxies, and an inner infinity comprising 37 trillion cells, which are replaced every 7–10 years. The internal world, our health, also impacts companies, though it is primarily explored by biologists and medical scientists. In this book, our focus is solely on external events that affect humans within organizations, which we will soon divide into a series of micro and macro factors. In this book, we are less concerned with various operations within a company, such as accounting, finance, marketing, and sales, which are well covered by other business disciplines. However, it should be noted that we rely heavily on the data they provide.

A business often originates from an individual with a product or an idea in mind. He writes a business plan and secures some initial financing. Later, this person begins to hire employees to fill various positions, not only technical but also managerial functions. Most of these roles have an internal focus, centered on production and management. However, as soon as the organization becomes operational—often even beforehand, like when researching data to answer the questions in the business plan—entrepreneurs start to direct their attention outward, beyond the organization, to their customers, competitors, and all who influence them (micro factors).

It's like a gigantic puzzle where intelligence is a main ingredient in all the three senses of the word: the intelligence process, the intelligence product and the intelligence faculty, the ability to think. The entrepreneurs who have started the company begin to consider possibilities for doing international business, gathering information about regulations for exports, social trends, and technical infrastructure like broadband speeds (macro factors) in specific markets, and all of this information must be gathered and analyzed, well, in theory. Traditionally, much of this outward focus was situated within the marketing function of the company, which explains why much of the initial research in business intelligence studies emerged from marketing research, but today this task has become so extensive that many companies of a certain size employ competitive or market intelligence experts, outside help. Many larger companies, like MNEs, go on to create entire intelligence departments, but these are still rare. From here on, every day is an opportunity to gain new insights and to act upon it. How we act will decide the future of our organization. This is the essence of intelligence work.

This, then, will define the scope of our lectures, which will begin with some background information and terminology more relevant to academics. For those who want to get started immediately and prefer not to delve into the theoretical framework, you can skip directly to Part 3 of the book, which introduces the intelligence framework, and Chap. 4, which delves directly into the science of intelligence.

A Short History of Intelligence in Organizations

2

This chapter is all about the terminology and history of our field of study. More importantly, it addresses the somewhat confusing landscape of different disciplines that study similar phenomena from varying perspectives. Our goal is to bring clarity and order to this theoretical landscape. Achieving this is crucial for ensuring efficient communication within the field, reducing misunderstandings, and increasing the effectiveness of intelligence work.

2.1 Origins of the Term 'Intelligence'

The term 'Intelligence' when used to describe an institution such as an 'Intelligence Agency,' is quite recent, first noted in the latter half of the nineteenth century. However, it has been used synonymously with 'information' for much longer, appearing as early as the middle of the fifteenth century. The first newspapers in Scandinavia were often called 'intelligense blader' or 'intelligence letters'. Their focus was on facts and objectivity, as opposed to the rumors one might hear on the street. It is this same meaning and alluding to accuracy that the field of Intelligence aims to bring to the subject in the sense of "need-to-know information" today.

We also note that "intelligence" has two other distinct meanings, in the sense of the cognitive ability (whether human or machine) and the organization and function of gathering valuable information. So, 'intelligence' has three meanings, and we will deal primarily with two of them in this book: intelligence as a product and as a function, process and organization.

K. Solberg Söilen, *Intelligence Studies in Business*, Management for Professionals,
https://doi.org/10.1007/978-3-031-76491-2_2

2.2 Early Intelligence Systems

The systematic process of what we now call intelligence is by no means new. The earliest and best literature, both from a practical and a theoretical perspective on intelligence systems, is still Sun Tzu's writings, like in the famous lines: "If you know the enemy and know yourself, you need not fear the result of a hundred battles. If you know yourself but not the enemy, for every victory gained you will also suffer a defeat. If you know neither the enemy nor yourself, you will succumb in every battle". He also said that what is most important in war is to attack the strategy of the enemy. Sun Tzu lived in China in the sixth century BC.

Alexander the Great had a well-organized intelligence system that included advanced cryptographic techniques and a systematic approach to handling and rewarding spies.[1] The Romans had their 'Speculatores,' foreign spies and soldiers who soon became elite Roman troops and personal guards—a tradition continued by the Roman Catholic Church in the form of the famous Swiss Guard.

However, it was the Venetian Republic that first developed an organized business intelligence system, educating young men as ambassadors to report home any piece of information that could give their employer a commercial advantage.[2] The Venetian model soon spread to other parts of the world during the Middle Ages and the Renaissance, notably to organizations in the places they traded with and among their competitors, such as the state of Dubrovnik, then called Ragusa. It was also in this very city where Stevan Dedijer, the father of intelligence studies in business, spent his last years and passed away in 2004.[3]

Early financiers like the Medici family in Florence, the Fuggers in Augsburg, and the Rothschilds in Frankfurt developed their own intelligence systems, creating news sources or newsletters like the 'Fuggerzeitungen' which kept them in the know about the important things regarding money in Europe. Until recently, the Rothschilds played an important role in the development and later overseeing of the newspaper 'The Economist,' now owned by another industrial family, the Agnellis. These news sources always aimed to be the fly on the wall in rooms where people of power meet. The same concept has given rise to a whole line of consultancies often referred to as 'those-who-have-been-in-the-room' consultancy, with companies like Hakluyt & Co. and WestExec Advisors, expected, I am sure, to be replaced by others in time.

In modern business organizations, intelligence departments have existed since at least the early 1900s. Stefan Dedijer tells us how the Swedish investor, Marcus Wallenberg Sr., established an Intelligence Department in his bank SEB as early as 1903. He supposedly appointed the 25-year-old R. John to head the department,

[1] See Krieger (2003).

[2] Relazioni (Italian for reports or accounts; singular relazione) were the final reports presented by Venetian ambassadors of their service in foreign states. Relazioni contained descriptions of the current political, military, economic, and social conditions of the country visited. In Ross and McLaughlin (1977).

[3] https://en.wikipedia.org/wiki/Stevan_Dedijer

which was called the statistical department, where he remained for 25 years. The Wallenberg family has been a dominant player in Swedish business for more than a century, and the investment company Investor AB today owns a significant percentage of stocks on Nasdaq Stockholm in companies like Ericsson, SEB, Saab AB, and EQT, largely because they have demonstrated an ability to handle information and build powerful networks. The concept of developing an intelligence function within specific companies began with SEB and fully matured more than half a century later in Ericsson.[4]

2.3 Evolution of Intelligence Studies

Next, we look at who the people, academics, and practitioners are who have shaped this study across different cultures since the Second World War. How is intelligence studies divided into its smaller parts, and how is it related to other disciplines in the social sciences that are part of what we call the information age? Where do its academics publish, and where do students go to get their intelligence education? More fundamentally how are we to understand the difference between a discipline aspiring to become a science and develop further as an applied field?

2.3.1 Academic and Practical Developments

A beloved child has many names, they say, but this is *not* a good situation to be in for a discipline, which demands clarity and precision, far less one that aspires to become a science. Intelligence Studies is an interdisciplinary field associated with journals such as Intelligence and National Security, International Journal of Intelligence and Counterintelligence, Security Studies, and International Security. For business applications there is the Journal of Intelligence Studies in Business, but also numerous sister journals in Business Intelligence, Information Science, Decision Support Systems, Foresight and Knowledge Management.

In the mid-90s, the field was simply known as Business Intelligence (BI) in English. As the software component developed, BI came to be referred to as the software used for doing intelligence in business. It encompasses tools, architecture, databases, and data warehouses so that everything works and is associated with companies and products such as Microsoft Power BI, Qlik, SAP BusinessObjects, IBM Cognos Analytics and Oracle Business Intelligence, just to mention some of the bestselling tools. BI is an umbrella term in which everything is integrated and works like a software unit managed through a dashboard.

The related field of Knowledge Management, which grew out of studies in organizational theory like Wilenky's Organizational Intelligence,[5] quickly became its

[4] Originally led by Göran Pagels-Fick, whose contribution to the development of business intelligence systems in Swedish industry was considerable, see e.g. Pagels-Fick (1999).

[5] See Wilensky (1967).

own separate study, dealing with how companies handle and manage information, rather than how they acquire and use it. Another direction in the literature focused on future predictions. Initially, this body of literature distinguished between forecasters and Future Studies, which use quantitative methods and are considered more scientific, and Futurology, where there is less demand for rigid explanations of cause and effect. There are also the areas of Foresight which is considered more practice-oriented. Forecasting overlaps with what is known as Marketing Planning. It differs from futures studies in that forecasting is more about predicting specific outcomes based on past and present data, whereas futures studies involve a broader exploration of potential futures, including scenarios that may significantly diverge from current trends, though not all would agree with that distinction.

So, the terms Future Studies, Futures Thinking, Foresight, and Futurology are often used interchangeably, but have distinct nuances and focuses within the broader field of anticipating and preparing for potential futures, as shown in Table 2.1:

By understanding these distinctions, organizations and individuals can better choose the terms, appropriate approach and tools for their specific needs in anticipating and preparing for future challenges and opportunities.

All these directions have their own scientific journals and groups of researchers that meet regularly at conferences around the world, illustrating the problem with overlaps, but also a fragmentation of research groups, or academic tribes, as they sometimes are referred to.

The three fields that once separated—all dealing with questions about predicting future events—are still developing mostly apart, at least for now: Intelligence, KM, and Foresight/Futures Studies/Forecasting.

2.3.2 Growth of Academic Programs

There has always been a demand for intelligence analysts, not only in the military but also in business. While I won't dwell on the case of Sweden too much in this book, it's worth noting that in 2002, there were 7 universities, 5 colleges, 4 private companies, and 5 state departments offering courses in Intelligence Studies.[6] Although there are fewer offerings today, few other subjects within the social sciences in Sweden have seen a similar surge in interest since the Second World War. Initially, in the 60s, the academic interest in this subject was typically Swedish, but in France, they studied much of the same material but from a different perspective, first of all, that of Geopolitics. Geopolitics was dropped in Germany after the war of obvious reasons, but not in France. In the 80s and 90s, Competitive Intelligence became popular in the US and the Anglo-Saxon world even though the first publication appeared almost two decades earlier.[7] The popularity in Sweden was likely due to the country's early industrialization and, even more so, its heavy reliance on

[6] "Omvärldsanalys".

[7] The first book on the topic may be Alden (1959). The first dissertation may be Albaum (1962). For a review model of contributions in Competitive Intelligence see Madureira et al. (2023).

Table 2.1 Disciplines focused on future predictions

#	Study	Explanation	Method	Focus	Journals or outlets
1	Future Studies, aka Futures Studies or Futures Research	An interdisciplinary field that seeks to systematically explore predictions and possibilities about the future.	Combines qualitative and quantitative methods from various disciplines, including sociology, economics, political science, and technology.	Broad examination of potential futures. Uses scenarios, trend analysis, and modeling. Often involves academic and scholarly research.	"Futures" and "Journal of Futures Studies."
2	Futures Thinking	A mindset and approach to thinking about the future.	Involves the ability to anticipate and envision different future scenarios and consider their implications.	Emphasizes the cognitive process of thinking about the future. Encourages creative and innovative thinking. Often used in educational and organizational contexts to develop strategic thinking skills.	Workshops and training sessions to develop futures thinking skills
3	Foresight	A systematic, participatory, and multi-disciplinary approach to exploring mid- to long-term futures.	Involves the ability to anticipate and envision different future scenarios and consider their implications.	Practical application in strategic planning and policy-making. Involves stakeholder engagement and participatory methods. Uses tools such as scenario planning, horizon scanning, and Delphi surveys.	"Foresight and STI Governance", Government foresight programs to anticipate and prepare for future societal challenges.

(continued)

Table 2.1 (continued)

#	Study	Explanation	Method	Focus	Journals or outlets
4	Futurology	Typically, with a focus on the development of theoretical frameworks and methodologies to predict future events and trends.	Often associated with a more scientific or speculative approach to understanding the future.	Theoretical and speculative exploration of future possibilities. Often involves bold predictions and visionary thinking. May include the study of emerging technologies and societal changes.	Works by well-known futurologists like Alvin Toffler and Ray Kurzweil. Books and articles that speculate on the future of technology, society, and the human condition.

exports, particularly of high-tech products as a subcontractor in a complex web of international business. This, coupled with the country's centralization of power and the close relationship that has existed between politics and industry since the time of Gustav Vasa, explains the emphasis on the Intelligence perspective. Today, the subject still receives less attention in other Scandinavian countries, like Norway and Denmark, which have different economic structures and a different industrial history.

Swedes are sometimes, and in my opinion correctly, referred to as the 'Japanese of Europe,' a nod to the two countries' homogeneous, conflict-averse, and somewhat authoritative cultures. Discussion is actively encouraged in Sweden (the "fika culture" by which workers meet several times during the working day to drink coffee and maybe have some cake). The function of these meetings is, except for the nice formalities, to create consensus around the direction taken out by the leadership. Although there are significant differences between Japan and Sweden, both cultures heavily rely on the export of high-tech products and are known for having developed sophisticated intelligence systems for business. For Japan economic growth through export became the way back to the central stage of power after the loss against the US at the end of the Second World War. The Japanese model is a true synthesis of private and public intelligence, coordinated by their Ministry of Economy, Trade, and Industry. The connection between private and public interests in Sweden is strong, albeit less formalized.

We should also note that the distinction between private and public sector intelligence is primarily a Western phenomenon, closely tied to our democratic systems, and does not exist in the same way in non-democratic and especially totalitarian states.

The countries that have developed the best practices for intelligence systems in business are typically major industrial producers and exporters, such as the United Kingdom, the United States, Germany, France, Japan, Sweden, the Netherlands, and

Israel (Group 1). New Asian exporters are now following suit, including countries like China, South Korea, India, Brazil, and Russia (Group 2). This does not mean that intelligence in business is less relevant for other countries; rather, it provides the best explanation for why both the theory and practice of Intelligence is more developed and emphasized in the two groups of countries mentioned above. Of course, the underlying mechanisms here are not static, so this is likely to change.

Many books have been written on intelligence operations in private companies over the last three decades— in French, English, and German. However, most of these books are more concerned with selling specific consultancy products, discussing problems, and telling stories based on personal experience than with trying to lay out a rigorous field of study. In the same way, most books on Business Intelligence from two decades ago were published by small and relatively unknown publishers and were intended to sell consultancy services. Today books on Business Intelligence are predominantly about technology, mostly software[8] and AI,[9] but also on management.[10] This is, as we shall see, all part of the natural evolution of the field.

In the United States, it was Michael Porter, influenced by contributions on entrepreneurship by figures such as Peter Drucker and Alfred Chandler, who, around 1980, reignited the spirit of Adam Smith and brought back attention to the problem of competitive advantage in academia. Porter's contributions to the applied field of what then became known first as Business Intelligence have been significant, even though his primary focus was on Strategy. Porter was the first to introduce models for understanding the forces influencing the competitive advantage of companies and to reemphasize a clear process-oriented approach to business issues lost since Henri Fayol, the father of Management. Porter presented his ideas in The Five Forces Model, The Diamond Model, Porter's Four Corners Model, and, notably, the Value Chain. Later, researchers in the US interested in the Intelligence function had a background in Strategy, while a large part of researchers in Europe came from Marketing, leading later to the popularity of Market and Marketing Intelligence.

Others influenced by Porter's work in the US appeared around the Society of Competitive Intelligence Professionals (SCIP), now the Strategic Consortium of Intelligence Professionals (SCIP). This association, along with contributors to the Competitive Intelligence Review and later the Journal of Competitive Intelligence and Management (JCIM), played a significant role in the development of the field. SCIP was founded in 1986 in part by consultants who were laid off from Langley after the end of the Cold War. These consultants believed that they could apply many of the same skills learned in State Intelligence organizations to the private sector. A key figure among them was Jan Herring, who had been an intelligence officer with the CIA for 20 years. He teamed up with Benjamin Gilad and Leonard M. Fuld, and their company soon faced competition from others with similar profiles as the topic caught the attention of managers. Today, SCIP is controlled by

[8] Warren et al. (2013).

[9] Zwingmann (2022).

[10] Munoz (2018) and Sharda et al. (2018).

David Frigstad of Frost & Sullivan, a market research company, through a non-profit entity.

The origins of Intelligence as an academic discipline can be traced back to Stevan Dedijer. In 1966, Dedijer founded the Research Policy Institute after being personally invited to Sweden by Prime Minister Tage Erlander in 1961. Before this, Dedijer had spent a year at the Niels Bohr Institute in Denmark on leave from his position as director of the Belgrade Nuclear Institute and working on the Yugoslav nuclear program. Stevan later developed a course he called Social Intelligence, which he held at Lund University in 1975.

His brother Vladimir was closely associated with Josip Broz Tito and instrumental in the formation and operation of Yugoslavia's intelligence and security apparatus. During the Second World War, Stevan served in the American army, where he was a paratrooper in the 101st Airborne Division, famously known for their involvement in the Battle of the Bulge. He was also recruited by the Office of Strategic Services (OSS) to work in occupied Yugoslavia. However, the OSS later released him, suspecting he was a Comintern spy, as he had been an active communist in the US after completing his PhD studies in physics at Princeton. He was also a friend of William Colby for many years. The two had similar views on the function and role of "intelligence as part of the knowledge industry".[11] The CIA was not there only to provide the president with briefings, but to help lead the country forward in terms of innovation, research and production, they thought. Seeing the power of the Dulles brothers, many presidents were weary of letting the CIA get the same amount of influence again that the organization enjoyed in the 50s. John Foster Dulles served as Secretary of State from 1953 to 1959, and Allen Dulles was the Director of Central Intelligence (head of the CIA) from 1953 to 1961. During their time in office, the President of the United States was Dwight D. Eisenhower who famously warned the public that too much power was being centered outside of democratic control.

Dedijer also had an influence on the development of 'Veille' (surveillance) and what later became Intelligence Economique in France, spurring, if not initiating, that country's occupation for assisting their industry abroad.

At the time the first course in Social Intelligence was introduced at Lund University, Wilhelm Agrell, tells the story of how he was working for a branch of military intelligence in Stockholm, noticed the course announcement in a newspaper and expressed interest in visiting Lund to learn more about it. However, his superior did not consider it worth the expense and believed that such matters should be left to the Swedish secret police (SÄPO). Other commanding officers reacted even more negatively; one went so far as to write a handwritten letter to Dedijer criticizing the appropriateness of the subject for an academic setting.[12]

The main idea behind the course Social Intelligence inspired by Fritz Machlup, an Austrian-American economist known for his work in information economics,[13]

[11] Dedijer and Jéquier (1987, p. 4).

[12] Agrell (1998).

[13] Machlup (1962, 1981).

but also by Peter Drucker,[14] and Marc Uri Porat,[15] was to elevate the field beyond just military and state intelligence services, transforming it into a discipline that serves the whole of society.

> Intelligence becomes the ability of [such] institutions to acquire new information, and knowledge, make judgements, adapt to the environment, develop new concepts and new strategies, and act in a rational and effective way[16]

Despite reservations, an agent was eventually sent to Lund to monitor Dedijer's course. The report sent back to Stockholm concluded that the course was "too theoretical to pose any security risk to the country". However, Agrell became intrigued by the course and moved to Lund and eventually followed in Dedijer's footsteps, ensuring the continuation of the study Intelligence Analysis in Sweden for the next generation (he has now retired). Agrell, who came from a military intelligence background and became an expert on the Middle East after living in Egypt during the 1970s, significantly influenced the field by steering it towards political science, which was his academic background. He made substantial contributions to its academic development by publishing numerous books in Swedish.

In 1996, Agrell taught his first course at Lund University, titled 'The Art of Guessing Right'.[17] He expanded this offering in 1998 with a course called 'Applied Intelligence Analysis',[18] and in the spring of 1999, he started a course at Malmö University named 'Intelligence Analysis'.[19] Agrell's successor at Malmö University, Katarina Kling, redirected the course back towards private organizations, drawing largely on American organizational theories, but left later for a career in consulting, as did other of Dedijers students, like Hans Hedin. Dedijer's tradition in academia has since been continued by others. Meanwhile, Dedijer continued his work as an international consultant also after he retired, until he passed away in his home in Dubrovnik in 2004.

Dedijer had an influence on two generations of practitioners and researchers in Sweden among them Lars Oxelheim, Hans Hedin,[20] Sven Hamrefors,[21] Katarina Svensson Kling,[22] Furustig and Sjöstedt.[23] Other Swedes who came later were inspired directly by American intelligence experts, first of all, Ben Gilad, who had already been an authority on intelligence-related matters for more than a generation and was running an international consultancy. Gilad inspired Anderbjörk and

[14] Drucker (1956).

[15] Porat and Rubin (1977).

[16] Dedijer and Jéquier (1987, p. Xi).

[17] 'Konsten att Gissa rätt' in Swedish.

[18] 'Tillämpad underrättelseanalys' in Swedish.

[19] 'Omvärldsanalys' in Swedish.

[20] Hedin and Sadström (2006).

[21] Hamrefors (2002).

[22] Borg et al. (1998).

[23] Furustig and Sjöstedt (2000).

Martell when they worked with the Intelligence function in Ericsson and later when they developed their own business intelligence software at Comintelli.[24] Another American influence was Robert D. Steele, who in the 90s inspired Swedish state intelligence services to focus more on Open Source.[25] Among those who Dedijer inspired in France was Philipe Clerc, who just retired from the Chamber of Commerce in Paris, but still teaches. Another group of business intelligence experts were centered in southern France first of all in Toulouse, around Prof. Bernard Dousset. These were often hard-core engineers and mathematicians. Henri Dou—another retiree—was among the first to develop software for the analysis of patents which is still used today.[26]

'Omvärldsanalys' literally translates to 'surrounding-world analysis,' referring to the analysis of the external environment. In English, we use the terms Environmental Scan (ES) and Environmental Analysis (EA).[27] An Environmental Scan involves gathering information from a broad array of sources but does not encompass actual analysis. While analysis is important, I will show later in the book that the exercise does not always bear any fruit. It is often more effective to allocate resources towards scanning and storing intelligence. The NSA's new facilities in Bluffdale, Utah, do exactly that, vacuuming the entire planet for data and keeping it. So far, they have had a problem of not knowing what they actually have, as it is simply too much data, but new LLMs (Large Language Models) are likely to solve that problem.

We will use the division into Private and Public Intelligence throughout much of this book, although it has not been widely adopted yet, as most professionals work in one domain or the other. Over the past decades, private contractors have been increasingly utilized by state intelligence services, though they are often considered contractors or outsiders, even when they hold high security clearances. In addition to Private and Public Intelligence, we will use the broader term 'Intelligence' and, more specifically, 'Intelligence Studies in Business' when discussing the private sector. This term was accepted by scholars and practitioners at a conference in Bad Nauheim in April 2011. It was coined by Sheila Wright and subsequently adopted for the new academic journal, the Journal of Intelligence Studies in Business (JISIB), which launched later that year as an open-access journal.

In Germany, where I wrote my doctoral thesis on Industrial Espionage,[28] the topic of Intelligence was for a long time studied under what is referred to as 'Wettbewerb,' the broader issue of competition. Today, many companies prefer to use the term 'insights' instead of 'intelligence' to avoid the military and espionage connotations associated with state organizations. There are also new emerging fields, such as Collective Intelligence[29] inspired by the study of biology and new

[24] Anderbjörk and Martell (2021).

[25] Rossander and Borg (1996).

[26] On Patent Intelligence see also Comai (2018).

[27] Corresponds with the terms 'omvärldsbevakning' and 'omvärldsanalys' used in Sweden. y

[28] Söilen (2004).

[29] Calof et al. (2022) and Söilen (2019).

topics such as Knowledge Hiding, which is attracting many researchers.[30] Related topics such as co-creation, the wisdom of crowds, complex systems, systems theory, and anticipatory systems have also gained traction. Anticipatory Systems comes from Robert Rosen's famous book. It is widely cited, but seldom read or understood, largely due to its mathematical complexity.[31]

To the knowledge of the author, there are currently no programs specifically on intelligence in business except for at L'École de Guerre Économique (EGE) in Paris led by a persistent Christian Harbulot. However, there are of course many programs in Intelligence Studies, with the most known being at Mercyhurst in the US, started by Robert Heibel in the early 1990s after he retired from the FBI and at Aberystwyth University in Wales. That does not mean that the subject matter does not exist elsewhere; rather, it is often taught under different terms, such as strategy, decision-making, and as part of international business courses. Today, about seven universities in Sweden offer courses in 'omvärldsanalys' or intelligence studies within the social sciences, but there are no programs. The focus of these courses has increasingly shifted towards technical topics, primarily forensics and IT Security, a trend that is mirrored in other countries as well. In France, the subject has traditionally been taught as geopolitics by legends like Yves Lacoste, Aymeric Chauprade, Joseph Le Bihan and Gérard Chaliand. These academics have educated generations of French intelligence professionals. By the turn of the millennium, the subject matter of Geopolitics was adapted to better fit the logic of the large MNEs, known as 'Geoéconomie', Geoeconomics in English[32].

In the United States, the field has also expanded, starting first as Corporate Intelligence, then Competitor Intelligence, and then Competitive Intelligence. Financial Intelligence has become an increasingly vital area today beyond mere credit card transaction checks as banks have become digital giants in their own rights. Banks have always required thorough analyses of foreign markets and major customers, wanting to know precisely who they are dealing with. These services continue to be offered today by consulting firms like Kroll and the four major auditing firms, sometimes as part of what is known as due diligence.

In the early days of the stock exchange, and before the invention of regulatory mechanisms like the SEC in the US, fraudsters were less easy to detect and caused considerable damage to investors, especially if they were rich and well-connected. One of the best examples was the Swedish investor Ivar Kreuger (1880–1932), who forged much of his accounting figures and saw his multiple businesses turn into a massive Ponzi scheme, leading to his tragic suicide in a hotel room in Paris. His empire was valued at around $600 million in the late 1920s, which is equivalent to several billion dollars today. He controlled a substantial portion of the global match production, holding monopolies in 16 countries and owning manufacturing operations in 36 countries. Intelligence services play an important role in the world of business among major players today to avoid dealing with the Kreugers of today. Of

[30] Oubrich et al. (2021).

[31] Rosen (1985).

[32] Söilen (2012).

course, that does not mean they do not appear from time to time. In many cases, fraudsters start out as honest, hard-working businesspeople, but circumstances turn them into criminals, as seen with Bernie Madoff and Sam Bankman-Fried.

In the world of academia, the discipline of Strategy soon started to have an influence on Marketing Academics, who were quick to include chapters on the "external environment" in their textbooks. All the major marketing textbooks by authors like Philip Kotler, David Jobber, and Svend Hollensen have increasingly included material on information gathering and handling.

2.3.3 Bridging Disciplines and Counter-Disciplines

The understanding of this book requires little previous knowledge of Economics or Statistics, but it will be advantageous if the reader has completed courses in Marketing, basic Algebra and Scientific methods for the Social Sciences.

The Scope of 'Intelligence Studies in Business' is broader than 'Competitive Intelligence' or 'Business Intelligence', but narrower than 'Intelligence' and 'Intelligence Studies', as it tends to exclude aspects unique to State and Military Intelligence. The disciplines that is the closest to Intelligence Studies in Business would be the more established Information Science.[33] Unlike Information Science, which can be said to have merged from Computer Science, Intelligence Studies in Business is interdisciplinary. Throughout the book, we will demonstrate how established subjects like Strategy, Entrepreneurship, and Marketing Research all contain elements useful to our study.

In the late '90s, Business Intelligence or Competitive Intelligence was often discussed alongside Knowledge Management.[34] Since then, aspects of the subject dealing with knowledge planning have gradually shifted back into the study of Strategy,[35] and those subjects dealing with the role of information have sometimes been merged into an Anthropology of Information.

Many universities, especially in Europe, traditionally approach topics of Intelligence under the banner of 'Geopolitics'. This study combines Geography, Economics, Politics, with History to reflect on the power of nations, and today, multinational organizations. In France, the subject has carried a strong military emphasis with a focus on history but also futurology.[36]

For the field of Intelligence to thrive and avoid the pitfalls seen in Knowledge Management, by becoming too narrow or Geopolitics, by becoming too normative, Intelligence Studies in Business must strive to be a practical science, that is instrumental, focused on solving real life problems and proving practitioners with a toolkit. It should conduct rationalist inquiries based on the Empiricist tradition,

---

[33] Intelligence Studies (IS) is defined as "The means by which people and organizations, utilizing technology, gather, process, store, and disseminate information," p. 3. Ward and Peppard (2009).

[34] Simon (1999). See also Liebowitz (2006).

[35] Neef et al. (1998).

[36] Loury and Le Bihan (1993) and Chaliand (1982).

acknowledging only verifiable facts and observable phenomena.[37] It should remain a positive science, not entangled with philosophy or wild speculations (educated guesses are ok, as we will see). Its scientific basis lies, in formal logic (reasoning, syllogism), communication theory (first with C. Shannon), organizational theory (setting up the function), organizational behavior (how to work) and the scientific method (working processes and methods).

Intelligence Studies in Business must consistently align with the practical roles and positions it aims to prepare students for. The study of Intelligence is designed to train analysts for specific and essential functions within organizations. Therefore, the emphasis should be on developing and managing efficient Intelligence Processes using available technologies, rather than limiting the discipline to normative or purely historical perspectives as has been the case in the past, especially on the European continent. A component of this constructivist approach must include continually testing new technologies from a user's perspective.[38]

This does not mean that normative aspects do not have a role to play in Intelligence Studies, just that they, in my opinion, should be handled separately. For my part, I have chosen to move the normative part over to the macro-level and the study of Geoeconomics, but it can also be treated within International Relations or as part of any discipline leaning on Critical Theory. I make it clear to my students that I have chosen Geoeconomics, based in evolutionary theory, because it promises the best theoretical framework for normative statements and maps open up for great illustrations of ideas. There is a need for nations to study the world from their own—subjective—reality, as it relates to each country's competitive advantage. Ignoring this fact—which has been a hallmark of the entire Social Science project since its inception after the Second World War—has rendered our studies of man and society fragmented and unrealistic, causing the further deterioration of our competitive advantage. Put differently, we need a social science located within business and economics that can study our own interests from the perspective of different groups, nations and cultures.

Similarly, companies need to understand how national interests affect their business. Most studies with a purely universalist assumption that ignore these interests ultimately fail because they become irrelevant and of no use to practitioners. This issue is particularly evident in a long line of business studies that, akin to Sociology, have chosen to focus on theoretical phenomena rather than practical applications. For example, they study 'about' entrepreneurship or 'about' accounting, not 'in' them. Consequently, we have a somewhat absurd situation in academia today where many teachers of Entrepreneurship have never started or worked in a company but claim expertise in how to do it, and numerous accounting professors lack basic

[37] Important contributions in this direction in the Anglo-Saxon world have been made by Prescott, Fleisher, Blenkhorn, Bensoussan and Gilad. Prescott and Miller (2001), Fleisher and Blenkhorn (2001), Fleisher and Bensoussan (2002), Gilad and Gilad (1988), Gilad and Herring (1996), Herman (1996).

[38] Agostino et al. (2013), Söilen (2012), Nyblom et al. (2012), and Amara et al. (2012), Using the SSAV model to evaluate Business Intelligence Software, and Söilen and Hasslinger (2012).

knowledge of how to prepare a cash flow statement for an annual report, yet they teach about different topics related to 'accounting.' This disconnect causes concern among major auditing firms.

Geoeconomics in the US meant something completely different at the turn of the millennium than it does today. It was originally conceived as a non-normative study, with the aim to identify relationships between geography and human economic behavior. It would engage in practical studies on infrastructure, like where to put a new Burger King given existing network of freeways and the location of its competitors by analyzing traffic and demographics. Geography naturally restricts economic activities: harbors cannot be built inland, and supermarkets cannot be constructed in rivers. By understanding these geographical constraints, we can predict human behavior, akin to how the study of economics considers the limitations imposed by scarce resources. The idea was not bad, but it had a narrow following.

In its normative version, Geoeconomics is an adaptation of the study of Geopolitics, which also meant that it struggled to establish itself as a university discipline. The study of Geopolitics comes with a heavy historical burden. During the Cold War, it was indirectly criticized for having provided theories that underpinned Nazi Germany's aggressive territorial policies aimed at creating a Lebensraum in Eastern Europe. However, when political discussions 'thawed' after the Cold War, it became evident that political interests and aspirations were not significantly altered—man was as he has always been, as were states; focused on their own self-interest. This led to a resurgence in the prominence of Geopolitics. This renewed interest later also extended to the United States, where Geoeconomics was welcomed through institutions like the Greenberg Center for Geoeconomic Studies at the Council on Foreign Relations.

Geopolitics starts with the simple acknowledgement that there is a correlation between geography and politics, illustrated by how national borders often align with natural features such as rivers and mountain ranges. The question of whether this alignment should persist also in the future is both a moral and political issue, reflecting normative considerations. Geopolitics is on everyone's lips now, especially since the War in Ukraine. Russia wants back what used to belong to the Soviet Union where history is used as the major argument, ignoring public opinion in the country being attacked. The resurgence of interest in Geopolitics, sparked by theorists like Carl Schmitt, is not unproblematic.[39]

A primary issue with Geopolitics is its tendency to overlook moral considerations and lean entirely on the approach of Realpolitik, focusing solely on the state's interests regardless of the consequences for other parties. In response, Critical Geopolitics emerged as a moral and political critique of traditional Geopolitics, consolidating an extensive body of literature that challenged the discipline after the Second World War. It serves as an antithesis to traditional Geopolitics—or like a counter-discipline—focusing on critiquing a specific area of social science, thus

[39]Among his more known books; Legalität und Legitimität (1932/1998) and Der Nomos Der Erde (1950/1997). Telos Press, under the leadership of Russell A. Berman, has published several articles related to Carl Schmitt's thinking as well as translations of his works into English.

defining its scope and applications. Many scholars regard Critical Geopolitics as an essential critique within the broader field of social sciences, yet it still attracts little interest outside of academic circles. Both the study of Geopolitics and Critical Geopolitics have been criticized for their inherent political nature, highlighting a broader issue within the social sciences. If we assume that human behavior follows laws generated by evolutionary theory, we must find a way to teach the social sciences as a branch of biology again, without becoming entangled in political biases.[40]

Other attempts to blend geography with social sciences, like Social Statistics, an interdisciplinary field intersecting sociology, economics, public health, psychology, and demography, are sometimes criticized for depoliticizing social issues, rendering it not much different from general statistics. Conversely, Human Geography, which focuses on the study of patterns and processes shaping human interaction with environments, is often criticized for being politically biased and overly subjective.

These experiences in academia suggest that disciplines should clearly define whether they are non-normative or normative and be transparent about it, just like any Intelligence discipline must be able to show that it can provide theories for training and educating a new generation of Intelligence experts and analysts. This then, is the ultimate test of any discipline. A discipline should primarily strive to be useful, that is, in demand and leading to job opportunities. If it can build its structure on universal principles, it can aspire to become a science. Otherwise, disciplines that do not meet the criteria of science are traditionally referred to in academia as an art. A discipline does not need to be a science to be taught as a social science at the university level. It can also be an applied field of study. It should instead prove itself to be useful in society, be taught in a scientific way, that is following scientific methods and with the potential goal of developing into a science.

2.3.4 A Case for Public Intelligence and NPO Intelligence

When Stevan Dedijer pioneered the first non-military course on intelligence, he named it "social intelligence", thinking it should aspire to be useful for all of society.[41] The course emphasized intelligence in corporations but also included public organizations. Social intelligence encompasses "government agencies, Industrial firms, political parties, trade unions, armies and political pressure groups".[42] This was an inspiration to create a true science of information gathering, analysis, and distribution to improve decision-making not only for key players in top politics like heads of states and ministers, or military leaders, but for all decision-makers, small and big, realizing that the fundamental process of handling information is the same in all organizations.

---

[40] Söilen (2017a).

[41] There have been few contributions combining intelligence to the larger social issue. One exception is Dedijer and Jéquier (1987), where the authors discuss the importance of a systematic approach to information gathering for economic development.

[42] Dedijer and Jéquier (1987, p. 22).

The argument is that a well-organized intelligence function at the state level can significantly benefit a country's innovation, competitive advantage, and prosperity by providing businesses, NGOs, and the public sector with valuable information. This information identification is termed "disruptive intelligence." Disruptive innovations are those that have the potential to transform entire industries by making products more accessible and affordable. Recognizing these innovations before they disrupt businesses becomes crucial. Incumbent companies can use this information to protect their operations, while others may leverage it to participate in the disruption. Therefore, gathering information about potential disruptive innovations is a vital activity at the state level.[43]

The Swedish state has had ideas of a centralized intelligence function for the purpose of the advancement of civil society several times. Numerous governmental reports have addressed the issue.[44] Although the decision to establish such a government agency for public intelligence was deferred following a comprehensive hearing that culminated in a 2000 report, the idea has not been abandoned, and the function remains active across various public organizations. According to a report by the Institute for Futures Studies (IFFS), an independent Swedish research institute established by the government in 1987, all government agencies monitor, analyse, and anticipate developments within their "environments". It is usual for designated state employees to use 5–25% of the time on intelligence analysis. In departments and government bodies where a dedicated unit exists, it often consists of between five and ten people. The report emphasizes the vital role of these activities in enhancing informed decision-making, particularly for strategic planning.[45]

We define these intelligence activities as Public Intelligence, which involves the collection of information for the interest of regional and local governments. In contrast, intelligence operations in the private sector, which we will refer to as Private Intelligence, are more straightforward in their goals, such as achieving a certain percentage increase in sales, return on investment or net profit to satisfy demands by investors. The objectives of political organizations are not always that clear and tend to change with new governments. There is also the risk that intelligence experts working for public organizations become derailed from what is best for the country in terms of the type of problems that they are encouraged to work on as they are easily influenced by political directives. Our political representatives systematically make decisions that harm the competitive advantage of the nation while facing minimal personal risk, as they are rarely held accountable for wasting taxpayers' money. This can be detrimental to the nation-state, as exemplified by Sweden's decision in the late '90s to dismantle a significant portion of its military, including strategic bases on the island of Gotland in the Baltic Sea or the dismantlement of nuclear power plants and research associated with this. A professional public intelligence function would undoubtedly have helped to bring to light the risks of these policies,

---

[43] Vriens and Søilen (2014).

[44] E.g. Fredriksson et al. (1999), Zanden (2003), and Björk (1997).

[45] Lundqvist (2010).

but it would not eliminate them. Moreover, these mistakes transcend political affiliations and are evident across the entire political spectrum.

A business is a more consistent entity when it comes to intelligence work as it often has clear (profit) goals. Organizations that do not have profit goals are defined as non-profit organizations (NPOs). NPOs present a unique case for intelligence activities as they often work for:

1. Mission-Driven Focus: Unlike private companies that prioritize profit maximization, NPOs aim to achieve specific social, cultural, or humanitarian objectives. Intelligence activities should therefore concentrate on identifying trends, risks, and opportunities directly related to advancing their mission.
2. Stakeholder Engagement: NPOs typically engage with a diverse array of stakeholders, including donors, volunteers, communities, and government entities. Intelligence gathering needs to cover the needs and expectations of these groups, assessing how changes in public policy, social attitudes, and economic conditions could impact stakeholder support and involvement.
3. Resource Allocation: NPOs often operate under more stringent budget constraints compared to for-profit entities. Intelligence efforts should focus on optimizing resource allocation, identifying potential funding sources, partnership opportunities, and cost-effective methods for mission achievement.
4. Regulatory and Compliance Monitoring: Since NPOs frequently benefit from tax exemptions and public funding, they must adhere to strict regulatory requirements. Intelligence activities should include monitoring changes in legal and compliance obligations to prevent any jeopardization of their status and operations.
5. Impact Assessment: Intelligence activities should include mechanisms to measure the impact of the NPO's programs and initiatives. This involves gathering data on program effectiveness, beneficiary outcomes, and the overall success in fulfilling the organizational mission.
6. Crisis Management and Sustainability: Given that NPOs can be highly affected by external shocks (e.g., economic downturns, policy changes, natural disasters), intelligence should include a strong focus on crisis prediction, preparation, and management, as well as strategies for long-term sustainability.
7. Collaborative Intelligence: Considering the collaborative nature of many non-profit endeavors, intelligence gathering could benefit from partnerships with other organizations, sharing data and insights to enhance overall sector effectiveness.
8. Advocacy and Policy Influence: For many NPOs, influencing policy and public opinion is crucial. Intelligence activities should therefore include analysis of policy developments, public opinion trends, and the activities of influential figures and institutions within relevant sectors.

NPO Intelligence can then be said to be a special topic within Intelligence Studies.

Public administrators often have vague, hard-to-measure, and hard-to-control goals. However, this is no value judgment on their importance. The work done by public organizations often triumphs over anything the private sector does, and that is by design, really. At the same time, public organizations frequently find themselves in situations quite similar to private organizations. For example, they need to raise their own taxes, maintain strict control over expenses, and balance their budgets. They also need to attract citizens and companies to settle in their area, competing with other districts and regions for educated employees and large private companies, both domestically and internationally. In essence, they often face competitive situations not unlike those of business organizations.

Like a business organization, a region needs to understand what drives its economy. Relevant questions might include:

1. What types of businesses are in our region by industry, size, and profit, and how much do they contribute to taxes?
2. Who owns these businesses, and where do these owners reside (within the region, in another region, or abroad)?[46]
3. What competencies exist in our region, and do they meet our needs (the knowledge management question)?
4. How are these competencies utilized?
5. Where does the income come from, and where do the expenses go?
6. What regions are we competing with, and what are their competitive advantages?
7. How is our region affected by macro factors (e.g., our dependency on the IT sector or changes in labour costs in neighboring countries)?
8. Which niche, if any, might our region fill in the global marketplace?
9. How adequate is our infrastructure for future needs?
10. How effectively do we utilize our suppliers?
11. What political groups and interests dominate the agenda in our region?
12. What organizations, if any, should we privatize, and why?

Every political organization is concerned with balancing the budget; thus, to be responsible, it needs to know how to increase revenues.[47] To do this effectively depends upon a well-functioning intelligence function. It's not enough simply to hire a strategist who walks around in the corridors like a black box version of a crystal bowl; all decision-makers need good intelligence, and there needs to be a process in place to assure that the municipality or government body actually receives it.

Public Intelligence operates on three different levels, each with its own constraints and possibilities for working with intelligence-related questions:

1. National,
2. Regional, and
3. Local.

[46] This affects factors like the likelihood of the owners' giving donations, their commitment to the local community. In the long run, it is more important to have the heart of the owners than their investments.

[47] On intelligence in municipalities see Ericsson (2003).

Local government is often too small to implement an intelligence system but will have employees working with strategy and planning, which entails a large part of intelligence work. The national government may find itself too large to gather detailed information about what is happening in all its regions. Compared to their respective information needs, national governments often produce an overload of less useful intelligence, local governments produce too little. For this reason, many nation-states try to position the intelligence function at the regional, or mezzo level, where it can be close enough to the action to know what is going on but also far enough away to gather necessary competencies and make comparisons to help numerous smaller communities and serve as an intelligence liaison in the public sector. Many strategic decisions are made at the regional level with the regional government, such as which industries to invest in, how to manage them, decisions about infrastructure, and K-12 education.[48]

2.3.5 The Case of Private Intelligence

Everything that is not public, NPO, state and military intelligence can be gathered under the term Private Intelligence. Together these different versions form the study of intelligence. To keep the different and most used terms in Intelligence separated and to understand their relations we can place them in a Wenn diagram[49] (Fig. 2.1).

The figure below illustrates the scope of the various intelligence functions within a private organization (Fig. 2.2):

Explaining the figure: 'Competitor Intelligence' is a subset of the 'Business Marketing Intelligence' function. 'Competitive Intelligence' analyzes all factors that contribute to a company's competitiveness. In contrast, 'Business Intelligence' unfortunately now has two meanings, which is confusing: one refers to software, and the other encompasses broader intelligence activities not directly linked to the organization's competitiveness, such as sourcing artists to decorate a new office building or finding employees who may want to join the company's soccer team.

Competitive intelligence addresses all elements crucial for the survival and prosperity of private organizations in the marketplace. Market Intelligence and Marketing Intelligence focus on intelligence functions related to activities in the marketing department, primarily concerning markets and customers. Competitor Intelligence is a more specialized activity that exclusively gathers information about the firm's competitors, it is sometimes outsourced. Although it is a smaller subset, it remains a priority in all medium to large companies. The question is only to what extent, with how much resources and analytical skills the questions are being pursued. The responsibility for this function is sometimes situated within the marketing department but may also be conducted by other members placed strategically in the

[48] The word 'region' comes from Latin 'region' and means "to steer". We may deduce that it was considered the ideal geographical unit for direct political control; not too small or too big.

[49] Jenster and Söilen (2009).

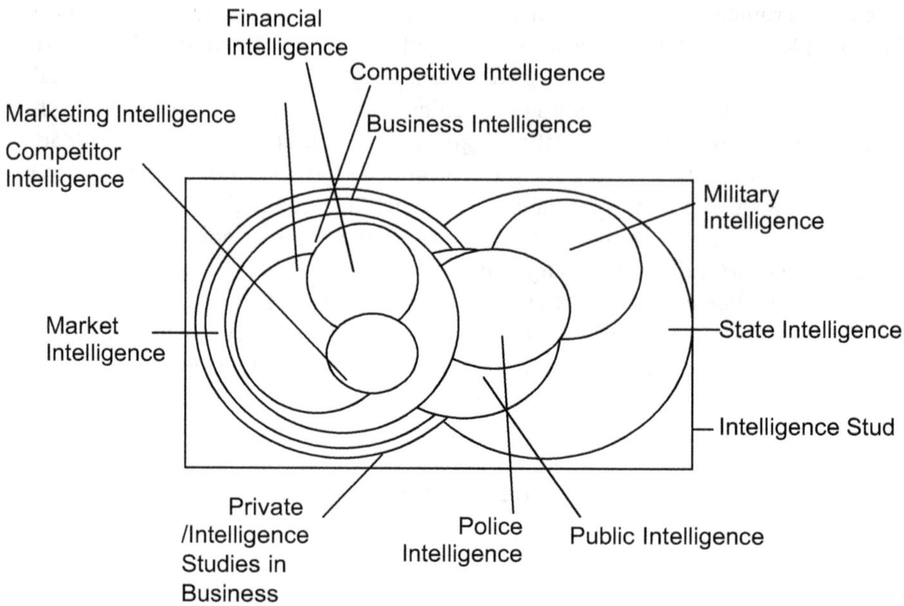

Fig. 2.1 An overview of the different intelligence functions in organizations

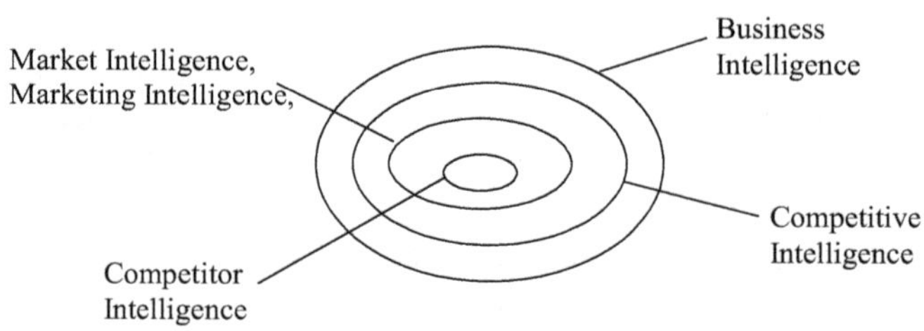

Fig. 2.2 Types of intelligence in a company

organization. Generally, the more specialized the intelligence operation, the lower it is positioned within the organizational hierarchy.

This says nothing about the popularity of each term or to which degree some have been outdated and are less used. The most used term in the existing literature, especially in the Anglo-Saxon world, is still 'business intelligence'. The early term 'corporate intelligence' has practically disappeared in recent years but is synonymous with private intelligence.[50] Competitive intelligence was popular, especially in Northern America, until the late 90s, but new publications are now fewer and seem often to come from Asian countries.

[50] Eells and Nehemkis (1984). Intelligence is a resource-intensive operation and, therefore, more relevant to 'corporations' than to a single person and less organized businesses. In this respect, it would have been more correct to stay with the term 'Corporate Intelligence'.

Besides all the terms ending with "intelligence" there is a whole list of abbreviations ending with INT, that originated much in the military and from state intelligence services: When business intelligence activities are performed by a nation-state, we refer to them as Economic Intelligence and Military Intelligence when the focus is military information. Gathering information using technology is termed Technical Intelligence, or TECHINT, primarily a concern for Military intelligence organizations, but increasingly also by private actors as in Digital Marketing. Anything not gathered by machines or through technology is known as Human Intelligence or HUMINT. It's important to note that information is not TECHINT merely because it is stored on a computer's hard disk; it becomes TECHINT to another person who discovers it there. SIGINT, or Signals Intelligence, refers to intelligence-gathering by interception of signals, whether communications between people (communications intelligence—COMINT) or from electronic signals not directly used in communication (electronic intelligence—ELINT). It involves collecting data from communication systems, radars, and other electronic systems. ELINT consists of Radar Signal Interception, Collecting data from foreign radar systems to analyze their capabilities, operational status, and deployment, and Satellite Reconnaissance, Monitoring signals from satellites to gather strategic information about other countries' space capabilities and intentions. To complete the list, there are also:

1. IMINT (Imagery Intelligence): Intelligence from satellite images, aerial photography, and other forms of imagery. This is useful for identifying and monitoring military installations, movements of troops and equipment, and changes in terrain or infrastructure.
2. MASINT (Measurement and Signature Intelligence): A technically complex form of intelligence gathering, MASINT deals with the detection, tracking, and identification of the unique signatures of fixed or dynamic target sources. This includes radar signatures, missile telemetry, nuclear radiation levels, and chemical composition of air samples.
3. GEOINT (Geospatial Intelligence): Intelligence that involves the exploitation and analysis of geographically referenced information about the Earth. This is derived from imagery, geospatial data, and imagery-derived products.
4. CYBINT/DNINT (Cyber Intelligence/Digital Network Intelligence): Intelligence derived from the cyberspace and information environment, including data about individuals, groups, and organizations' cyber operations and capabilities.

But more importantly for intelligence studies in business:

5. OSINT (Open Source Intelligence): Intelligence collected from publicly available sources such as newspapers, blogs, public data databases, and other openly available materials.
6. FININT (Financial Intelligence): Involves gathering information about the financial transactions and financial state of entities of interest, often to track illegal activities like money laundering or funding of terrorism.

7. SOCMINT (Social media intelligence) refers to the process of collecting, analyzing, and interpreting data from social media platforms to gain insights that can inform decision-making in various domains such as marketing, public relations, security, and competitive intelligence.

The list of abbreviations is of course continuously under development, where SOCINT is just a more a recent addition.

2.3.6 The Special Case of Business Relationship Management (BRM)

Some readers hesitate to use the term 'Intelligence' for information-gathering activities in private companies. The association with military intelligence and 'spying' is off-putting to some, preferring the term 'insights', although the meaning is largely similar. Insights is sometimes referred to as a deep understanding derived from intelligence that leads to actionable conclusions. For example, realizing that the competitor's new product targets a specific market segment suggests a gap that our company can exploit. From this perspective, the intelligence part would be more about market research data indicating a competitor's new product launch.

The adoption of 'intelligence' in business mirrors a historical trend where military terms are repurposed for corporate use. For example, in the 1960s, the term 'strategy' was initially used to describe a company's plans.[51] Today, it is probably more used in business than in a military context, showcasing how definitions can rapidly evolve. This tendency to borrow military terminology reflects the competitive nature of business, akin to organizational warfare. However, such comparisons should be approached with caution. Overly aggressive business tactics can backfire, and it is important to remember that competitors can also be potential partners. We operate as competitors in some areas and collaborators in others. In business, you want to avoid making enemies.

Studying relationships and networks is key in Intelligence for business leaders and heads of states alike. In business, we are used to studying customers, like in Customer Relationship Management (CRM), but not people of power. There is something called Stakeholder Management, but most people of power and influence will not be part of this group. Instead, this special type of relationships and networks is covered by what is called Business Relationship Management (BRM). BRM is a formal approach to understanding, defining, and supporting inter-business activities related to business networking. This discipline emphasizes building and maintaining relationships with other business entities and influential individuals, such as industry leaders, partners, and key influencers. Owners of large companies which are not involved in the day-to-day business but have delegated this to professional

[51] Alfred D. Chandler first applied the term to the conduct of business in 1962, in his book "Strategy and structure". A year later Drucker thought of using the word, but together with the publisher found that it risked being misunderstood. See Drucker (1985), footnote p. 209.

management can spend most of their time practicing BRM. This means that they spend a large percentage of their work time enlarging and refining their network of contacts in order to nurture existing relationships and find new business opportunities. The Intelligence function is central in this process.

2.3.7 Progress and Decline in Academic Disciplines

From one perspective, particularly for outsiders or practitioners, the field of study appears to have an overwhelming number of terms. However, each discipline has its own history and evolution that contribute to this terminology. There is a method to the madness, as it continually evolves over time. Ultimately, the terms used are primarily decided by practitioners rather than academics, which isn't always advantageous. Consultants often coin new terms to market 'new' services, and academics frequently adopt these terms too eagerly, further complicating the understanding of the phenomena being studied. This tendency has led to a proliferation of terms such as corporate intelligence, business intelligence, competitive intelligence, and market intelligence, often without significantly altering the meaning of the concepts being studied. The primary role of academia should be to make sense of these terms, to explain and bring clarity, and also to question their validity and utility.

Academic fields evolve, which is the main reason why names and labels change. 'Competitive intelligence' has mainly been an American-led approach. In the late '90s and early '00s, the number of articles on competitive intelligence declined, but discussion of the same phenomena under new terms continued. This led some academics and practitioners to wrongly believe that 'competitive intelligence is dying', implying a reduction in research within this field. While it was true that during this period fewer contributions came from academics in the US, maybe due in some part to the economic downturn caused by the 2000 and 2007 financial crises, which led some to leave the field and change jobs, the intelligence field itself was not diminishing. In many ways, the demand for Intelligence professionals was increasing, but in other areas, first of all, related to new technology. Today it is the prompter who is in demand. Prompt Engineering has become a part of Intelligence Analysis or what a Data Scientist does.

Consultants are often obsessed with the coining of new terms. So, how can we create clarity and lack of overlap in the terms we use? It shall be suggested here that we need stricter standards when accepting new terms, much like in the German academic tradition. If a new term is not precise and sufficiently distinct from existing terms, it should be rejected. The focus should be on what German colleagues have focused on at least since the nineteenth century as 'Verstehen'—the 'interpretive or participatory' examination of social phenomena—not on coining new terms. A new critical process of thinking needs to be instilled by asking: What problem does this field of study claim to address? Are there other studies that claim to address the same problem? Are they solving it? If yes, revert to the existing field. In reality, though, this hardly ever happens; instead, disciplines die because the academic tribes become too small, attract too little attention internally, cannot recruit enough new researchers, and their once-strong defenders change direction or leave academia altogether. All that is left in the end are their books and articles. Academic tribes can also in many cases continue even though the outside interest among practitioners is close to non-existent. That something is not proven to be useful is, unfortunately enough, not always a criterion in academia. So, we always need to check with practitioners in our field of study.

Much of what we call Intelligence Studies in Business in this book was inspired by visionary businessman and futurist Alvin Toffler,[52] mathematician Claude Shannon, Igor Ansoff, the Russian-American applied mathematician who became known as the father of strategic Management, and Gabriel Naudé, the father of library sciences. They all wrote books that were useful. The most successful academic projects are those that align with developments in business life. More importantly, the focus should shift to discussing the problems being solved, rather than merely discussing what is being written about. This approach will clarify which bodies of knowledge make the most significant contributions. Additionally, it is often beneficial to have conferences that include both practitioners and academics, as both groups can learn from each other and help keep each other on track. The conferences organized by SCIP in the US and ICI in Europe have been instrumental in achieving this balance.

Part of the fault lies with academia itself, which since the 1950s has focused on the number of new research publications, less on its quality. Scientific journals often work too much like clubs. The number of scientists and researchers in the same period has increased by over 1000%, but the number of new inventions has decreased. Its apparent that academia, and especially the social science and parts of the humanities, has become too much of an intellectual playground of no particular use to others than academics, academic institutions and local communities. To change this, we need incentive systems that award real contributions, not the number of papers published. Academics need to start engaging with and discussing each other's works again, rather than focusing on bibliometrics and exploiting the publication game.

We also need larger, more comprehensive monographs that outline the core of each discipline, aiding in the creation of more robust courses and helping business professionals solve real-life problems. This is the aim of the project presented in the next seven chapters: to lay out a logical plan for the techniques and skills needed to become an intelligence analyst. I also encourage you, the reader, to provide feedback on how it can be improved as all knowledge production is a collective effort.

This concludes the section dealing with the definitions, roles, and justification of the study of Intelligence in Business. In Chap. 3, we continue by introducing the reader to a few basic frameworks for environmental scanning as we try to get a grip on all the things that can happen to an organization.

---

[52] Credit should rightly also go to his wife Heidi, whom he was writing with, for example, in his best-selling book Future Shock. See Toffler (1970).

Environmental Scanning 3

All organizations seek to gain an overview of their environment, but the question of where to start is crucial given the myriad of dimensions and variables to track. In this book, we will examine each of these variables in detail. To begin, it is useful to adopt the funnel approach, starting with the broadest perspective possible to ensure no important variables are overlooked. As we progress, we can gradually eliminate dimensions that prove irrelevant, narrowing our focus effectively. This method helps minimize the risk of overlooking critical factors that could later cause surprises. In state and public intelligence organizations, such oversights can lead to a loss of trust and, in some cases, the replacement of responsible staff. In the private sector, the consequences are much more severe, and the entire function or department may be shut down.

3.1 Macro and Micro Perspectives

To avoid being surprised we begin by considering all the potential events that can impact an organization, taking the widest possible view. The field of Global Catastrophic Risk (GCR) focuses on the study and mitigation of risks that could cause severe harm to human civilization on a global scale. We then proceed to examine the macro factors surrounding the organization and continue with the micro factors, building on Porter's Five Forces model, working our way down the funnel.

3.1.1 Global Catastrophic Risk (GCR)

Some readers may object at this point, asking, 'How do the stars affect our business? That sounds almost like astrology, which is not a science' Well, very little in our day-to-day business is affected by the stars, of course, but there are other objects

K. Solberg Söilen, *Intelligence Studies in Business*, Management for Professionals,
https://doi.org/10.1007/978-3-031-76491-2_3

and factors in space that do, like the fall of meteorites that are fragments of asteroids or comets. They do not need to be the size of the Chicxulub impactor to deserve our attention.[1] More importantly, there are other forces of nature that affect our organization. A nation-state must keep track of these phenomena.

In general, we want to know how nature at large affects our organization, including earthquakes, tsunamis, and extreme weather due to global warming. All these events consist of a special area studied under the umbrella of Global Catastrophic Risk. They are not so much the concern of smaller companies on a day-to-day basis, not because they do not affect them, but because they simply have limited resources to study them. GCRs are, first, the concern of nation-states and are studied by Academic and Research Institutes, like the Future of Humanity Institute (FHI) at Oxford led by talented professor Nick Bostrom,[2] Non-Governmental Organizations (NGOs) and Think Tanks and International Organizations.

A research article by Söilen and Alipour[3] show how to try to detect what may happen in a surveillance model that classifies emerging risks prior to occurrence, named The State Intelligence Model, receiving its name because these impacts are mostly studied for nation-states and international space organizations.

GCRs belong to groups of macro factors (here labelled Ecological for natural phenomenon and Political and Technological for man-made risks). *Macro factors* are defined as the events that affect organizations but which organizations do not have much influence over, in many cases, none. *Micro factors*, like customers and suppliers, on the other hand, are actions, behaviour, or events that organizations—depending on their size, of course—have some influence over (Fig. 3.1). *Outside influences* are events that affect organizations, but which are non-human, like the weather or a volcano eruption. *Inside influences* are events that originate from humans (Table 3.1).

Given the risks listed in Table 3.1 we can start to do probability calculations of each type of risk happening. It may look something like in Table 3.1 but will change over time, also depending on the level of technology and competence at the times of measurement (Table 3.2).

The research presents a methodology for conducting risk analysis by identifying trigger points that link internal and external influences, potentially signaling existential catastrophes. To make it more realistic, the authors' analysis is grounded in a classification of current risks rather than speculative distant future risks. To effectively predict potential occurrences, a surveillance model must classify emerging risks before they manifest. The model aids in the survey of potential macro factors, focusing on the classification of immediate, tangible risks over those that may lie in the distant future.

[1] A large asteroid or comet struck the Yucatán Peninsula approximately 66 million years ago, leading to the mass extinction of the dinosaurs and many other larger life forms.

[2] Which was just closed as I wrote this, but I am sure there will be others.

[3] **For a full overview, see Söilen and Alipour** (2011).

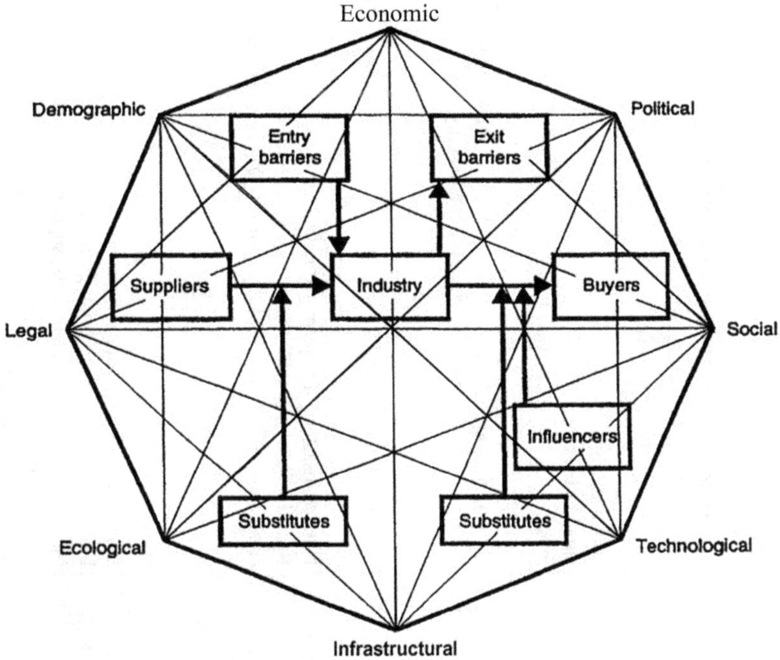

Fig. 3.1 The company's micro and macro environment

3.1.2 Micro and Macro Factors

If we take a closer look at the daily realities of organizations, they are primarily concerned with events that can be classified as macro and micro factors defined above. Jenster and Söilen show a model that presents these factors in a single view (Fig. 3.1):

This model builds on an earlier model by Michael Porter, who introduced the Five Forces model in an influential article in the Harvard Business Review in 1979, focusing on micro factors. A company must pay attention to its customers, of course, but also to those who influence them, referred to as influencers, though note, not in the narrower sense we associate with social media influencers today, but as Trade Associations, Industry Analysts and Media, Investors and Shareholders. Our customers, or buyers, may choose to go elsewhere, to competitors, so it's crucial to keep an eye on all our competitors. Further upstream, we need to develop strong relationships with suppliers and sub-suppliers, both existing and potential (a second form of substitutes in the model). And companies must continually monitor the costs associated with starting and ending a business.

Students are often surprised to learn that there are costs involved in ending a business until they see the full picture of long-term contracts, such as renting office space or machinery. Sometimes, it may be more profitable to continue operating than shutting down the business, at least for a while. We can control these factors to

Table 3.1 Outside and inside influence or risks

Surveillance/ risks	Outside influence (non-human)		Inside influence (human)	
	Risks	Surveillance	Risks	Surveillance
1	All the risks below with/without one another, collaborating in small or bigger groups	Detect via all methods below	All the risks below with/without one another, collaborating in small or bigger groups	Detect via all methods below
	Average $P \geq 0.28$	–	Average $P \geq 0.4$	–
2	Multiple-large scale natural disasters: *hurricanes, fires, Atlantic Tsunamis, earthquakes, acid rains, virus attacks, pandemic, etc.*	Metrological satellites, geological and seismic sensors, medical surveys, etc.	Human climate footprint (*current*)	Industrial BI reports, consumer-producer, ecological effects, biodiversity reports, etc.
	Average $P = 1.0$	OIR^- 4, 5, 6, 7 and/or 1 IIR^- 2-5, and/or 1	Average $P = 1.0$	OIR^+ 2 and/or 1
3	*Hostile extraterrestrials or a cosmological catastrophe (e.g., an ultimate space-time dimensional rip)*	Could happen anytime by altering space-time fabric; we refer to speculative reports, hypotheses, observatories or other means of current space and time technologies	Nuclear disaster footprint (*less concurrent*)	Frequent geopolitical, and real-time security reports, via surveillance, intelligence organizations, databases, etc.
	Average $P = 0.5$	OIR^+ 8 and/or 1	Average $P = 0.75$	OIR^+ 2 and/or 1
4	*Super-volcanoes*	Detect through geological sensors and current reports on surface + underground Earth activities	Synthetic biology (*less concurrent*)	Medical reports and current biotechnological hazardous developments, super bacteria, etc.
	Average $P = 0.00000082$	OIR^+ 2 and/or 1; OIR^- 2, 5 and/or 1	Average $P \geq 0.5$	OIR^+ 2

5	*Asteroids or deadly impact*	Detect through satellite before impact; non-compensable after impact relative to reduction risk reports like Matheny (2007), or migration to elsewhere, below surface or other planets	Physics experiments (*less concurrent*)	Energy physics reports, probability impact reports on subatomic strangelet possibilities (*strange matter*)
	Average $P = 0.00000002$	OIR^{+} 4, and/or 2	Average $P = 0.08$	OIR^{+} 1
6	*Sun's death or a nearby collapsing star (supernova)*	Detect through satellite telescopes; non- compensable on a global scale after death.	Machine Super Intelligence or AI (*N/A to current, or to be in a distant future*)	Currently unavailable or sci-fi material, but might be developed in the future as a new risk; academic research reports and patented inventions on paper
	Average $P \approx 0$	OIR^{+} 1–5 and/or 8	Average $P \approx 0$	IIR^{+} 1
7	*Anomalies between all the above and below risks, their correlation and time/order of occurrence!* $P > 0$		Psychological large-scale mass suicide/ systematic or collective genocide (*current*)	Psychological profiles and cases of mass suicides via e.g., psychological warfare, media, religion, etc.
			Average $P = 0.0000277$	IIR^{-}1 and/or OIR^{-}1
8	*Other unknown outside risks*	Hidden	*Other unknown inside risks*	Hidden
	Average $P = 0.5$		Average $P = 0.5$	

This is a 8-by-8 summary surveillance table on risks as inside and outside influence, their trends and relationships
Legend: OIR^{+} could result in one or more outside influence risk(s), respectively, IIR^{+} is for inside influence risk, OIR^{-} could be triggered by certain outside influence risk(s), respectively, IIR^{-} is for inside influence risk, P probability

Table 3.2 Disaster-related issues with probabilistic impacts, indexed in our real-time surveillance system

No.	Disaster-related issue	Causes issue	Global impact	Concern level	Impact probability	Occurred	Controlled
1	Asteroid *a.* size = 10–50 m	0	0%	2	0.2	+	+
	b. 100 m	0	1-to-1.66%	3	0.001	+	–
	c. 1–2 km	{2,3,4,7}	100%	4	0.00001	+	–
	d. 15 km	{2,3,4,7}	∞	5	0.00000002	Δ	Δ
2	Large-scale earthquakes *a.* Average of 2.7 years (1968–1987)	0	0.01%	5	1	+	–
	b. Average of 2.4 years + hurricanes (1988–2005)	0	1%	5	1	+	–
	c. similar frequency with more coincidence 2005–1010	0	5%	5	1	+	–
	d. similar frequency with greater human population under effect (2010…)	0	5%$^{+}$	5	1	+	–
	e. So many earthquakes consecutively	{3,7}	∞	5	1	Δ	Δ
	f. So many earthquakes simultaneously	{3,7}	∞	5	1	Δ	Δ
3	Super-volcano *a.* Every 60,000 years	{4,7}	∞	5	0.0000014	+	–
	b. Yellowstone	{4,7}	∞	5	0.00000024	Δ	Δ
4	Climate Change *a.* 1960	{2, 7}	10%	4	1	+	–
	b. 1970	{2, 7}	25%	4	0.8	+	–
	c. 1980	{2, 7}	50%	5	0.3	Δ	Δ
	d. 1990	{2, 7}	75%	5	0.05	Δ	Δ
	e. 2000	{2.7}	90%	5	0.25	Δ	Δ
	f. 2005	{2, 7}	100%	5	0.1	Δ	Δ

5	Human Footprint *a.* 1975	{4,6,7}	100%	2	1	+	–
	b. 1985	{4,6,7}	110%	3	1	+	–
	c. 1995	{4,6,7}	124%	4	1	+	–
	d. 2000	{4,6,7}	129%	4	1	+	–
	e. 2005	{4,6,7}	145%	5	1	+	–
	f. 2008	{4,6,7}	151%	5	1	+	–
	g. 2012	{4,6,7}	175%	5	1	Δ	Δ
	h. 2014	{4,6,7}	200%	5	1	Δ	Δ
	i. 2014^+	{4,6,7}	∞	5	1	Δ	Δ
6	Nuclear Disaster Footprint *a.* Hiroshima and Nagasaki	0	1%	5	1	+	–
	b. Chernobyl = 400 Hiroshima bombs	0	1%	5	1	+	–
	c. Global Nuclear War = 30,000 warheads	{2,3,4}	∞	5	0.5	Δ	Δ
	d. Instant human annihilation = 1.24 million warheads	{2,3,4}	∞	5	0.5	Δ	Δ
7	Other probabilities: Multiple large-scale *hurricanes, fires, earthquakes, acid rains, pandemic, etc.*	0	∞	5	1	Δ	Δ
8	Earth's collapse as a black hole (*physics experiments*)	0	∞	5	0.08	–	Δ
9	Sun's death or nearby supernovae or black hole	{1-to-6, 8}	∞	5	0.5	–	Δ
10	Cosmological impacts	{1-to-6, 8, 9}	∞	5	0.5	–	Δ

Legend: (–) = No; (+) = Yes; Δ = Not yet or circumstantial; ∞ = Infinite impact or a set of effects indicating a global catastrophe; 0 = Yields no other issue or the consequent global impact is minute otherwise infinite

Note: The numbering (No.) is not based on risk priority like Table 3.1, since Table 3.1 is the deduction summary of the analysis made in Table 3.2. Therefore, the current table representation is of probability analysis leading to the classification of risks based on priority as well as the acquisition of incoming information on risks for the KOS

a smaller or larger extent. Normally, we have more control upstream since this involves our suppliers, compared to downstream, which involves our customers.

When it comes to macro factors, companies must constantly monitor new and existing laws and regulations that affect their business. In marketing, we identify the potential of new markets using demographic data, social trends, and developments in technologies, such as a new plugin for an AI service. Macro factors, like the change in interest rates by a central bank, infrastructure developments that may impact our supply lines, and political factors, such as the potential for a new government with different agendas, are crucial. As seen above, we must not overlook the growing concern over ecological issues, as human activities increasingly impact our natural environment. Larger companies, in particular, need to vigilantly monitor all these factors to survive and remain competitive in the marketplace.

We are now ready to leave the overall perspectives and start the sometimes-tedious work of learning to gather and analyze data.

4 The Science of Intelligence Studies

After we have obtained the perspective of what it is we are going to look at—the variables—we want to get down to the actual details of what to do as fast as possible, to the analytical work. To help with this, this chapter presents a number of components of what is meant by and is needed for performing intelligence analysis. We call this the Top-Down Analytical Approach.

4.1 The Distinction Between Intelligence, Information and Data

As Shapiro reminds us, it is uncommon to find a company that fully understands the implications of the Information Age: companies gain their competitive edge based on how well they handle information.[1] The marketing department prefers to focus on marketing activities, and the production department focuses on manufacturing products; neither is particularly eager or equipped to specialize in information management. Most employees view their roles through the lens of daily tasks such as meetings, purchasing new equipment, and monitoring competitors' advertising. The information is often unstructured and seldom analyzed formally. Businesspeople are typically action-oriented, which has its advantages and disadvantages. Many avoid or dread the moment they must sit down to write a report to meet a specific deadline. As such, we could say that many have not fully embraced the Information Age, despite being a part of it for decades already and spending a significant amount of their time exchanging information.

In Intelligence Studies we make a clear distinction between intelligence, information and data:

[1] Shapiro and Varian (1998).

K. Solberg Söilen, *Intelligence Studies in Business*, Management for Professionals,
https://doi.org/10.1007/978-3-031-76491-2_4

- Data: Loose bits of communicative sign, reduced to sentences, numbers, codes: in writing, visual or verbal.
- Information: Gathering of data to sentences which express ideas.
- Intelligence: Actionable information, (the veins in an organization)

One of the main problems in any organization, whether private or public, is that there is too much information and too little intelligence, or, said differently, too much *nice-to-know* and too little *need-to-know*. A major task for any intelligence organization is to make sure that employees are not wasting valuable time *discussing* information. Information should instead be seen as something that is discarded—*set aside* —through a process of sorting and analyzing. The product, or what we want to end up with, is called Intelligence. Think again about the Venetian ambassadors as the Doge acquires what is happening in England. Imagine the situation: There is no time for small talk; we have to cut to the chase as we look up at this man in his richly decorated robe and distinctive corno ducale.

To differentiate between the intelligence gained from simply reading information versus the intelligence derived from a detailed analysis of that information, we use the terms 'raw intelligence' and 'analyzed intelligence', respectively. Raw Intelligence (RI) refers to data or information collected from various sources that has not yet been processed or analyzed. It includes the direct information obtained from reading, observation, or initial reports. Raw intelligence is unprocessed, possibly unverified, and may include a mix of relevant and irrelevant data, focusing primarily on gathering and compiling. On the other hand, analyzed Intelligence (AI) refers to the intelligence produced after raw data has been processed, evaluated, and analyzed to extract actionable insights. This form of intelligence is refined, contextualized, and often synthesized to reveal trends, patterns, or insights not apparent in the raw data alone.

Data are simple elements like '2', 'k', and 'p'. Information is data composed into meaningful constructs, such as 'Dell is today the most successful American PC company.' (true, or not). However, intelligence aids in making strategic decisions, potentially reading as 'Dell's competitive advantage lies in cost cutting.' Note that what constitutes intelligence for one organization may not do so for another. If your organizational decisions are unaffected by such information, it is not intelligence for you. However, this could be vital intelligence for a company like HP or any of Dell's competitors. Knowing that Dell's primary competitive advantage is pricing could prompt further strategic questions like: 'Can we produce computers at the same price?' or, if not, 'Can we identify other competitive advantages that may increase our sales, such as better service, faster machines, or better color screens?' In intelligence work, we engage in a sort of Socratic dialogue, which involves a series of simple yet pointed questions and answers.

Data, information, and intelligence can collectively be referred to as Intelligence Products, or simply as Intelligence, each associated with specific actions: Collection, Sorting, Analysis, and Decision-making. The relationship between these stages can be illustrated as follows (Fig. 4.1):

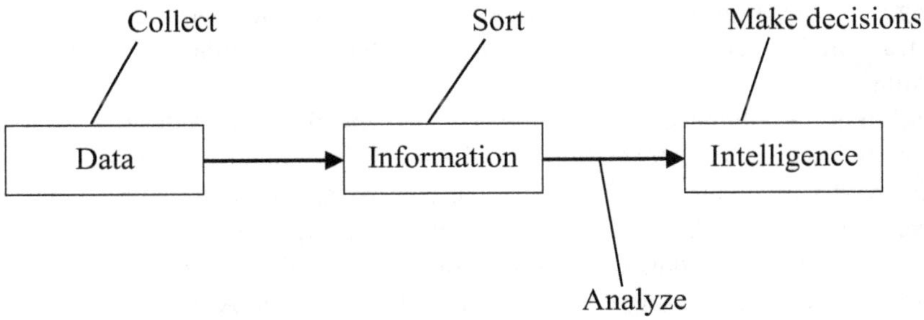

Fig. 4.1 From data to intelligence—with corresponding activities

We begin by posing questions. Data collection follows, driven by the investigative problem at hand. These data are transformed into information and sorted. The information deemed valuable progresses to analysis. The conclusions derived from this analysis are termed 'intelligence,' serving as the foundation for decision-making. If the intelligence is robust and the leadership competent, the organization can make more informed decisions.

Ideally, leaders should not exhaust time seeking information; their primary role is decision-making. However, it often happens that leaders act more as intelligence officers than decision-makers due to the lack of a supporting system that provides relevant intelligence. This may be because the organization believes it cannot afford such a function, lacks the necessary expertise, undervalues its importance, or struggles with organizational setup. It may also be that some managers or leaders simply enjoy finding the information themselves and do not rely on or trust others to do it.

4.1.1 Principal-Agent Model (PAM)

Intelligence involves defining questions and seeking answers. We can describe this interaction using the Principal-Agent model (PAM), where the principal poses questions and the agent responds. These roles might exist within the same organization or encompass a customer and client relationship. The questioning process typically initiates with the principal, who contacts the agent to discuss an area of interest, usually framed by several questions. The agent records these and engages in a dialogue to pinpoint the exact questions needing answers.

It often surprises students (less often practitioners) to learn that the principal will not always understand his or her own informational needs. This reality underscores the agent's crucial role in helping refine and sometimes redefine the questions, reflecting the principal's underlying concerns. The principal may also alter his or her focus during the intelligence process, underscoring the importance of formulating the right questions rather than hastening to answer less relevant ones.

The agent must resist the temptation to shape the questions based on personal knowledge or bias, particularly when less familiar with the problem than the principal. This influence can skew the intelligence process. Often, the principal involves the agent in question formulation to leverage his experience and judgment, reflecting trust in his analytical capabilities. This delicate dynamic requires careful handling.

In foreign intelligence services, the agent is typically an outsider who resides in the country where the information is gathered. This individual may collect intelligence overtly as a consultant or covertly as a secret agent, often risking their career or even life if detected. In these cases, the principal typically risks little or nothing personally, except for damage to their conscience if the agent is sent to jail, or worse. An agent may be active or a so-called Sleeper Agent: A spy placed in a target country or organization but not activated until needed. If the agent is active he may become a mole, an insider within an organization, typically a government agency, military, or corporation, who is secretly working for an adversary. Moles are often recruited and placed in their positions because they have access to valuable and sensitive information. Active agents may take years to get similar access.

When an agent secretly switches allegiance without revealing it, they are called a double agent. Double agents are extremely harmful as they can access and exploit the intelligence systems of the country they pretend to serve, while actually providing information to the adversary. Such agents are often subject to severe punishments by their intelligence services, including assassination, even on foreign soil, as seen in the case of Alexander Litvinenko, who was poisoned in London. Operations involving assassinations are often referred to as wet work.

An Intelligence Team (IT), group or unit, especially in state intelligence services in general, whether international or domestic, consists of two distinct roles that we call intelligence agents and intelligence officers (handlers). The agent is a front-line worker whose job is to gather information, often using HUMINT, located in a foreign country or working domestically but in charge of a specific foreign country, industry or market. In the public sector, the agent often works without disclosing his identity. In private organizations, this practice is mostly considered immoral, and many companies have conduct guidelines that try to regulate the practice. In the chapter about ethics at the end of the book, we will revisit PAM in connection with the larger moral questions and what is called the 'Diversification of Moral Risk'.

PAM operates as an ongoing process, not a one-time activity. It is often likened to a dance, where questions are sent and answers are received, which in turn generate new questions. This back-and-forth interaction is facilitated by technology today, allowing us to define the main roles as follows:

1. Principal (Manager): Requests specific intelligence or data insights.
2. Agent (AI-driven Database): Acts on these requests by querying relevant data from business intelligence technologies.
3. Intelligence Technology (IT): Processes data and returns analyzed intelligence back to the principal.

In today's IT-driven organizations, the IT function very much resembles a Help Desk, and the agent will be an AI-driven database, much like Wikipedia, Google, or ChatGPT. As always, ITs are only as good as the people who work there. However, a structured approach to the intelligence function will increase the team's performance and enable them to provide management with better grounds for decisions.

This "dance" represents a continuous flow of information and intelligence between the requester (principal) and the provider (agent), facilitated by the technology. The principal makes decisions based on the intelligence received, which can involve strategic business moves or operational adjustments.

To express the Principal-Agent Model (PAM) mathematically, we can define it in terms of functions and variables that represent the interactions between the principal and the agent. Here's a simplified representation:

Let's denote:

- P as the Principal who initiates the query.
- A as the Agent who processes the query.
- Q as the Query or intelligence request from the Principal.
- I as the Intelligence or output generated by the Agent.
- f as the function representing the Agent's process of converting the query into intelligence.

Mathematically, the interaction can be described by the function: $I = f(Q)$

Where:

- Q is input by the Principal P.
- f represents the process where the Agent A processes Q and produces I.
- I is the output used by the Principal P to make informed decisions.

This function f encompasses the data querying, analysis, and intelligence synthesis processes undertaken by the Agent. It simplifies the conceptualization of how requests are transformed into actionable intelligence within an organization.

4.1.2 The Intelligence Cycle in Its Different Forms

Intelligence teams are composed of various specialized functions working together in a process called the intelligence cycle. This cycle involves different roles: some team members collect intelligence, others perform analysis, and dissemination can be handled by an agent, a dedicated person, or via a webpage.

The most common form of dissemination in state intelligence is the briefing; a concise, structured presentation of information and analysis, typically delivered to decision-makers or stakeholders to inform them about specific topics or issues relevant to national security, military operations, or other critical areas. The purpose of a briefing is to ensure that the recipients are well-informed and able to make decisions based on the most current and accurate information available.

An intelligence briefing is characterized by its focused content, centering on a specific topic, issue, or threat. It provides relevant background information, analysis, and implications. The briefing is concise, presenting key points clearly and efficiently, often using visual aids like slides or charts to enhance understanding. Clarity is paramount, with the information presented in a logical manner. Additionally, the briefing includes actionable insights, offering assessments, recommendations, and potential courses of action based on the analyzed information.

Intelligence briefings are used in various contexts. During crisis situations, they provide critical updates and assessments to guide immediate decision-making. They are essential in operational planning, ensuring all relevant parties are informed about current intelligence, potential risks, and strategic options before launching military operations or strategic initiatives. There may also be briefings when a military operation fails, what is called Blowbacks (like the Bay of Pigs in 1961). Policymakers rely on briefings to stay updated on the latest intelligence concerning national security, foreign policy, or economic stability. Routine updates keep leaders and stakeholders informed about ongoing intelligence assessments and developments. In advisory meetings, such as those of national security councils or defense committees, briefings offer the necessary context and information for informed discussion and decision-making.

There are compelling arguments for assigning the same person the responsibilities of both planning and dissemination. This approach helps close the loop in the intelligence cycle, ensuring that the individual responsible for dissemination remains closely connected with the decision-maker, thus enhancing the overall effectiveness and coherence of the intelligence process. Besides that, an intelligence team may consist of anything between 2 and 100+ persons, as when a nation faces a major and specific threat, like when a foreign nation directs cyber-attacks to steal sensitive information or disrupt critical infrastructure.

Once the agent has documented the questions, he should review them with the principal to ensure his or her understanding of what is expected. This step helps prevent miscommunications. If the initial questions are incorrect—common when the principal and agent lack rapport—the entire effort may be wasted. Only when the correct questions are confirmed should the organization proceed to the next stages of the Intelligence Cycle: Collection, or Information Gathering (Fig. 4.2).

The "Mission" in the center is a parallel to a company's strategy.[2] The work with the cycle is improved by a continuous process of evaluations and feedback.

There are many versions of the intelligence cycle. The simplest one consists of four parts:

(1). *Direction*, the determination of requirements and preparation of the plan for information gathering. (2). *Collation or Accumulation*, the actual gathering and delivery of information to analysts. (3). *Incubation or Elevation*, the extracting of intelligence from information through analysis, and (4). *Presentation or Dissemination*, the delivery of intelligence to decision-makers. It is often illustrated as a wheel or circle to make a point out of the fact that it is an ongoing

[2] In business life a mission has a completely different meaning, namely what the values of the company are, what it believes in.

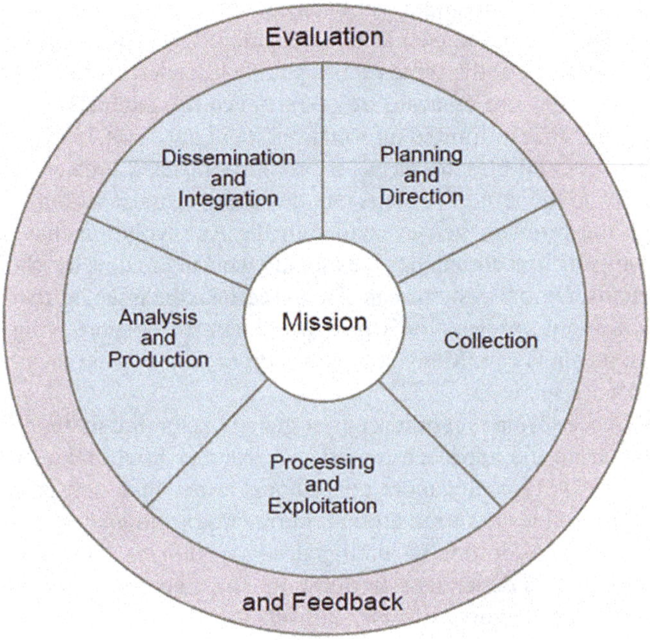

Fig. 4.2 The intellgence cycle. (Source: Joint Intelligence/Joint Publication 2.0 (Joint Chiefs of Staff))

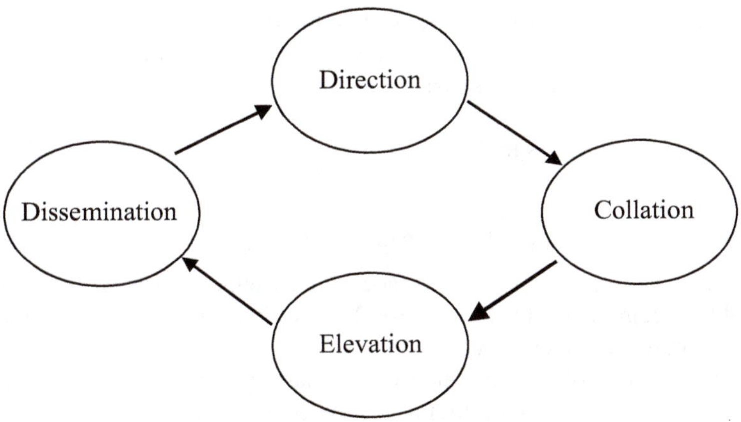

Fig. 4.3 The intelligence cycle

process, and that the analyst takes his experience with him or her for each new turn (Fig. 4.3).

One of the most challenging aspects of the Intelligence Cycle is ensuring that intelligence reaches the right person at the right time. Often, the necessary intelligence exists within the organization but fails to reach those who need it most. The complexity of this issue cannot be overstated. Organizations frequently purchase multiple versions of the same report, yet the intended manager may never see it simply because they are unaware of its existence. Economists often discuss the concept of 'asymmetric or limited information.' In many cases, knowing what information we possess and how to access it promptly poses a greater challenge than gathering it. While modern IT systems are designed to assist with this, they do not entirely solve the problem yet, even though the AI revolution that we have just entered is promising and companies are already working to develop their own internal LLM systems. Digital systems can also exacerbate the issue, as there is no physical indication of the information's presence, such as a report lying around that might catch someone's eye. Many companies do not know what they have because they simply cannot see it.

The Intelligence Cycle is reminiscent of general scientific methodologies, yet it differs notably from the approach a market researcher might take. In intelligence work, the process is typically more continuous, rather than consisting of one-off assignments. It is often structured around routine tasks and includes more stringent control mechanisms. Additionally, intelligence work utilizes a broader array of analytical methods, is less dependent on questionnaires, encompasses a wider scope, and generally demands a more diverse skill set.

There is another aspect that plays in here, time. There is a time lapse between when a piece of intelligence is created or recorded and when it is used to consider. A source may sit unused for an extended period, merely as information. When it is finally utilized, time is required to produce the report. After the report is made, additional time is needed for it to be read and understood, and from reading to its actual application in decision-making. This timeline, which represents a process, can be expressed mathematically as:

Equation 4.1 Time lapses in the intelligence cycle.

$$\Delta t_{\text{total}} = t_{\text{creation}} + t_{\text{storage}} + t_{\text{processing}} + t_{\text{reading}} + t_{\text{decision-making}}$$

Where each term represents the time spent in different stages of the intelligence cycle, adding complexity to the process. By the time the report is completed the intelligence may no longer be required.

We refer to this problem as "Intelligence Latency" or "Temporal Delays in the Intelligence Cycle." This issue highlights the time lapse between the creation or recording of intelligence and its eventual application in decision-making.

Intelligence Latency encompasses several stages:

1. Creation and Recording: The initial generation of intelligence information.
2. Dormancy Period: The time during which the intelligence remains unused.
3. Processing Time: The period required to produce an intelligence report from the raw data.

4. Dissemination and Comprehension: The time needed for the report to be distributed, read, and understood.
5. Decision-Making Application: The final stage where the intelligence is actually utilized in decision-making processes.

Each of these stages adds to the overall delay, which can result in the intelligence becoming outdated or irrelevant by the time it is used. This latency poses a significant challenge in maintaining the effectiveness and timeliness of intelligence operations.

To conclude, the practical application of the Intelligence Cycle varies from one organization to another, influenced by the industry, whether it is private or public, and whether it pertains to state or military sectors. However, the level of commitment and effort invested in the intelligence function is the most critical factor. Less ambitious organizations might apply the Intelligence Cycle on an ad hoc basis, allowing significant autonomy to individual analysts. Another problem with the IC is that it is not always used in practice, not in a structured way.[3] Instead, it often serves more as a mental map, in a fuzzy-logic kind of way.

An organization's success in the Information Age depends crucially on its ability to distinguish between mere information and actionable intelligence. Implementing an effective intelligence system, where establishing a robust process is just one component, is essential. The ability to filter information—identifying what is relevant and what is not—is key to strategic decision-making and gaining a competitive advantage. Our discussion in this chapter starts with global events, which we interpret as pieces of intelligence. These events are significant when they serve as causes that lead to effects, akin to the scientific method. We analyze these events across different timelines—past, present, and future—to fully grasp their implications, but to get there we must first try to handle events in a more structured way.

4.2 The Science of Events[4]

Understanding the structure or Science of Events in intelligence involves analyzing occurrences and their implications systematically. Events, in this context, refer to significant happenings that can impact the operational environment of an organization or state.

[3] Hoppe (2015) suggests that "the IC follows a political logic, not the logic of empirical description. As with the IC, the idea of an ideal informative flow has political value, and it will also most likely live on for a long time", p. 54.

[4] A special thanks to my former student, Philip Baback Alipour, for valuable input to this part of the book.

4.2.1 Evaluating Future Outcomes

We want to know the likelihood of something happening, expressed as events (E).

We start with a present event (PEn), like a specific news story (PE^1). Events can be manmade or the result of nature, PE^M or PE^N. Natural events are easier to predict because they follow the laws of physics, like a weather forecast.

Events can be classified as either essential or trivial, depending on their importance to an organization. What is critical for one organization may not be for another, as they typically have different strategies and objectives. We are not concerned with trivial events here. Significant events are referred to as 'intelligence,' meaning events that affect an organization's strategy, such as if a competitor raises their prices. If a junior employee in a large organization is late for work because his car broke down, this event is trivial for the organization but may be crucial, for the individual, as he risks getting a warning if it is repeated. However, the latter case is not considered 'intelligence' for the organization.

We can take a different approach to determine whether an event is a piece of intelligence for the larger society. We can ask: How many people (x-axis) does it affect in a given geographical location (region, country, globally)? To what extent does it affect each person (y-axis)? Thus (Fig. 4.4):

In the figure above, we see three examples of present events (PE). The facts, effects, pieces of intelligence, or events (E) themselves can be categorized into economic, political, and social (1) and security (2). The first category can jeopardize our comfort, while the second can threaten our very existence. Although the first event can lead to the second, in most cases, it does not. For example, severe economic depression can lead to starvation. It's crucial to distinguish between these types of events, as nation-states have different organizations to address various problems; for instance, in the US for example, the Treasury handles the first type of issues, and the War Department manages the second.

There is another way of determining what constitutes intelligence for a society from an economic perspective, used throughout this book. It involves asking to what

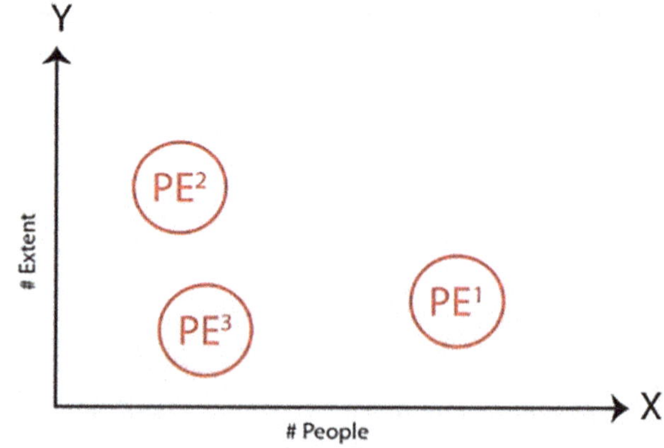

Fig. 4.4 Assessing if an event is important for an organization or society

extent an event affects the competitive advantage of that country. A country may not have a written strategy, but it will have national interests that align with the interests of its major companies. This alignment is because all countries depend on the output of their factories and the services they sell and products exported to achieve a certain standard of living (if it does not depend on foreign aid and loans, that is).

Then there are historic events (HE^n), what have happened earlier. This is what we find in our history books and in old newspapers we may have kept, things that have happened in the past, which may or may not be relevant today. Then there are Future events (FE^n), that may happen in the future. HE can be found to the extent that they are recorded. Given that they have been proven and are not just speculations, the probability that they happened is 1,0. FE are unknown as they have not happened yet. As soon as they happen, they become PE and then HE. For the sake of simplicity, we can say that PEs become HEs when they are no longer current events that are discussed or when new, more significant effects of the same causes arise. We may be talking days or weeks, but it can also be longer, like in the case of a war. A war affects the whole of society for as long as it continues, but there will be events in that war that are no longer discussed and thus passed over as HEs as new and larger events take their place.

In a much-mentioned example, the US claimed Iraq had weapons of mass destruction, $P = 1$, which led to the war in 2003. The intelligence was wrong, so the value was actually zero, or close to zero. There must have been some analysts within the CIA who knew this, probably many, but they were overruled, for political reasons, we must assume. It could be argued that this claim was based on 'groupthink,' and the absence or refusal to allow for a scientific method to forecast events. A scientific method would have detected whether what was claimed to be events was merely speculation, even with what probability it was a speculation. The intelligence report, when done properly, classifies information as false intelligence for lacking the elements necessary to counterargue the event as hypothetically nonexistent, P as $P = 0$, or for failing to prove the existence of those weapons, $E(t < 0)$ to be $E(t < 0)$ to be $P = 0$. This approach is also known as the null hypothesis, denoted by H' (or H_0). This hypothesis asserts that the quantity to be measured is zero (null). This quantity, when measured, represents the difference between two scenarios. For instance, it is used to determine if there is positive proof that an effect has occurred or if samples originate from different batches (Fig. 4.5).

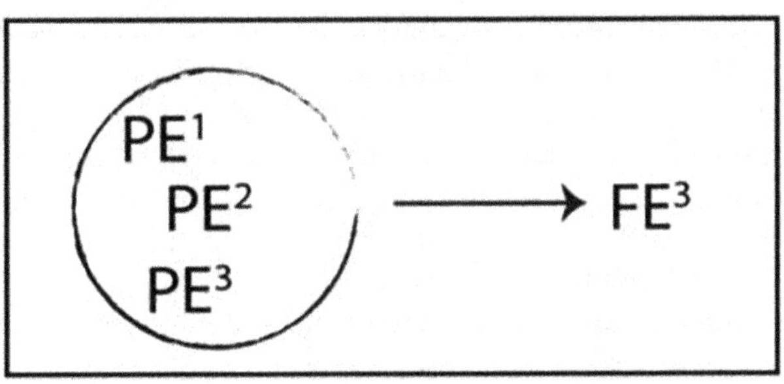

Fig. 4.5 Trying to predict future events (FE)

In the figure above, we see three observations of present events that lead to a future event. We use the term 'predicting,' not 'guessing.' Guessing would be akin to randomly drawing ideas out of a hat without any systematic method of analysis. In guessing, we rely entirely on our imagination. (Let's set aside 'educated guessing' for now.) As such, guessing has no place in intelligence work. What people often refer to as guessing is, at best, based on some underlying ideas and experiences that have not yet been clearly articulated. This is normal; the brain works quickly and produces what seem like hunches before we can articulate those reactions in words. So, these 'guesses' are—hopefully—not truly guesses, but due to a delay in time, the time it takes us to express our ideas when it is shown that they are supported by arguments.

To predict the likelihood of a future event (FE[1]), we first need to consider as many possible future events as we can related to the area of interest we are examining. These events should be realistic; we are not interested in merely generating any kind of ideas. To determine if they are realistic, we engage in a work process where we initially come up with ideas independently, and then, in the second phase, sit down with colleagues who have done the same. Together, we discuss which future events are realistic, named Realistic Possible Events or a Realistic Possible Future Event. For practical reasons, we shall simply call them Future Events as an event that happens immediately becomes a Present Event. Said differently all possible future events regarding human behavior are speculations. For natural phenomena, we can make accurate predictions, or very close to it, like for the weather or the impact of a comet on its way towards the earth. To come up with a set of realistic events to a discussion requires that all participants have completed some groundwork before coming to the meeting rather than during it, to avoid the risk that the outcome will resemble a compromise between group members, which would undermine the value of having independent experts.

When group members meet, no one member should request another expert to dismiss a possible future event; however, an expert may choose to withdraw a possible future event themselves upon hearing counterarguments from other group members. We aim to compile as large a database of potential future events as possible, provided they are realistic. We call this process Collaborative Scenario Exploration.

We then assign a weight (w) to each FE depending on its importance, as previously described. This importance varies depending on whether it impacts our strategy as an organization, or in the case of a state, how many people are affected and to what extent. Note that this is not the same as the probability of the FE occurring.

Much discussion of cause and effect in the social sciences, shows how one cause leads to one effect. This is not realistic, of course. Instead, an effect is often the result of several causes and one or several causes result in one or several effects. For example, a company decides to increase the price of a good because of higher salaries, higher costs of electricity and higher interest rates on bank loans to the company. It's not the higher salaries by themselves that lead to this consequence, but in the end, adding one cause to another, the decision is made. Technically, it's the one last cause (triggering cause) that becomes too much, forcing the company to increase the process of a good, but it's not the triggering cause that leads to the decision by itself; they do so jointly. The other causes are referred to as "supporting causes". Supporting causes plus triggering cause is what causes the decision or the event (pundit intended):

Equation 4.2 The relationship between causes and events.

$$C^{s} + C^{t} = E^{1}$$

These causes and effects are also events to the extent that they happen. So far, we have classified Events into historic, current and future events.[5]

4.2.2 Advancing Event Prediction: Integrating Human Experience and Potential Events with Advanced Computing

Computers are good at gathering, storing, and analyzing large amounts of HE, PC and possible FE. With Large Language Models (LLM) they can speculate or suggest possible FEs. To reduce the amount of uncertainty and information in predicting events, we can use computation of events using quantum and classical computers via hybrid computers.

A case example: The invasion of a foreign power is defined by the country attacked as:

$$PE^{1}$$

Using the scale of weight:

$$PE^{1} : g^{1}\left(8-10\right)$$

And if it has not yet happened:

$$FE^{1} : g^{1}\left(8-10\right)$$

Meaning for the event (invasion), the value is for a given geography (g^1) defined as the country attacked, an 8 for "economic, political and social" impact and a 10 on "security" impact, on a scale from 0 to 10. The weight (w) is the consequence of something happening, not the likelihood of it happening (p).

Many social sciences, like Economics, look at events separately. This leads to the researcher quickly losing the realistic perspective (despite the *ceteris paribus* warning), and our results are less likely to be valuable. Instead, we encourage another method whereby events are studied together, both HEs and PEs to predict FEs. The reason is that this is the way our brain works when making decisions. It also means

[5] Per Frankelius goes further in explaining the different kinds and nature of events in a chain of events in what he calls Factor X-modeling. See Frankelius (2001).

that we can only operate with a limited number of variables. With the increasing use of computers, humans are expected to make decisions based on complex datasets, but this not true yet, even though large databases are used. However, this will change with the development of AI in the years to come. We do not like making decisions out of a black box but want to grasp the essentials ourselves. In future, we may have to rely more on our confidence in the system and the method, which is not an ideal situation, but we will have to build in numerous checks and balances and some sort of clearinghouse control mechanisms for AI-generated content.[6]

A thinking process may look like this, considering both HEs and PEs (Fig. 4.6):

Based on two historical events HE^1 and HE^3, and a present event PE^1 we make a prediction about a future event FE^1. This is simple enough. The value of the model is that it helps us communicate to others what events we are choosing in our reasoning and which once we are discarding. This makes discussions easier and more structured, like "why did you not consider HE^2, PE^3?". You then have to defend your choice with real arguments.

4.2.3 The Likelihood of an Event

There is no 1.0 likelihood of a future event for human behavior (M), that is PE^M, but only for nature (N), PE^N, as we can never be fully certain of anything that includes human behavior, because it is too complex, at least for human mental abilities. Thus, there cannot be a science for man as there is for nature done by man, but we can come closer to finding future events by following certain rules of thinking. If an event is more likely not to happen, we say:

$$FE^1 < 0.5$$

Or, the probability that FE^1 happens is less than 50%. We shall use a division starting with Sherman Kent to denote grades of certainty, using a seven-grade scale to allow for neutral value (Table 4.1):

A nine-grade scale allows for more exact numbers with a difference of 0.125, but it is also more difficult to assess the difference between a level 6, 7 and 8, and a 2, 3 and 4.

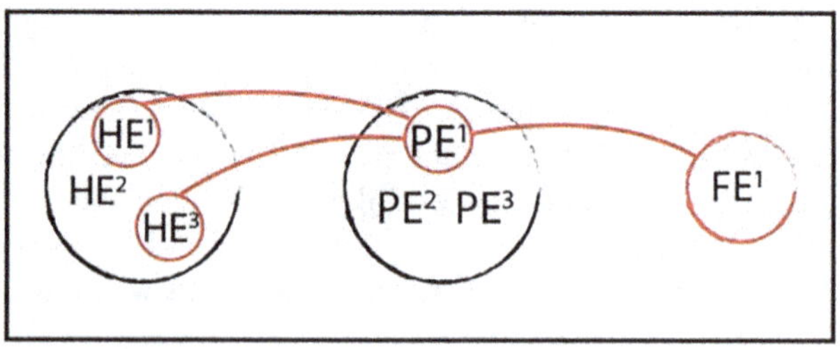

Fig. 4.6 Studying events in relation to each other

[6] Söilen (2024).

Table 4.1 Grades of certainty

#	Probability	Term	Description
1.	1,0 = 100%	Certain	There is absolute certainty. The event will happen without any doubt.
2.	0.875	Almost certain	Extremely high likelihood. While not absolutely guaranteed, it is expected to occur in nearly all scenarios.
3.	0.75	Highly Likely	Significantly more probable than not. The event is expected to occur in most situations but is not a foregone conclusion
4.	0.6125	Probable	More likely to occur than not. There is a better than even chance that the event will happen.
5.	0.5	Probably not	There is a 50-50 likelihood. The event is just as likely to happen as not to happen.
6.	0.375	Possibly Not:	Slightly more unlikely than likely. There is a small tendency towards the event not occurring, but it's close to even chances.
7.	0.25	Probably Not	More unlikely than likely. While there is some chance of the event occurring, it is more expected not to happen.
8.	0.125	Almost Certainly Not	Extremely unlikely. While not completely impossible, the event is expected not to occur in nearly all scenarios.
9.	0	Impossible	There is absolute certainty against. The event will not happen under any normal circumstances.

4.2.4 Using Probability Calculations

The Brier Score is a measure used to evaluate the accuracy of probabilistic predictions.

Example: Weather Forecasting

Imagine you're a weather forecaster, and over a period of 5 days, you make predictions about whether it will rain or not. For each day, you provide a probability of rain.

Predictions and Outcomes:

Day 1

Prediction: 70% chance of rain (0.7 in probability terms)

Actual Outcome: It rains (represented as 1)

Day 2

Prediction: 20% chance of rain (0.2)

Actual Outcome: It doesn't rain (represented as 0)

Day 3

Prediction: 60% chance of rain (0.6)

Actual Outcome: It rains (1)

Day 4

Prediction: 30% chance of rain (0.3)

Actual Outcome: It doesn't rain (0)

Day 5

Prediction: 80% chance of rain (0.8)
Actual Outcome: It doesn't rain (0)

Calculating the Brier Score:
The Brier Score is calculated by taking the mean of the squared differences between predicted probabilities and the actual outcomes. For each prediction, calculate (*predicted probability – actual outcome*). Then, average these values over all predictions.

Let's calculate this:

Day 1: (0.7–1)2 = 0.09(0.7–1)2 = 0.09
Day 2: (0.2–0)2 = 0.04(0.2–0)2 = 0.04
Day 3: (0.6–1)2 = 0.16(0.6–1)2 = 0.16
Day 4: (0.3–0)2 = 0.09(0.3–0)2 = 0.09
Day 5: (0.8–0)2 = 0.64(0.8–0)2 = 0.64
Average of these values: [(0.09 + 0.04 + 0.16 + 0.09 + 0.64)/5] = 0.204

Interpreting the Score:
The Brier Score ranges from 0 to 1, with 0 being a perfect score (perfect predictions) and 1 being the worst score. In this example, a score of 0.204 suggests a reasonable level of accuracy, but there is room for improvement. If we were 100% correct the Brier score is 0. If we are 100% wrong, it will be 1,0.

The Brier Score is useful because it considers the magnitude of errors and whether the predicted events occurred. The Brier score tells you how good you are at predicting; it does not tell you how to predict. We can't know exactly what the likelihood of something happening is because human behavior is, as said before, simply too complex; there are too many variables and options for each step in the line of cause and effect, but we can do some estimates. These estimates must be based on present and past events:

Equation 4.3 Calculating events using the Brier score.

$$\mathrm{FE}^1 = \mathrm{PE}^1 + \mathrm{HE}^1$$

The events must be set in a context. To access this context, we use our previous knowledge.

4.2.5 Using Previous Knowledge to Estimate the Likelihood of Events

Previous knowledge can be divided into primary and secondary sources, where the primary is our own experience, and the secondary is the experience of others. The experiences of others come mostly in the form of books and writings, which we gain access to primarily through our education, but we can also be self-taught (autodidact). The education most useful for predicting future events is, in my opinion, history (past events), literature (possible events), and news (current events). Literature also teaches us much about human psychology, which is important when we analyze decision-makers, like the heads of foreign states (profiling). We need geography to put knowledge into perspective and draw up constraints. For example, human behavior is restrained by natural barriers, like rivers and mountains, but also by climate. Politics and law are useful for understanding how societies work administratively, and economics and management to know how money and wealth are created and used.

It is against this backdrop of knowledge that we evaluate events. Our own experiences stem from what we observe ourselves while interacting with others as we live our lives. We can note these observations down, like in a diary or notebook, but most of us probably just try to remember, which is difficult and prone to errors due to memory biases, especially as we get older.

What is of interest to intelligence professionals is not to try to impress others by having opinions about the future, as we often see in interviews with experts in the media. In the first instance, it is not even about having or pronouncing our guesses and ideas about what we "think" will happen, but about starting to talk about our sources. What we claim to know is most often simply a set of sources, and most of those sources, at least when it comes to macro factors, are simply a list of what we have read. In my experience, less than one in a gazillion sits down and analyze what they read, so our opinions carry very little analytical intelligence. Most opinions we have about the world are just infantile adoptions of the sources we happen to have come across and read recently, also because we tend to forget what we read, sometimes only a month ago or even shorter. The brain tends to discard anything we do not use, that is, anything we do not repeat in conversations. Instead, we believe something because it's expected of us; it makes us feel good, and we are afraid of being seen as ignorant. So, we adopt a series of "opinions" on major issues, everything from wars to the economy and immigration, so we are ready to share them in future conversations. Most of this is just mimicking what we think we remember we have heard or read.

So, instead, on any topic, we are better served by starting with the exchange of lists of the sources we have consulted. "This is what I have read; what did you read on this topic? What did you get out of it?" When we exchange lists of what we read, we can together start to dissect the content of what we have read, or as Confucius reminds us (loosely translated):

> When gentlemen meet friends, they present a book or an essay. Through their discussion, they gain understanding and respect for each other.

This is a far better method to get to the truth. When we can agree upon a set of events that we have read about that we think are true, we can start to use these pieces of intelligence for probability calculations about the future. Probability calculations mean exactly what they imply: sitting down and weighing factors, not pulling figures out of a hat. So, to abstain from having "opinions about the future" is not only a brave step, but a necessary first step for any intelligence professional.

There is another perspective to consider when evaluating what is being said, namely to make an estimate of what the source could possibly know. Senior employees will use this method with younger staffers, often without thinking about it. They know that the person who just walked in the door cannot know much about the industry, and most often they are right. Experience takes time. If we know something about the actual expert or author, we can ask simple questions like, "When did this person sit down and read the many books required to have the required knowledge in this field?" There are basically two periods to do this in life: at university and before you get married and have a family. There are some cultures where young people actually read a lot before they go to university, but they can be counted on one hand. France is one of them. China used to be another, but that was before the Cultural Revolution. Most Chinese who are my age today only know what they should have read when it comes to the humanities. In the natural sciences, though, they are often already ahead of us, who live in the Western world. So, most Chinese cannot tell you much about their national poet, Du Fu, but everthing you need to know about Algebraic Topology. It's not their fault, not even their parents'. With Mao, most reading was seen as bourgeois culture. Students should instead be sent to work in the fields, in the countryside, the conviction went. Bourgeois culture was shunned. The younger generation should study engineering, toppled with some Marxist theory. The current president, Xi, was one of those students. It will take time for China to rebuild their cultural knowledge, but they are already at it. The only other way to gain knowledge, apart from reading, is through experience. By the same token, we can ask: how and when did the person acquire the necessary experience to become an expert?.

When we have estimated what the person could have learned, we move to the next step, which is to ask what the person can learn now: "When during the day does he sit down and read for an hour or two?" Most professionals have very little time to read up, as they are drowned in meetings, conversations, travel, and commuting while at work, and have other interests when work is done. Most of what they read are snippets of information from the media, what they hear in the corridors, or at best, a summary of some report. Deep knowledge require concentration and plenty of time to read and digest. Very few of us have that time once we are working. It is simply the wrong time in our lives. At best we will get this time back later when we retire, or maybe when the children grow up and move out.

Believing that one can become an expert in anything intelligence-related without investing significant time in reading, traveling, and working is an illusion. There are no shortcuts. We live in an era where an entire generation reads far less compared to college students two generations ago. The so-called experts we see on TV often resemble a scene from the metaphorical expression ‘the blind leading the blind,’ though there are of course exceptions. Fortunately, cultures have the capacity to improve and self-correct; otherwise, they cease to be great nations. So, in conclusion, evaluating a source also involves understanding what the source may know by gathering information about their education and background.

Now, for primary sources, the big questions are:

1. If what you think you saw is what actually happened.
2. If what you saw or heard can be generalized to a whole group, organization, culture, or nation.

If we think it can be generalized, we should state why. It’s not enough to say ‘because I saw it twice.’ Then it is better to have support from secondary sources. To strengthen our conclusions, we should look for patterns and corroborate our observations with documented evidence or expert analysis. Furthermore, understanding the context in which the primary source was obtained is crucial, as it influences the reliability and interpretation of the information. This methodological rigor ensures that our intelligence assessments are both credible and actionable.

We often tend to forget the importance of traveling as a primary source. Traveling has many advantages. If we travel and stay in foreign countries over time, we do not only observe events, but can also learn something about culture—how others behave compared to us—especially if we stay long enough to learn the language. What is more important, when learning about other cultures, we also learn about our own. That is, using an old Greek motto, you cannot ‘know thyself’ if you have not absorbed at least one other foreign culture because you have nothing to compare to what it is that you are.

4.2.6 How We Assess the Value of Each Probability

The method described here builds on a collective approach to individual assessments and what we have chosen to call “the wisdom of the wise” to separate it from another more known method by Galten, “Wisdom of crowds” (relying on averages of all those asked regardless of knowledge), which we shall argue is a type of “group thinking”. These notions, by the way, has given rise to a whole new field of research called Collective Intelligence.[7]

We do not assign a probability to each event here separately, but only to outcomes, FE. In the example below this is 0,4, meaning a 40% chance that FE^1 will occur. In theory, the number is found by considering all historical events (HE) found to be relevant for a given situation A, plus all the current events, like in the figure below (Fig. 4.7):

[7] Calof et al. (2022) and Söilen (2019).

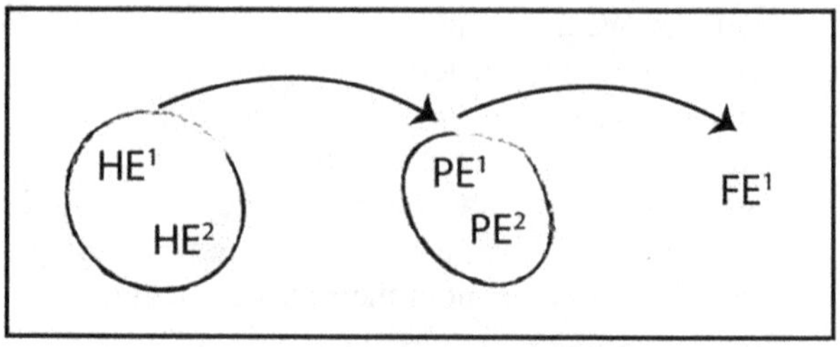

Fig. 4.7 Theoretical framework for calculating probabilities of future events from individual assessments

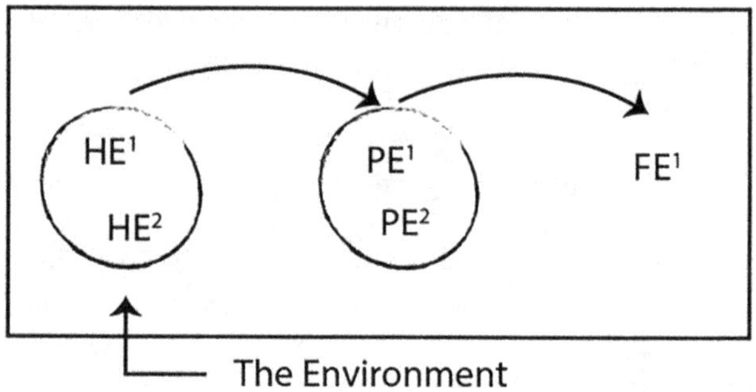

Fig. 4.8 Theoretical framework for calculating probabilities of future events from individual assessments with a context

To this, we must add context. Events do not exist in a vacuum but within a given environment (Env), consisting of a number or amounts of resources (R), which we evaluate based on their abundance or scarcity. This environment is denoted by the box, and the resources are represented by whatever we choose to fill the white space within the box, in addition to the events that we have already drawn up. When certain resources are plentiful, there is no pressing need to act, as more or less everyone can access them. Like in the study of economics, we are particularly interested in scarce resources. Scarce resources lead to higher demand and more competition. The environment is modelled by a single box surrounding the events. As we proceed with the analysis, we denote the scarce resources by names inside the box (Fig. 4.8):

The events combined with a specific environment make up what we call a situation (Sit), in the case of the war example, expressed as Sit^a. Situations do not exist in a vacuum and influence each other, but we can as humans cognitively only analyze one situation at a time.

In the example above, we have analyzed the probability of one specific event happening, FE1. In most situations, we will have no idea of how many critical future events there are.

4.2.7 Working with Multiple Future Events

In many cases, we want to test several possible outcomes: FE^1, FE^2, FE^3, as in the figure below (Fig. 4.9):

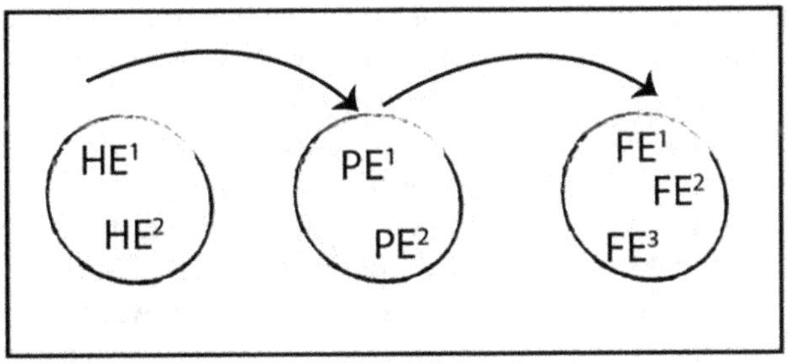

Fig. 4.9 Theoretical framework for calculating numerous probabilities of future events from individual assessments

Calculating the probabilities of our FEs.

In the example above, we just said a probability of 0.4 for FE1. However, in reality, we need to calculate this value. The suggested method involves a collective approach, which includes numerous individual assessments by experts. The process is defined as follows:

Work independently and assign a probability to each FE based on historical events (HE) and present events (PE).

Meet with other experts to discuss any potential events you may have overlooked that could be relevant to your assessment but avoid discussing the probabilities. This is crucial as it prevents influencing others regarding the value you place on each event, which could alter their own assessments. Return to your work and adjust your probability estimates for each FE. Once everyone is finished, calculate the average probability of all experts for each FE. Use the Brier score to monitor results and discuss why certain probabilities were incorrect. Or as expressed:

Equation 4.4 Use the Brier score to monitor results.

$$\frac{\mathrm{Sit}^{a}\left(e1+e2+e3\ldots e^{n}\right)}{n}$$

This will give the collective probability in Situation A for the assessments of all the experts. I will give us one result for each FE. The weight (w) of each FE will tell us which ones are more important.

Now to how to calculate the individual probabilities using the critical thinking approach:

To think critically means to try to find counterarguments for why something will *not happen or is true*. Critical thinking requires deep and extensive knowledge because, if we do not have it, we will not find the counterarguments, because we simply cannot imagine them, so they will never occur to us.

A working process for deducting them may look like this:

1. Start by giving each FE a probability of 1,0 (certain it will happen)
2. Use your critical sense and find arguments for why this will *not happen.*
3. For each counterargument you redraw a number between 0,001 and 1.

4. For example, "I do not think that country A will attack B because that country has never gone to war before, they have a history of being non-violent...", 1,0–0,75 = 0,25, so "probably not".
5. When you find no more counterarguments, you have your individual probability for FE[1], "there will be war".
6. When you meet with other experts, you can calculate your collective probability of FE1, which could simply be the average score of all experts divided by their number. You can also assign different weights to each expert's probability, depending on their previous successes, success rates, seniority, or years of experience.

Other methods, like Tetlock's 'superforecasting,' start with a baseline of 0.5 and add likelihoods on top of that. They seek arguments for why an event will happen. ChatGPT, in its current form, also calculates like this if asked to speculate about future events. The problem with this method is that it's easier to find arguments for why existing ideas *are* true, rather than for why they *are not* true. This is primarily because it is more challenging to be critical and find critical arguments than supportive ones once we have an idea.

Several biases are identified here, including confirmation biases, as we might ignore counterarguments, and anchoring bias, where initial estimates, or 'anchors,' overly influence final assessments and decisions. To mitigate this bias, we can involve other experts to identify counterarguments, assuming they can do so fairly. Sometimes, experts may be motivated to undermine others' arguments to highlight their own, which is an example of hostile attribution bias.

In an ideal world, you could have intelligence teams working in parallel on the same problem without contact with each other. You could then see which team makes the best predictions. However, a problem with this approach—besides the obvious fact that it is time demanding, so costly—is that individual experts may not be as critical as they could be because they want their own group to win, a phenomenon known as in-group bias. Optimism bias also exists, and biases will always be present. Our role is not to eliminate them, as that is impossible, but to reduce them as much as possible, given the resources at hand. Not even MNEs have the resources to have multiple teams work on the same problem, although we can imagine that computers will do this in the future by working with different datasets or programming. Computer power and AI are set to revolutionize intelligence in the decades to come.

So far, we have assumed that Events are all true, but that is, of course, not true. So, what do we do when the information is false or 'fake', as people say today?

4.3 False Information

For our theoretical framework, an event (E) has to be true. If not, it is not considered an E. We shall label everything we cannot prove as Speculations (Spec), which may be true or not. Pieces of Intelligence (I) can either be Es or Ss (Table 4.2).

Table 4.2 The difference between intelligence, speculations and events

Information	Intelligence	
Strategic Information	Speculative Intelligence (Spec Int)	Verified Intelligence (Ver Int)
Non-Strategic Information	Speculation	Event
	May happen	*Have/Will happen*

All data gathered by an organization that makes sense can be defined as information. Initially, the organization tries to distinguish between what is strategic and what is non-strategic. Anything non-strategic can be discarded to save time. In the next phase, we must differentiate between information based on verifiable facts and that which cannot yet be proven. The inability to prove something does not mean it is not of interest. In an organization, the most intriguing intel will likely be speculative. In a world where information is abundant and high-quality intelligence can be purchased from large providers, it is the handling of speculations that distinguishes us from the competition, which can give us a competitive advantage. We need to foster an organizational culture where speculation is encouraged but have systems in place to manage these processes.

It has been noted that a piece of intelligence for one company or organization is not necessarily a piece of intelligence for another because organizations have different strategies. Put differently, a piece of intelligence is only relevant for two organizations to the extent that their strategies are similar. Since the variables or key success factors that make organizations competitive tend to be somewhat similar, what constitutes intelligence for one organization may also be so for another, like, for example, the value of the USD, for two companies engaging in international trade.

Events (E) are either known by persons/organizations or they are not. That is, there are some events that are facts not yet known by anyone, as illustrated in the now well-known formula made famous by former U.S. Secretary of Defense Donald Rumsfeld:

1. Known knowns: These are things we know that we know.
2. Known unknowns: These are things we know we don't know.
3. Unknown unknowns: These are things we don't know that we don't know.

   We could also add that there are:
4. Unknown knowns: Things that we don't know that we know.

Sometimes, in organizations, it can make sense to talk about things we don't know that we know because we had a report that we forgot about or similar situations of forgetting or misplacing. A second explanation for this fact is that they are unconsciously known but not actively at the forefront of our thoughts.

Staying with the concept of "knowing" it makes sense to know (pundit intended) the following terms:

- Assumed knowns: These are things we assume we know but haven't verified. These can lead to overconfidence and errors.
- Misidentified unknowns: These involve situations where we incorrectly believe we understand something, but our understanding is flawed or incorrect.
- Taboo knowns: Knowledge that is avoided or not discussed openly due to cultural norms, political pressures, or social taboos.
- Unknowable: Information that cannot be known now or ever, often due to limitations in scientific understanding or technological capabilities.
- Ignored knowns: These are facts or pieces of information that are deliberately ignored or overlooked, often because they conflict with strategic goals or personal beliefs.

To minimize the likelihood that a speculation is false, we should test the Specs against all known biases. These can include, but are not limited to:

- Confirmation Bias: The tendency to search for, interpret, favor, and recall information in a way that confirms one's preexisting beliefs or hypotheses, while giving disproportionately less consideration to alternative possibilities.
- Anchoring Bias: The common human tendency to rely too heavily on the first piece of information offered (the "anchor") when making decisions, even if subsequent information suggests other alternatives.
- Availability Heuristic: This bias occurs when people overestimate the importance of information that is available to them. A person might argue a point based on an example that readily comes to mind, rather than examining a wider range of examples or statistical data.
- Overconfidence Bias: This is the tendency to hold a false and misleading assessment of our skills, intellect, or talent. It can cause one to overestimate their own abilities in predicting accurate outcomes of events.
- Status Quo Bias: The preference to keep things the same or maintaining a previous decision. People with this bias resist change and prefer the current state of affairs.
- Affect Heuristic: The inclination to make decisions based on emotions and feelings rather than factual information. This can heavily skew one's judgment in forming opinions based on how one feels about the topic at hand, rather than the evidence.
- Bandwagon Effect: The tendency to do (or believe) things because many other people do (or believe) the same. This can lead to 'groupthink' where individual critical analysis is sacrificed for cohesion within the group.
- Dunning-Kruger Effect: A cognitive bias wherein people with low ability at a task overestimate their ability. This arises from an inability of individuals to recognize their lack of ability.
- False Consensus Effect: The tendency to overestimate how much other people agree with us. This can lead to a belief that our opinions, beliefs, preferences, values, and habits are "normal" and that others also think the same way.

- Hindsight Bias: Sometimes called the "knew-it-all-along" effect, this bias leads people to perceive past events as being more predictable than they actually were before the events took place. It can alter one's memory of their own predictions.

We shall come back to many of these types of biases in the next chapter when we present different analyses. For now, this may be a bit too much to digest in one go, but learning the terms saves a lot of time when a bias is first thought to have been identified.

To minimize the likelihood that speculation or a piece of intelligence from secondary sources is incorrect, we can, in addition to applying a checklist for the various biases mentioned, conduct an evaluation of both the source and the intelligence itself.

In a classroom exercise I have used for over 25 years now, students are required to complete an assignment using a form divided into two sections: one is fact-based and objective, while the other is assessment-based or speculative. An intelligence report can also be submitted in essay format, similar to most academic reports, possibly including a summary that highlights the key findings. However, this format still may not meet the rigorous standards required for intelligence reporting. It is essential to classify and rank all gathered intelligence, distinguishing between Raw Intelligence (RI) and Analyzed Intelligence (AI), and to document the source and the assessments made (Table 4.3):

The table consists of two parts: one more objective (blue) built on observations that can easily be stated. The other is open for human interpretation (red), and extensive analysis is more subjective. Thus, we have:

1. The objective part:
   A. 'Intel #' is the identifier.
   B. Then comes the actual intelligence, enclosed in quotation marks, followed by the source cited in a standard format like APA style or other.
2. The subjective part:
   A. The value of the intelligence is determined by comparing it to the company's strategy and assessing how important this intelligence is for the given strategy.
   B. Confidence in the source is evaluated by asking to what extent we trust this source, for example, a specific newspaper or a Walk-in, an individual who voluntarily offers to provide intelligence to an agency without being recruited.
   C. Confidence in the intelligence is determined by questioning how much we believe this intelligence to be true, regardless of the source.

Table 4.3 The intelligence report format

Observation			*Assessment*		
Intel #	The Intel (RI/AI)	Source (APA style)	Value of intel (1–10)	Confidence in Source (1–10)	Confidence in intel (1–10)
1	"Nn" (RI)				

It may be that the intelligence is reliable even though it is published in a newspaper with low credibility. In other words, a source with low credibility does not only publish untrustworthy intelligence. If you trust the intelligence despite not trusting the source, you need solid arguments for why it is true. Also, you cannot assert that something is true simply because it's printed in a source you trust, such as the New York Times (NYT), which, like all major international newspapers, has its biases. The paper is often viewed as having a left-center bias, generally supporting liberal perspectives and the Democratic Party. Although known for its credible and reliable reporting, its editorial and opinion sections often exhibit a moderate liberal bias. This bias is reflected in the language used and the selection of stories covered, which tend to favor progressive causes and viewpoints.

As readers, we must identify these biases. To take another example, when reading The Economist—a newspaper I read every week and thoroughly enjoy, not least because of its eloquent language—I put on my 'The Economist glasses,' a filter I use specifically for this source. I have identified several biases in this publication: it is pro-English, pro-free trade, anti-Chinese (the loss of Hong Kong), anti-French (engaging in "frog-bashing"), and generally against most countries that left the Commonwealth and revolted against Great Britain. If I draw my conclusions without wearing these glasses, I risk misperceiving reality. These biases do not make The Economist a poor newspaper, as all sources are to some degree biased. Historically, The Economist is also of interest to the study of Intelligence as it was one of the early adopters to start its separate division dedicated to industry and company analysis in 1946, called The Economist Intelligence Unit (EIU).

Sometimes the source is simply a person. In the secret service, the process of verifying the reliability and value of an intelligence source is known as Asset validation. This involves conducting background checks, cross-referencing information with other sources, and continuously monitoring the asset's behavior and information over time to ensure credibility and access levels are maintained.

If we do not trust a piece of intelligence, it must be because we have counterarguments. These counterarguments must be listed and discussed with others. Eventually, a conclusion must be made on whether to use this intelligence. As discussed above, we can attempt to translate these arguments into probabilities, turning all the arguments into a likelihood of the intelligence being true or false. For simplicity, we can set the threshold to $P > 0.5$, meaning we will use the intelligence if the probability is greater than 0.5 (Table 4.4):

Table 4.4 Classifying sources according to risk groups

Quality of Peer Review	*Commitment to truth*		
		Low	High
	High	Biased academic journals, Reports by Think Tanks	Unbiased academic journals, Reports by Research institutions
	Low	Gossip magazines, Internet	National and International Newspaper, Investigative journalism

We are always looking for organisations and sources with a high commitment to truth that has a high degree of quality control. However, this is no guarantee that the intelligence will be true. In the same way, we can note that most scholars who do peer review are not the most senior or competent researchers but often up-and-coming ones. The real experts often do not have time to do reviews or have other priorities that actually remunerate work, so they decline requests for reviews. Peer reviewers are often selected from a group of researchers who have simply published on a similar topic before or who are part of a group of researchers within a certain field, for example, those who participate at specific conferences. As such, they are very often victims of group thinking and consequently, it's very difficult to get truly new material published. So, as a group, scientific journals that publish findings in the social sciences are inherently conservative and resistant to change, which is quite a contradiction to what scientific journals should ideally represent.

In the other corner of the table above, anyone can publish anything on the internet regardless of whether it is true or false, and the fact that it is published online carries no inherent credibility. On the other hand, many experts have their own YouTube channels, including leading scholars. Listening to these channels is often more valuable than all other sources. For all practical reasons, we can say that linear TV programs and news have become less important as customers today prefer on-demand tailor-made subscriptions and alerts. In practice, the internet leads to a situation where the smart are becoming smarter and the ignorant more ignorant. (On the topic of manipulation see further down).

Belief has no place in science and no place in intelligence studies. That someone believes something should trigger all the alarm bells, especially if it's not followed by arguments as to why someone believes something. I prefer to use classic syllogism here and say that a piece of intelligence is a conclusion and that we must list our premises to see if the argument is true or false. If the conclusion follows from the premises, it's true. We have known how to do so since the Middle Ages, but somehow it has been mostly forgotten in schools today. This is the classic example that students have learned for centuries, and it is still as relevant as ever[8]:

Major Premise:	All men are mortal.	(Premise: P1)
Minor Premise:	Socrates is a man.	(Premise: P2)
Conclusion:	Therefore, Socrates is mortal.	(Conclusion: C)

In logical symbols:

P1: $\forall x(M(x) \rightarrow D(x))$
P2: $M(S)$
C: $D(S)$

[8] My favorite book in this area is still Jevons (1919). *The Elements of Logic*. T. C. & E. C. Jack Ltd. and T. Nelson & Sons. As a young man studying in Paris, I translated it into Norwegian, and many years later it was published as *En liten bok i Logikk. Hvordan lære å tenke* (2016).

Where:

$M(x)$ $x$is a man
$D(x)$ $x$is mortal
S: Socrates

So, the syllogism reads as follows: For all x, if x is a man, then x is mortal.

Socrates is a man. Therefore, Socrates is mortal.

If a conclusion in a syllogism is true, we say that the conclusion is valid if it logically follows from the premises, and it is sound if the premises are also true:

Valid: The conclusion logically follows from the premises.
Sound: The syllogism is valid, and the premises are true.

So, if a conclusion in a syllogism is true, and it follows logically from true premises, we describe the syllogism as both valid and sound.

It's important for us to detach ourselves from the intelligence we are presenting. Saying we believe something signals the opposite, that it is an opinion we hold close to our heart. Some scientific training helps here. Speculations are like hypotheses; we hold ourselves detached and unemotional towards them. When conducting our statistical analysis, as when testing a hypothesis, we may come to two possible outcomes, either Reject (R) or Accept (A). It should be the same with speculations. For all practical purposes, hypotheses, speculations, and guesses are here treated as the same thing, as synonyms.

Speculations without any argument are sometimes called "wild guesses"; they have no place in intelligence studies. The opposite is often called "educated guessing," meaning we can show, at least, some arguments.

4.3.1 The Notion of One-Truth in Organizations

Organizations struggle when employees have different ideas about what is true, for example about markets or competitors. It's not uncommon for employees to have found different figures and to try to defend them. Often, we argue about nothing, creating unnecessary discussions and, in the end, wasting large amounts of time and resources. Thus, the importance of the one-truth system in the organization. The one-truth system means that employees agree that certain sources or authorities provide the truth and that all employees should use these figures when making decisions. It becomes like a common language within the organization, one could say.

The challenge arises when determining which information sets represent the 'one-truth.' It may seem easier to purchase intelligence from a major vendor like Gartner, agreeing to accept everything from them as truth, although this approach carries significant risks. As Pagels-Fick, former head of intelligence at Ericsson in the 1990s, highlighted in his book, outsourcing your organization's knowledge asset is precarious.[9] Furthermore, if all your competitors also source their intelligence

[9] Pagels-Fick (1999).

from say Gartner, you end up with the same information sets and are likely to make similar decisions. While Gartner may make fewer mistakes than the average company and provide more accurate intelligence, they are not infallible. Building your own 'one-truth' system, though more costly and time-consuming—sometimes even impractical due to the level of detail required—avoids this pitfall but can lead to internal conflicts and rivalry over whose 'one-truth' should prevail. Thus many companies, realizing that the external one-truths they buy are not perfect and may include mistakes, they are rational to use, given the alternatives and costs.

One-truth systems can become problematic when salespeople, who have direct contact with the market and customers, gather information that contradicts data obtained through the one-truth system. It's not uncommon for large companies to prefer not to 'contaminate' their purchased data with insights from their own employees. To address this, a system of exceptions needs to be established, which is both complex and challenging. Verifying the intelligence before it enters the system is time-consuming and costly, leading companies to often disregard data from their employees. However, ignoring insights from salespeople or those closest to the market can be detrimental to a company's competitive position. Sony-Ericsson is a prime example, having ignored customer preferences for touchscreens, which proved to be a significant oversight, eventually leading to the break-up of the company.

If all multinational enterprises (MNEs) rely solely on purchasing the same information from the same vendors and instruct their employees to use only this data, they will inevitably end up with nearly identical information sets. This homogeneity can lead to similar decisions across companies, making it more challenging to achieve a competitive advantage. This phenomenon resembles groupthink, specifically the Bandwagon Effect, where individuals align their decisions based on the majority. It can also be seen as a form of self-manipulation, as companies limit their perspective and potentially miss out on unique insights from within their own ranks.

The opposite of truths are lies. Lies are also information, just false. People, organizations, and states lie all the time, but more often they refrain from telling the truth or the whole truth. On the organizational level, we talk of deniability—the ability to deny knowledge of or responsibility for any actions. I guess it sounds better if we are being asked to deny something for our employer than if we are being asked to lie. ("You have full deniability" VS. "Please just lie, Joe"). If the lie is part of an organized scheme, we talk about disinformation, false information spread deliberately to deceive. We also talk about deception, deliberate misrepresentation of information to mislead adversaries. On the receiving end of all of this is someone being manipulated.

4.3.2 On Manipulation

If we rely on incorrect or outdated information, whether it has been intentionally manipulated by others or has become outdated due to our own negligence, we risk being manipulated. This manipulation can lead us to make poor decisions based on sub-optimal information. While it cannot be entirely avoided, it is a pervasive issue that requires vigilance and continual verification of the information we use.

Consider advertising, where companies often present their products in an overly favorable light. This systematic embellishment in marketing can border on dishonesty. For example, a billboard shows a big, juicy hamburger that looks more appealing than the actual product we receive at the restaurant once there. While we immediately notice this discrepancy as soon as we sit down and get ready to take the first bite, our frequent exposure to such tactics has desensitized us, and we may not react strongly unless the difference is stark. In such cases, feeling deceived, we might complain or express dissatisfaction.

The boundary between acceptable marketing and illegal deception is nuanced and varies by jurisdiction. Most countries have regulations mandating truthful advertising, but enforcement can be lax, and consumer protection laws often lack teeth. In the United States, companies may face lawsuits over misleading advertisements, but such legal actions are less common in other countries.

Similarly, the internet is rife with erroneous information. Despite the absence of transactions, the spread of such information rarely faces accountability—except through the critical thinking skills fostered by a good education.

State intelligence organizations have historically sought to influence adversaries' perceptions. Today, much of this manipulative effort has been industrialized by 'troll factories,' which produce disinformation to deceive or scam citizens. Sometimes backed by governments and sometimes operating independently, these entities engage in activities ranging from political manipulation to cyber piracy, including credit card theft and identity fraud. We are indeed living in a golden age of manipulation and misinformation.[10]

Organizations do sometimes attempt to manipulate the information sets of their competitors as a strategic advantage, a practice falling under the broader category of counterintelligence. Counterintelligence involves protecting against and exploiting intelligence activities from adversaries, and in the business context, this can include activities designed to mislead competitors. For example, companies may use tactics such as exaggerating public relations statements or manipulating trade show appearances to project false optimism about their future sales.

The goal of such actions is to influence competitors into making poor decisions based on incorrect or misleading information. This approach, however, raises significant ethical concerns. While some companies adhere strictly to ethical guidelines and maintain rigorous standards, others may only profess to do so for appearances or may disregard such considerations altogether.

Effective counterintelligence involves not only the defensive measures to protect sensitive information but also the strategic dissemination of misleading information to gain a competitive edge. These practices are complex and often necessitate a balance between ethical considerations and strategic benefits.

Sometimes, we become so accustomed to manipulation that we fail to recognize it and, in some cases, accept it as part of the trade. For example, investors often

[10] See Söilen (2016a, 2021a).

believe that summaries of accounting figures from organizations reflect reality accurately, such as the income and balance statements found in annual reports and presentations at shareholder meetings. However, as anyone who has worked with accounting knows, this is seldom the case. Organizations manipulate their figures to produce annual reports that appear most favorable, often benefiting the CEO, whose salary is often directly tied to share prices. This manipulation frequently includes techniques like timing investments when cash flow is strong or delaying them when it is not, known as periodization or revenue recognition timing. Companies can also increase short-term profits by capitalizing costs, spreading them over several years as depreciation, using off-balance sheet entities to keep debt and other liabilities off the primary financial statements, and manipulating the timing of write-offs to reduce the immediate impact on earnings. These practices are referred to as 'engineering the books.' When such practices break the law, it is referred to as 'cooking the books.' The difference is determined by the auditor if they spot and report it.

Companies often engage in strategic deception to mislead competitors about their true intentions, capabilities, or plans. Some examples to help illustrate this:

1. Disinformation through Media and Press Releases: Companies may release misleading information through press releases or media interviews, suggesting they are heading in a particular strategic direction while actually pursuing another. This can divert competitors' attention or resources away from critical areas.
2. Leaking False Information: Deliberately leaking false information through what appears to be accidental or unofficial channels can be an effective way to mislead competitors about a company's future plans, such as new product developments or market expansions.
3. Feinting Operations: In this deceptive practice, a company might start a project or initiative only to draw attention and resources of competitors. Once the competitors have committed to countering this initiative, the original company pulls back or redirects resources elsewhere.
4. Overstating Capabilities: Companies might boast about the capabilities of their products or services more than what is actually true to mislead competitors into overestimating the company's competitiveness or technological edge.
5. Understating Capabilities: Conversely, a company might downplay its abilities or withhold information about successful developments to catch competitors off guard with sudden advancements.
6. Misleading Financial Reports: While financial reporting must comply with legal standards, companies can sometimes present data in ways that emphasize certain positive elements or downplay negative aspects, leading competitors to make incorrect assumptions about the company's financial health or strategic priorities.
7. Fake Products at Trade Shows: Displaying or announcing products and services at trade shows that are not actually intended to be developed can mislead competitors about a company's strategic focus or technological advancements.

8. Strategic Litigation: Engaging in legal battles, such as patent disputes, can be used to distract competitors or create an illusion of possessing certain proprietary technologies or rights, thereby misleading others about the company's actual competitive position.
9. Partnership and Alliance Misrepresentations: Announcing strategic partnerships or alliances that are less substantial than claimed can create false impressions about a company's market strength or global reach.
10. Misleading Recruitment Ads: Posting job ads for positions or projects that don't actually exist or are different from the actual job can be a way to confuse competitors about the company's new projects or the direction they are taking.

When we dig deeper, most communication is manipulation: We are constantly trying to convince not only others but even ourselves of what is right, regardless of whether it is true. It seems to be a part of our nature, our survival techniques. What seems to matter most to humans as living organisms is what we benefit from. This isn't a cynical view, but a realistic and scientific one. It does not mean we cannot be wonderfully honest at the same time. Paradoxes are no problem for humans. Ultimately, it comes down to a matter of degrees.

Research in the neurosciences over the past two decades has shown that the human brain is a fantastic lawyer but a poor scientist. That is, we are very good at defending ourselves, regardless of the situations we find ourselves in, but not so good at telling the truth. Said differently, we have to train ourselves to be scientific, to tell the truth, especially when it is not in our interest, while lies often come naturally. From an evolutionary perspective, we seem to have little preference or trouble distinguishing between the two. This, of course, is worrying and a major problem for a study like intelligence studies, as it is with all kinds of scientific thinking and inquiries. For companies and organizations, it simply means that we have to be very critical of everything that is said and written. This is easier said than done.

4.4 Information Sets

The sum of all that is true is much larger than what all organizations and individuals know. Instead, individuals and organizations possess what we can call information sets, several pieces of information related to what the organization is doing. These information sets can be small or large, and they can overlap with the information sets of other individuals and organizations. The information listed only consists of the intelligence that is relevant to the organization, which is just a part of what all the individuals who work in the organization know. Employees usually have most of their lives outside of the organization; thus, most of what they know is not related to work.

We can utilize set theory to describe the same idea, which is useful for illustrating how different collections of information (sets) relate to one another. Here's how we might conceptualize and formulate this:

1. Universal Set (U): Represents the sum of all truth or all possible information.
2. Individual Information Sets (I_i): Each individual or organization has their own subset of the universal set, representing the information they know. This is represented by $I1$, $I2$, …, In, where each subscript denotes a different individual or organization.
3. Organization Information Set (O): This set consists of all the information relevant to a specific organization, which is a subset of the information known by all individuals within that organization. If we consider an organization with members 1, 2, …, n, then the organization's information set could be represented as:

$$O = I1 \cup I2 \cup \cdots \cup In$$

This expression states that the organization's information set is the union of the information sets of all its members.

4. Work-Related Information Subset (W): Within the organization's information set, there is a subset of information that is strictly relevant to work:

$$W \subseteq O$$

This subset is only part of the organization's overall information set and represents strictly work-related knowledge.

5. Non-Work-Related Information (N_i): Represents the information that each individual knows that is not relevant to their work. This can be represented as:

$$Ni = Ii - W$$

Here, Ni is the set difference between an individual's total information set Ii and the work-related subset W.

6. Overlap Among Information Sets: The overlap between the information sets of different individuals or organizations can be described using intersections. For example, the information shared between two individuals $I1$ and $I2$ is:

$$I1 \cap I2$$

7. Relative Size of Sets: To express that the sum of all truth is much larger than what all organizations and individuals know, we use the relationship:

$$|U| \gg |I1 \cup I2 \cup \cdots \cup In|$$

Here, $|U|$ represents the cardinality or size of the universal set, and $|I1 \cup I2 \cup \cdots \cup In|$ is the size of the union of all individual information sets, indicating that the total possible knowledge (U) far exceeds what is collectively known by all individuals.

The mathematical formulation using set theory shows the relationships and relative magnitudes of different types of information in organisations and among individuals.

The study of knowledge management is about how we handle and try to use and enlarge our information sets in an organization. The aim of the organization is not to make the information sets of the company as large as possible—that is the aim of an encyclopedia—but to enlarge it to the extent that is defined by what the company is trying to achieve.

To obtain a competitive advantage is relative, meaning we only need to know more than our competitors. Some industries are low-intelligence-based, like some retailers. It's enough to be smarter than the shop on the next corner, whereas other companies, like software producers, need to be smarter than companies that are already very competitive, and there are many of them competing on a global scale. The topic of intelligence is more important for the latter organization, and they tend to invest more in the knowledge of intelligence, setting up special departments or functions defining each player's information sets. In plain English, we want to have an idea what our competitors know as compared to what we know.

4.5 Types of Intelligence in an Organization

So far, we have treated intelligence as one type of information within an organization. In reality, different types correspond to different intelligence receivers at various levels in the organization. We may say that the more important the decision, the more valuable the intelligence.

The intelligence function is typically performed by an individual with a position in say marketing, such as a market researcher, or by a data scientist or a librarian. In some companies in the Anglo-Saxon world, these professionals are still referred to as CI analysts, meaning Competitive Intelligence analysts or Market Intelligence experts. A number of companies are replacing the term 'intelligence' with 'insights,' but the meaning remains much the same. In larger companies and organizations, intelligence professionals work in teams, not only in the public sector, where thousands of employees can work for the same state intelligence service. In the private sector, it's unusual to have intelligence teams that are larger than 20 employees. However, if you include all those who work with intelligence-related matters, the numbers quickly rise into the hundreds and sometimes even the thousands. In other words, it depends on how we define 'intelligence.' On one side of the scale, it includes anyone working most of the time as a knowledge or information worker. On the other end, it refers to someone specifically assigned as an intelligence or data analyst.

To get a quick grasp of the numbers, if we look at the major secret services, the CIA (foreign intelligence) is estimated to have more than 20,000 employees, the NSA (signals intelligence) more than 30,000, and the FBI (domestic intelligence) about 35,000, creating a community of about 100,000 employees. The SVR (foreign) and FSB (domestic) in Russia do not have publicly available figures, but they are substantial. The same is true for the MSS (foreign and domestic) and the PLA SSF (military intelligence) in China. The BND in Germany employs about 6500, as does the DGSE in France. The Mossad (foreign) and Shin Bet (domestic) in Israel do not disclose their figures either, but the numbers are also substantial, especially as compared to the country's population is of ten million. Other Anglo-Saxon countries have employees in the thousands, and smaller countries often have a maximum of 1000 intelligence professionals on their payrolls. That is an estimated 268,000 intelligence personnel globally just in the state and military intelligence here mentioned, what is sometimes referred to as the Global Intelligence Community (IC).

In comparison, the estimated numbers worldwide of market researchers run into the hundreds of thousands. Data scientists in the US alone accounted for about 170,000 employees in 2022. There are tens of thousands of business intelligence consultants globally. Therefore, the total number of employees in the private sector working with intelligence-related tasks far surpasses those working in state intelligence departments. Thus, the relevance of treating the topic of intelligence from a business perspective.

4.5.1 Operational, Tactical and Strategic Intelligence in Organizations

In the private sector, we sometimes call the teams *Business Intelligence Teams* (BIT).[11] BITs have three types of customers each with their specific needs: (1). Top management, (2). Middle management and (3). Front line management. Top management often seeks strategic intelligence, while front-line management seeks *operational intelligence* (Fig. 4.10).

Strategic intelligence is handled by top management, tactical intelligence by middle managers, and operational intelligence by those who work closest to customers, such as in sales. In reality, the picture may not be this clear-cut, but theory here teaches us important distinctions.

Tactical Intelligence: A good way to understand the difference between tactics and strategy is to consider that tactics are the small steps, while strategy is the plan.

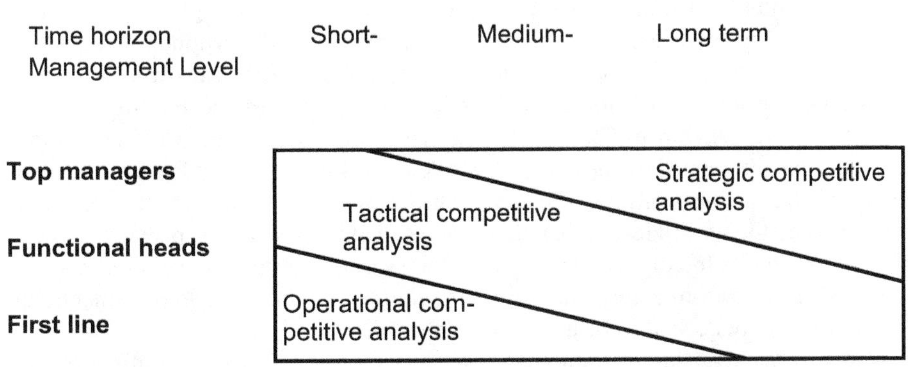

Fig. 4.10 Management levels and scope of analysis. Modified version of Jenster Customer/Market Scope. (Jenster & Söilen, 2009)

[11] Also called CIT for Competitive Intelligence Team. BITs are nothing new but have existed in larger private organizations under other names. For public organizations, we call them Public Intelligence Teams (PIT). For the neutral form, we shall use Intelligence Teams (IT) in this book.

A good analogy is a football match. If the offensive player number 7 on the white and red team (Arsenal's Liam Brady, for those old enough to remember, and have an interest in soccer) has a role in pushing the ball on the left flank as soon as he gets it and runs towards the goal, that is a tactic. On the opposing team, they may anticipate this because they have seen him play many times before, so number 3 on the blue team has the job of stopping number 7. This would be the equivalent tactic on the other side. The overall strategy for the red and white team might be to play offensively, positioning more players at the top, whereas the blue team, having lost more matches, decides to play defensively, placing more players on their own half of the field. The behavior and roles in organizations can be reduced to similar groups using the same allegory.

4.6 Defining the Unit of Output in Intelligence Work and Tracing the Intelligence in the Decision-Making Process

The farmer produces crops, and the industrial worker produces material goods and services, both of which can be quantified in terms of output. However, what does the knowledge worker produce, and how can their production be measured? More importantly, how can it be traced in the decision-making process?

If we cannot trace it, there is no way to measure its relative contribution, thus no effective method to measure the value of the intelligence. This represents a significant challenge to the intelligence profession, and explains why intelligence organizations, especially in the private sector, are not more recognized. Their input often remains unmeasured, either because decision-makers prefer to take all the credit themselves, or because it was not practical to measure it.

Today, intelligence analysts must argue for their value through documentation and traceability. By keeping records that can demonstrate the originality and added value of their insights at the time they were provided. They must try to quantify contributions whenever possible to highlight the impact of the intelligence provided. Sometimes, they use benchmarking, which involves comparing the outcomes of decisions influenced by the analyst's work against industry standards or competitors who did not use similar intelligence. They also must demonstrate that decisions informed by their work lead to better outcomes than those made by peers, which can underscore the value of the intelligence. However, this process is very tedious and takes time away from actual intelligence gathering and analysis, so documentation of the work may be said to be a two-edged sword.

Now, with advances in computer systems, we can begin to solve this problem. We have previously seen that intelligence can be divided into Raw Intelligence (RI) and Analyzed Intelligence (AI), but it's still an unclear measure of output. An intelligence output can be a report, or it can be a single piece of advice (unit of output). In this case, it's a report and that report will consist of numerous pieces of intelligence.

Intelligence in the form of an output can be defined as:

> Actionable insight, intelligence,
> meaning, and implications
> derived from data and information. [or, in short as] Future-oriented, Accurate,
> Resource-efficient, Objective,
> Useful, and Timely (referred to as FAROUT). p. 5[12]

A report can consist of an Executive Summary, Background or Context, and a summary of sources used—each potentially subject to selection bias. The empirical data presentation section displays the actual raw intelligence gathered. The analysis section follows, where again, selection bias can occur depending on the analytical tools used.

It is advisable to employ several analytical tools, a method referred to as redundancy in the method. If one analysis yields a particular result with one tool and a different result with another, a third analysis using an additional tool is recommended. The conclusions that follow are derived from the analyzed intelligence. It's useful to consider each conclusion as needing support from several arguments or pieces of raw intelligence, which are termed premises in logic and can be structured into a syllogism, as shown earlier. An intelligence report may also include policy recommendations at the end, which should logically follow from the analytical intelligence presented earlier.

Overall, an intelligence report can be divided into numerous raw intelligence arguments (premises) and several pieces of analyzed intelligence. The policy recommendations should be tested to see if they logically follow from the conclusion, or if other recommendations might fit better. Computer systems are already assisting us in this process.

To illustrate with an example, imagine a scenario where all major decisions are predefined in a computer software system. Here, managers simply read the intelligence related to each decision and select an option on a screen, say decision C from options A to F. If the decision proves to be successful, the analysts who provided the intelligence are rewarded. Additionally, if we understand the consequences of a particular situation, we can trace back to our potential decisions and the underlying intelligence to determine if we had the necessary information to make a good decision, and whether any of the alternatives was a better choice. This allows us to evaluate both the decision-makers and the intelligence analysts in one go. Technically, this is already feasible, but it has yet to be widely implemented because it is still considered somewhat cumbersome.

In a sense, we might not even need decision-makers anymore, as this could all be managed based on the strategy and intelligence risk provided. The computer system could itself determine which decisions correspond to the available intelligence. If we can calculate monetary outcomes for each decision, like pay-offs in a decision tree in game theory, then it would be clear for the computer which decision to make. In other scenarios, we might only need a manager to set the risk level, but even this could be standardized across the company for any given year. For example, the

[12] Bensoussan and Fleisher (2013).

board of directors could decide to choose risk level 3 out of a scale from 1 to 5 for a given year, and the software would handle the rest based on the intelligence entered into the computer. This is no longer fiction. Organizations are already planning AI factories much according to this logic.

As production increasingly relies on robots, the critical resources in this system become: (1) The investment, or capital required; (2) The competence of the employees; (3) The raw materials needed for production; and (4) The selection of intelligence put into the system. This signifies what we may call the Maturity Stage of the Information Age. We may go there very soon.

4.7 From Information Asymmetry to Intelligence Asymmetry

It is often said, that to achieve a competitive advantage for a company during the information age implies information asymmetry; that is, the company wins over its competitors because it possesses a superior information set. This is common sense.

But this view is too simplistic, much like when a teacher in entrepreneurship tells a student that they will succeed if they have a good idea. Any successful entrepreneur knows that the difficult part is realizing the ideas—getting through all the rounds of financing needed, living on little money for many years, working around the clock, postponing family life, and navigating all the conflicts that arise in the work environment. It is this hardship that makes or breaks the entrepreneur, not the lack of good ideas.

A competitive advantage is not found by having all the information available but by having the right kind of information. The notion of "asymmetry" in the study of economics does not consider this.

Let's consider this scenario instead: Most companies today are overloaded with information. Many purchase the same kind of external information so they could potentially know the same if they knew what they had and could use it better. Most companies have no clear idea how much information they possess, and in many companies, you will find several versions of the same expensive reports. From this perspective, the challenge is not in information asymmetry but in intelligence asymmetry—distinguishing the 'need to know' from the 'nice to know' and acting upon it, getting it to the people who need it and in time. Many companies know what to do but still don't do it. Very often, this is related to the human element; employees struggle among themselves to advance their careers within the organization, are unwilling to share, and often care more about their own interests, which do not need to be those of the company. This is part of human nature and can be expected to some degree, but it also sets limits for the company to the possibility of a competitive advantage.

To identify intelligence asymmetry, we need to ask what information is required in each process that leads to a competitive advantage. It's not enough to have this information somewhere in the organization; we need to be able to make it available and act upon it. Only then do we have a situation of intelligence asymmetry.

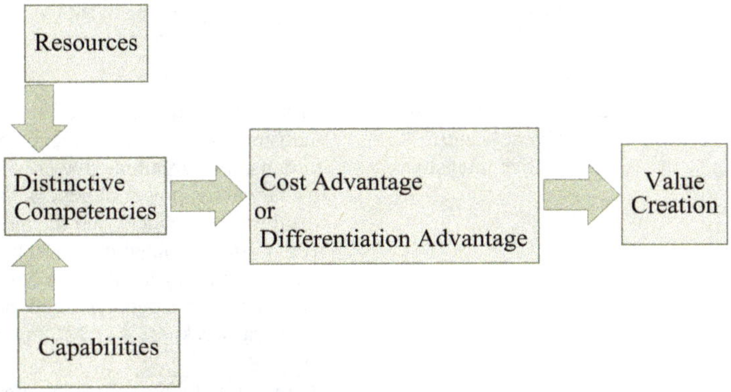

Fig. 4.11 Porter's model of competitive advantage. (Porter, 1980)

Let's expand on this idea by taking the example of Michael Porter's models. Porter identifies two kinds of competitive advantage: cost advantage and differentiation. That is, there are, in general, two ways to be different and win market share: either by offering a better price or by offering a better product. Porter's model for competitive advantage illustrates this (Fig. 4.11):

From the model we learn that Resources and Capabilities form the Competence of the organization. This competence is used to implement at least one of two strategies: Cost advantage or Differentiation Advantage. Thus, we have Cost Advantage Intelligence and Differentiation Advantage Intelligence as two major distinct types of activities.

In Porter's model, information and intelligence are not just supportive elements but foundational components that inform and guide the strategic direction and tactics of a company. They help the firm to exploit efficiencies, create unique offerings, and effectively compete in its chosen markets (Table 4.5).

To achieve a true competitive advantage, we must ask ourselves what information needs we have for each of the steps in the models used to gain a competitive edge. Obtaining intelligence asymmetry means that the organization is capable of gathering the right kind of intelligence related to what makes it competitive. Porter's models help us define these focus areas.

In many cases, the problem is that the company has chosen the wrong strategy, one that does not lead to a competitive advantage. If this is the case, the company will also gather the wrong kind of information. By focusing on intelligence asymmetry, the focus shifts away from the quantity of information needed—moving away from the phenomenon of information overload—and towards the quality of the information needed to achieve a competitive advantage for each type of analysis. Ultimately, like an entrepreneur, we need to act on this intelligence, put in the hours, and endure the hardships. Without this effort, the outcome will inevitably be zero.

Table 4.5 The role and purpose of intelligence in gaining a competitive advantage

#	Type of analysis	Purpose	Role of Intelligence
1	Industry Analysis	Used to assess industry attractiveness and competitive intensity.	Information and intelligence are vital to analyze these five forces: the threat of new entrants, the bargaining power of suppliers, the bargaining power of buyers, the threat of substitute products, and the intensity of rivalry among competitors. Detailed and accurate industry intelligence helps a firm understand these dynamics and identify the structural weaknesses and strengths of the industry.
2	Competitor Intelligence	Used to assess competitors' strategies, strengths, and weaknesses, allowing a company to strategically position itself to exploit opportunities and mitigate threats.	Gaining intelligence about competitors' strategies, strengths, and weaknesses can provide a significant advantage. This enables a company to position itself optimally by exploiting competitors' vulnerabilities and defending against their strengths. Accurate intelligence is key to predicting competitors' moves and reacting strategically.
3	Customer Understanding	Helps in segmenting and targeting markets more effectively, enabling the creation of products and services that meet specific customer needs and preferences.	Intelligence about customer preferences, behavior, and trends helps in better segmentation and targeting. This is particularly crucial for the differentiation strategy, where understanding nuanced customer needs and preferences can lead to the development of products and services that are perceived as unique.
4	Operational Efficiency	Enhances process optimization and cost reduction, contributing to better resource management and improved profitability.	Information systems play a pivotal role in achieving cost leadership by optimizing operations and reducing costs. Effective data management can lead to improved supply chain efficiencies, better inventory management, and overall operational improvements that reduce costs while maintaining quality.
5	Strategic Decision Making	Informs the formulation and implementation of business strategies, supporting decisions on market entry, product launches, and other crucial business activities.	Broadly, the internal and external intelligence feeds into strategic decision-making. This can involve deciding on entering new markets, timing product launches, investment in technology, and other strategic moves. The quality and timeliness of the information can determine the success of such decisions.
6	Innovation and Learning	Drives the development of new products and improvements, fostering a culture of continuous improvement and adaptation to changing market conditions.	Information and intelligence gathering are integral to fostering innovation and continuous learning within an organization. Understanding technological trends, regulatory changes, and market needs can drive innovation that underpins both cost leadership and differentiation strategies.

4.8 The Tripod: Intelligence, Security and Counterintelligence

So far, we have only discussed Intelligence. There are two other topics associated with our study: Security and Counterintelligence. While Security often has its own dedicated literature and courses, Counterintelligence is an important aspect of intelligence studies that is also highly relevant for private organizations.

Counterintelligence, as briefly introduced earlier, involves creating an organizational and technical system designed to construct counterattacks without the awareness of a potential attacker. This often includes disseminating false information to exploit the attacker's reliance on their new information set. As a method, it can be likened to the Japanese sport of Judo, where the aggressiveness of the opponent is used to their disadvantage.

The role of Counterintelligence is still perceived to be relatively unimportant in business. However, larger deals and advances in intelligence technology are convincing companies of the necessity of Counterintelligence measures, at least in certain situations. For instance, the media reports a new scandal involving bugging almost every week, yet relatively few of these incidents, which are leaked to the press, involve private organizations. The stance taken by private organizations is often that revealing the incident to the media will harm the company more than it will aid in repairing the damage caused by the incident. Thus, most companies choose to keep the details of the breach confidential. Larger companies with connections to national intelligence services might convey information through their designated channels but are often wary of Government Leakage Risk. To prevent eavesdropping, many companies conduct regular technical sweeps before discussing any sensitive matters in a foreign meeting room, or in some extreme cases, may choose to discuss certain issues during a walk outside rather than in the office. We often assume tape recorders are used—even within the company—making much of the actual working environment distrustful. It's difficult to speak your mind freely anywhere.

Negotiations are particularly sensitive to intelligence activities because there is so much at stake during these meetings.[13] Companies are also on their toes when they attend trade shows, being careful how much they disclose and to whom.

These situations are associated with different types of Intelligence Risks. It is a risk, not an uncertainty, as a well-formed Counterintelligence Plan can help eliminate at least some of the risk.[14] The Counterintelligence Plan is a way to work to reduce this risk and a part of the organization's Intelligence Strategy. It may look like this:

1. Identification of essential items that are most at risk.
2. Identification of essential situations that are most at risk.
3. Identification of competitors and their assumed capabilities.

---

[13] Söilen (2004).

[14] The distinction between Risk and uncertainty has been explained by Knight (1971).

4. Identification of vulnerabilities to competitors' assumed collection capabilities.
5. An assessment of the degrees of risk to those competitors and their capabilities.
6. Design of cost-effective countermeasures, which can range from education to perception management.[15]

Protecting all information and all facilities is both expensive and unnecessary, but all companies spend resources on security, protecting premises, buildings, and laboratories, but also intellectual property.

Also private companies can use safe houses for security. These safe houses are typically used to protect employees, executives, or clients in situations where their safety is at risk. These locations can be utilized during business travels, in regions with political instability, or in cases of kidnapping threats or other security concerns. Safe houses offer a secure environment where individuals can stay until it is safe to return to their normal activities.

For instance, large multinational corporations, particularly those operating in high-risk areas or industries, often have contingency plans that include the use of safe houses. These companies may collaborate with private security firms to establish and maintain these kinds of secure locations.

By its very nature, counterintelligence is about the perception of how the other party—the competitor or the supplier—thinks. We try to anticipate their moves and counter them by our own moves to decrease the damage they would otherwise inflict on us. Some companies, like banks, hire consultants or hackers and ask them to try to steal information from them in order to uncover weaknesses in their own security systems.[16] To get a more colorful perspective on what we are talking about, let's look at some famous examples from history:

In the literature, it is popular to trace the start of Counterintelligence activity back to Sir Francis Walsingham, who cracked the secret code of Mary Queen of Scots, thereby strengthening Queen Elizabeth's charges against her, which, as we may remember, led to her beheading; but he is of course not the first to have used such techniques.[17] Walsingham is also interesting for other reasons, as he is said to have dispatched students from Cambridge to infiltrate the French court, unaware of course that the Russians would use students from the same university to spy on their own centuries later (irony of history). He is said to have been inspired to build the intelligence system surrounding the Queen Elizabeth by Henry VII, who, by sheer necessity, had to construct an elaborate security and intelligence system just to prevent himself from being assassinated. Life as head of state was truly different in those times, even though parallels can be found today too, mostly in non-democratic developing countries. There is a reason why Vladimir Putin travels with his own personal chefs wherever he goes and a part reason why he would sit on a ridiculously long table when receiving guests. Not contracting COVID may have been another part reason.

[15] Based on Nolan (1995).

[16] See e.g. Winkler (1997).

[17] See e.g. Haynes (2001).

If a company has reasons to believe that one of its suppliers or competitors is using dishonest means of gathering information about its operations, it potentially has the possibility of preventing these acts. Let's say the company believes its competitors are tapping our phones. Phone security is a function which is no longer limited to state intelligence, but which anyone can buy, often from old spooks. Phone hacking has also been used by many journalists as an offensive strategy to get information. The most well-known case in recent years is the Mirror Group Newspapers (MGN), which includes publications like the Daily Mirror, Sunday Mirror, and The People. Although the scandal did not result in the total collapse of Murdoch's media empire, it had substantial repercussions. Murdoch had to withdraw his bid to take over the broadcaster BSkyB, resignations of top executives followed, and there were arrests of key personnel involved.

Counterintelligence may be used as a defensive strategy whereby a company goes in and "hijacks" the intelligence operations of another organization. Other examples are more offensive strategies. At the end of the last century, a company in the arms industry intercepted a fax from a competitor and quite cleverly changed the numbers in an offer to win the bid for a contract.[18] Companies must always determine what the intelligence risks are in any situation, especially when operating in foreign environments and different cultures, but we must also assess the vulnerability of all the equipment we use to send information.

After the Second World War, the size of the economy of many private companies had outgrown that of many nation-states. Multinationals today are more involved than ever in world politics as private interests merge with national interests. Large corporations maintain close ties with politicians through the activity known as lobbying, which often takes the form of exchanging funding for future favours. Lobbying as an intelligence operation is not only a problem in the American political system but is also an issue in the EU and in most other parts of the world. Foreign companies and nations are continuously trying to influence our politicians and the electoral base, called foreign interference.

Security is the building of an organizational and technical system to prevent a potential attacker from gathering information. As private organizations expand their operations to other countries, they often need even more security: for their employees, but first and foremost for their plants and equipment. Companies can be especially ruthless to competitors on their own home soil, in the worst case helped by their domestic security services.

The fact that the police are unable to meet these new demands for increased security has opened up an enormous market for private security companies. In 1934, Erik Philip-Sörensen founded "Hälsingborgs Nattvakt" in Helsingborg, Sweden, focusing mainly on Office Building Security. Today, his company is the largest security company in the world under the name of Securitas AB, employing some 300,000 people in 53 countries. The security industry primarily includes markets for guarding roads, buildings, parking lots, private homes, and for cash handling. To a lesser degree, it includes the guarding of employees and people, as that is

[18] On Offensive Strategies see Dylewski (2023).

considered an especially dangerous job. A number of smaller firms specialize in this niche of personal or executive protection. They also handle cases of certain types of fraud and theft in foreign countries.[19] This is where private intelligence started, with the security guard and detective agency Pinkerton in 1850, protecting the railroad companies as they fought their ways through new states and territories. Today, the company is part of Securitas AB.

We are nearing the end of this chapter, but before we are ready to discuss the different forms of analysis used in intelligence, there are a few other distinctions we need to explain about different types of intelligence.

4.9 Push and Pull Intelligence Proactive- and Reactive Intelligence, One-Time and Continuous Intelligence

By Push Intelligence, we refer to the dissemination of information to employees who have not requested it, but whom the intelligence officer believes might need it. Conversely, Pull Intelligence involves employees seeking out information themselves. In the latter case, we know the employee needs the information. However, it would be unfortunate if useful information existed within the organization but remained unknown to those who could benefit from it. This raises the issue of finding the right balance between push and pull intelligence in all organizations. Needless to say, this is a major topic in the discipline of digital marketing.

Early systems of business intelligence often relied on push intelligence, where the intelligence officer writes a report and sends it out to the organization. Pull intelligence is often cited as a drawback of a centralized intelligence model where Intelligence Teams produce copious reports that go unread.

Push intelligence is time-consuming, costly, and risks missing key issues as it typically begins without a clear understanding of the receiver's real information needs. On the other hand, some senior analysts may possess better insights than decision-makers and need to inform them about specific issues without a prior request. An intelligence system based solely on pull risks leading to what we call bottlenecking. Bottlenecking can severely limit an organization's efficiency and responsiveness, as a single manager becomes a bottleneck that delays decisions, restricts information flow, and potentially causes the company to miss opportunities or fail to address issues promptly.

The most common form of Push Intelligence is the newsletter, today often delivered by email or similar. These are often regarded as nice to have but peripheral to the employee's needs and relatively unimportant. Other forms of push intelligence with dubious value include mass emails sent by some central function in the organization or emails that are forwarded because they might be nice to know. This type of information often irritates employees when they realize the content is irrelevant as they have to spend time opening, deleting, or, in the worst case, replying to thank

[19] See e.g. Roberts (2004, pp. 11–25).

the sender. Therefore, we should be cautious with what we send as Push Intelligence to avoid alienating our audience.

An alternative is to develop a system for Pull Intelligence, where employees, depending on their security clearance, search for the information they need themselves. Pull intelligence is often considered more efficient and cost-effective and have become much easier to do now with larger and more advanced computer systems.

Most companies with well-developed ITs today use a combination of push and pull intelligence. The actual mix depends on factors such as the industry in which the company operates and the prevailing company culture. Tech companies, with employees skilled in computer use, may lean more towards pull intelligence, assuming employees will seek out necessary information via the computer. However, larger companies, especially those frequently interacting with new and diverse companies from other cultures, may find it both affordable and necessary to develop a system of push intelligence to ensure all employees are informed about critical issues.

There are two types of requests in pull intelligence: proactive and reactive. Proactive intelligence consists of information that the IT already has available, while reactive intelligence requires the IT to perform primary research to obtain the necessary information. This latter form is very costly. Most information for company analysis will be proactive as it already exists within internal systems such as accounting, financial reports, and marketing reports. Reactive intelligence tasks must be carefully managed to control costs.

Some assignments are one-time intelligence tasks, such as determining the impact of a political election on a country's economy (political dimension). Other issues require continuous monitoring, like tracking competitors' financial figures (competitor dimension), or customers' purchases (customer dimension). We call this Continuous Intelligence. One-time intelligence often requires initial investments in time and resources. If such intelligence is not sought again, initiating it can be costly, thus ITs strive to minimize major one-time intelligence assignments.

This chapter concludes the book, where we lay out the elements that constitute the basis for intelligence as a science. In the next part, we will present a number of analytical techniques. Note that while few of these techniques are unique to intelligence studies, they are used across many of the social sciences. However, certain analyses are more pivotal and commonly used in intelligence studies than in other disciplines, such as battle cards, win-loss analysis and wargaming.

Intelligence Analysis

5

The term "analysis" has an almost magical sound to it. There is an expectation that problems will be solved and that we will find the answers. Some try to learn as many types of analysis as possible, but it is more important to learn which analysis fits with what kind of problem and, on a more fundamental basis, what analysis actually is and what the value of analysis is. This, then, is the ambitious goal of this chapter.

5.1 The Intersection of Strategy and Public Policy in Intelligence Analysis

Intelligence gathering and analysis begin by finalizing, or if the company does not have one, writing a company strategy. The strategy should outline how the company intends to gain a competitive advantage.

A well-defined strategy is crucial for several reasons (Table 5.1):

Together, these objectives ensure that the company or organization does not derail. If we can gather intelligence for each objective, we have come a long way in creating a sustainable competitive advantage. This strategic focus not only guides day-to-day operations but also shapes the company's decisions about future growth and development.

Competitive advantage refers to the attributes that allow a company or organization to outperform its competitors. These attributes can include a variety of factors such as:

1. Cost Structure: Being able to produce goods or services at a lower cost than competitors.
2. Product Offerings: Providing superior products or services that meet customer needs better than competitors.
3. Brand Strength: Having a strong, recognizable brand that inspires customer loyalty.

K. Solberg Söilen, *Intelligence Studies in Business*, Management for Professionals,
https://doi.org/10.1007/978-3-031-76491-2_5

Table 5.1 Objectives, reasons, and effects of a strategy document

#	Objectives	Reason	Effects
1	Clear Direction and Focus	A strategy provides a clear roadmap for the organization, outlining specific goals and the means to achieve them.	This focus helps to align resources and efforts across the organization towards common objectives, maximizing efficiency and effectiveness.
2	Resource Allocation	By defining a competitive strategy, a company can make more informed decisions about where to allocate its resources, such as capital, talent, and technology.	This ensures that the most critical areas that can provide a competitive edge receive the necessary investments.
3	Differentiation from Competitors:	A strategic plan focused on competitive advantage helps a company differentiate itself from its competitors.	Whether through cost leadership, product differentiation, or niche markets, a clear strategy helps a company stand out in the marketplace.
4	Anticipation of Market Changes:	A strategy that includes a focus on gaining a competitive advantage requires an understanding of current market trends and potential future changes.	Whether through cost leadership, product differentiation, or niche markets, a clear strategy helps a company stand out in the marketplace.
5	Long-term Sustainability	By aiming for a competitive advantage, a strategy ensures that the company not only focuses on immediate gains but also considers long-term sustainability.	This can involve innovation, strengthening customer relationships, or improving operational efficiency, all of which contribute to enduring success.
6	Attracting Investment	Investors are more likely to put their money into a company with a clear, viable plan for achieving a competitive advantage.	This demonstrates to investors that the company has a thoughtful approach to overcoming market challenges and capitalizing on opportunities.
7	Motivation and Employee Engagement:	A clear competitive strategy can motivate employees by providing them with a sense of purpose and direction.	Understanding how their roles contribute to achieving a competitive advantage can enhance employee engagement and productivity
8	Risk Management:	A strategic approach to gaining a competitive advantage often includes identifying potential risks and developing ways to mitigate them.	This proactive risk management can protect the company from potential downturns and ensure stable growth.
9	Market Positioning	Clearly defining how to achieve a competitive advantage helps in positioning the company in the market.	This involves not only targeting the right customers but also communicating the unique benefits of the company's products or services effectively.

(continued)

Table 5.1 (continued)

#	Objectives	Reason	Effects
10	Enhanced Customer Value	Strategies focused on competitive advantage often lead to improvements in products or services, directly benefiting customers.	This could be through better quality, lower prices, or more innovative products, which can increase customer satisfaction and loyalty.

4. Technology: Utilizing superior technology to improve production processes, products, or services.
5. Distribution Network: Having an efficient and effective distribution network to reach customers quickly and reliably.
6. Customer Service: Providing outstanding customer service that enhances customer satisfaction and loyalty.

Competitive advantage allows companies to generate greater value for their stakeholders, resulting in higher sales, margins, and customer retention compared to their competitors. While the competitive advantage is a well-known concept in the business world, it is equally crucial for nation-states. Here's why:

1. Economic Growth: Nations with competitive advantages in key industries can boost their economic growth. For example, countries with advanced technology sectors, like the United States or South Korea, can lead in global innovation and economic performance.
2. Employment: Competitive industries can create jobs and reduce unemployment rates. Countries that lead in automotive manufacturing, for instance, provide extensive employment opportunities, from production to sales.
3. Global Influence: Nations that excel in certain areas can exert more influence on the global stage. For example, Saudi Arabia's competitive advantage in oil production gives it significant geopolitical leverage.
4. National Security: A country with a strong industrial base and technological edge is better positioned to ensure national security. Technological superiority in defense systems, for instance, can deter potential threats and ensure a nation's sovereignty.
5. Trade Balance: Countries with competitive industries can achieve a favorable trade balance by exporting more than they import. This leads to a stronger national currency and economic stability.
6. Innovation: Competitive advantage fosters innovation, as nations invest in research and development to maintain their leading positions. This innovation can lead to new industries and economic diversification.

In summary, competitive advantage is vital not only for companies but also for nation-states as it drives economic growth, enhances employment, influences global politics, ensures national security, improves trade balances, and fosters innovation.

The opposite of competitive advantage for nation-states can be considered decline, both economically and socially. Without a competitive edge, nations struggle to attract investment, foster innovation, and maintain high levels of productivity, leading to economic stagnation or regression. Socially, a lack of competitive advantage can result in reduced quality of life, higher unemployment rates, and greater inequality, eroding social cohesion and stability. Thus, sustaining a competitive advantage is crucial for nations to ensure ongoing economic growth and social well-being, avoiding the pitfalls of decline. This process is best explained through evolutionary theory, which emphasizes adaptation and survival in changing environments. Just as organisms must adapt to external pressures to thrive, nations must innovate and evolve their strategies to maintain competitive advantages and avoid decline.

In the public sector, the equivalent of 'strategy' used in business contexts is often referred to as public policy or strategic planning. Public policy involves the actions and decisions taken by government bodies to address public issues. It serves as a strategy for governing and is intended to solve problems efficiently and effectively, enhance public welfare, and achieve objectives that benefit the community or nation as a whole. Similar to business strategies, public policies are developed based on research, public needs assessments, and goals. They are designed to guide the public sector on how to allocate resources, implement plans, and measure outcomes. Strategic planning involves setting long-term goals and determining the best strategies to achieve these goals within public sector organizations. It aligns with the broader goals of public administration, such as improving public service delivery, increasing transparency, and promoting sustainability. It includes defining clear objectives, understanding the needs of the public, and planning how to use resources to achieve desired outcomes.

Both public policy and strategic planning in the public sector focus on creating public value, analogous to creating shareholder value in the private sector. They aim to enhance the quality of life for citizens, ensure effective management of public resources, and achieve sustainable, equitable development. Unlike private sector strategies, which primarily aim for competitive advantage and profitability, public sector strategies strive for social progress, equity, and the effective delivery of services to the public.

Gathering intelligence requires a defined strategy, but defining a strategy also necessitates gathering information. While this may seem paradoxical, in practice it seldom is. To complicate matters further, strategies evolve and change, rendering much of the collected intelligence outdated or merely informative rather than actionable. Despite these challenges, intelligence gathering remains a continuous effort, as social and economic events flow like a river, requiring constant filtration and analysis to remain relevant and useful.

An operating strategy defines the day-to-day work of the intelligence function. The overall strategy should ensure that the operating strategy is optimal at all times. An operating strategy is not a static tool and will change frequently. It must be revised regularly to remain relevant as the environment is continuously changing. As a consequence, an intelligence function cannot exclusively focus on its operating strategy for the gathering of information but must continuously search among a broad span of information sources to define and redefine future operating strategies.

The bias that otherwise occurs is called strategic blindness or confirmation bias in a strategic context. Strategic blindness occurs when an organization's predefined strategies and goals hinder its ability to see and respond to new information, trends, or threats that fall outside those strategies. The focus on existing strategic frameworks can limit the scope of intelligence gathering, causing the organization to overlook or dismiss important data that could suggest a need for strategy adjustment. It's also a form of confirmation bias. This happens in the context of strategic planning and intelligence when decision-makers or intelligence functions pay attention only to the information that confirms their pre-existing beliefs or strategies. This can limit the effectiveness of intelligence activities by narrowing the range of data considered, potentially leading to strategic missteps or missed opportunities.

5.2 The Time Perspective in Intelligence Studies

The true aim of intelligence activities is to achieve foreknowledge. However, we understand that human and social behavior is exceedingly complex, with numerous possible outcomes, making it impossible to predict the future. What we can do is map certain causes and effects and try to assign probabilities to various outcomes. With the advancement of AI, our ability to analyze and predict will improve significantly, but we will still be far from real-time mapping of social behavior in the foreseeable future.

Many are trying. The investment industry is a good example, but 'quants' can only take advantage of small discrepancies in the immediate future of markets. They have, at least so far, poor performance when it comes to long-term investments. Imagine, even if you specialize in the product of gold, chances are you have very little certainty as to the price of gold tomorrow. If you did, you would go out and borrow all the money you could get your hands on and make your bet today, either by buying or selling gold. The fact that no one does this just shows how difficult foreknowledge is. The manager who hires an intelligence analyst to gain this foreknowledge is at best overly optimistic. What we can deliver are scenarios, payoffs, and probabilities, in short, estimates for selected series of events.

We need to start any discussion about possible future events with a time axis. First, the longer into the future we want to see, the more uncertain our results are likely to be. The more specific answers we seek about events that have not yet happened, the more difficult our assignment is. This means that we have greater possibilities of making accurate predictions about general occurrences taking place in the immediate future, like the 'quants' have shown in finance, (assuming, of course, nothing major happens, like a market crash, then the quants fail too).

On this topic, the study of intelligence draws on the study of economics, which despite some of its irrelevance, at least aims to follow a strict scientific trajectory. Good economists never express themselves with certainty about the future. Instead, they start with a number of assumptions and axioms, much like in the natural

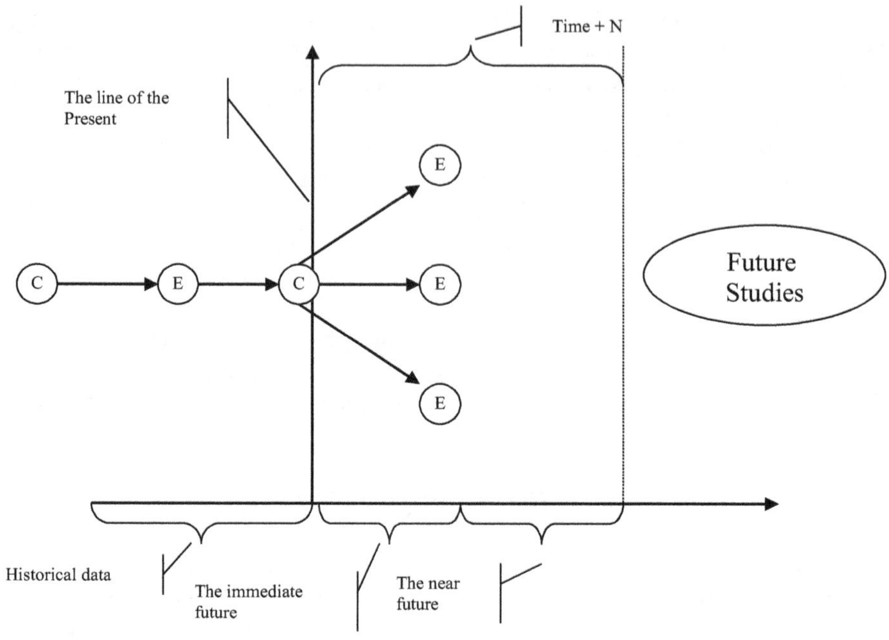

Fig. 5.1 The time perspective in intelligence studies

sciences. Based on these assumptions, they set up models and simplifications of our social reality, which are then tested, often by the use of statistics or modelled with econometrics. This is not a flawless method, but it allows for certain careful statements about human behaviour, which are far better than having no statements at all.

In the conclusions, economists may say that something is 'likely' to happen, that there is a certain chance for the appearance of an incident, and they may even sometimes specify a degree of certainty in the form of a careful probability calculation. This vagueness may be annoying to some, even suspect. Still, it is formulating predictions to the furthest extent that the scientific method allows for. No one can give a clear prediction about future human action: often not even about their own behavior. Those who do—and we see them every day in the media—are either tempted to promote themselves, feel forced, or act out of ignorance.

The example in the Fig. 5.1 shows a row of causes (c) and effects (e). The last cause has three effects. In most cases, each social fact (event) as a cause has a number of effects. This is what makes social facts and social predictions—and indeed the social sciences—so complex and difficult: some would say interesting, others impossible. In the natural sciences, we know that all water consists of two hydrogen atoms and one oxygen atom no matter if it comes from the Amazon River or from the Pacific Ocean. In the human sciences, we know that not only do human beings act differently from one culture to another, but also the same human being may act differently (effect) from 1 day to another, given the same action (cause). In fact, to show how complicated social reality really is for social scientists, a human being may want to act in one way—she may even pronounce her intentions of doing so in public—only to actually act in a completely different manner (a problem of Rational Choice). In some cases, it may be a lie—as when a politician says what she wants to do once elected president—but most of the time there are other reasons for why we change our behavior. Changes in actual behavior may be more or less conscious, that is, in many cases we mean to do something when we think of it, but our poor habits take the upper hand over our good thinking and our intentions. Human beings also tend to change roles depending on who we talk to; we wear different hats, so to speak. We are one person when we talk to our boss, another when we talk to the children or to the wife. We change hats as naturally as we mix vegetables in a salad. What version of reality we present depends on what hat we happen to be wearing at the time. We can even be in meetings wearing several hats at the same time, depending on whom we are addressing. All this makes mapping causes and effects very difficult, to say the least, but not impossible. Returning to the topic of water, while the molecular structure of water (H_2O) is always the same, at a higher level, all water is different because it contains varying levels of dissolved salts and minerals. For example, seawater has a higher salinity, averaging about 3.5%, due to the presence of dissolved salts like sodium chloride, magnesium, and calcium. This variation in composition can be seen as an allegory for human behavior, where the fundamental aspects are similar, but the details and complexities vary widely.

In intelligence studies we need to make a simple model by excluding a number of effects for each cause. The risk now is that the model loses more predictive power than it gains in insight. To exclude all additional effects will be too simple; to hope to catch all the effects and evaluate them accurately is too difficult. We have to settle for something in between, like selecting what we see as the most important effects for each single cause. We may help ourselves a bit further by setting up a number of assumptions for the model, describing under which conditions the model will be true. We refer to these as axioms in the natural sciences.

In mathematics and logic, axioms are foundational statements or principles that are accepted without proof and used as the starting points for further reasoning and arguments within a theoretical framework. Axioms are typically presented in a clear and concise manner, outlining the conditions or premises that are assumed to be true within the context of the model. These statements serve as the basis upon which the model is built and from which further propositions and theorems are derived.

Here is an example of how axioms might be presented:

1. Axiom 1: If two quantities are equal to the same quantity, they are equal to each other.
2. Axiom 2: The whole is greater than the part.
3. Axiom 3: A straight line can be drawn between any two points.

In the context of our statement, the axioms might look something like this:

1. Assumption 1: The model assumes that all input data are accurate and reliable.
2. Assumption 2: The relationships between variables are linear and additive.
3. Assumption 3: External factors influencing the model are constant and unchanging during the analysis period.

By clearly stating these assumptions, we define the scope and limitations of the model, ensuring that any conclusions drawn are understood to be valid within the specified conditions.

Another way to see the problem, but which will not give an answer to the practical question at hand, is to say that we must consider and accept our cognitive limitations as human beings, as we are not intellectually able to follow more than a few effects for each cause over time. Even with the use of computers, this will not be an easy task, but now with AI, we are making progress. The question will be more, how much progress we will make.

Today we are able to analyze a problem very much by studying the way the brain works. If we know how the brain works, we will probably be able to construct better methods because we will have a better understanding of what we are actually able to do. This was what brought forward the breakthrough in AI, making a program that mimics the brain in the way we translate language. Future advances in Behavioral Neurology and Neuropsychology are likely to provide significant contributions to the further understanding of social behavior, which will also improve the study of Intelligence.

But let's get back to the timeline. Any student involved in Intelligence should respect the line of the present. Once we cross this line, most social facts become uncertain or mere speculations and guesses. Ignoring this boundary often leads to hubris and incorrect predictions. Every day, the media entice experts to appear on TV and predict the future. A few weeks later, when the actual outcomes are known, these experts often seem untrustworthy due to their earlier mispredictions. Simply put, most experts do not show respect for the line of the present. It's always tempting to step over this line and downplay its significance, but it is a big deal. Fortunately for the experts, most viewers will have forgotten their advice anyway, and if one expert happens to be correct once, they will remind us of it forever, even though it was likely due to luck.

Intelligence is primarily concerned with what may happen in the immediate future and, at most, what will happen in the near future. How long these time periods last depends much on the kinds of questions asked and the type of industry we are in, but normally we are talking about an interval of 0–3 years. To take an example, it may be possible for the marketing research department to say what the trends are going to be in youth clothing next year, maybe even the year after—based on historical data and some early warning signals from the fashion industry—but difficult and almost impossible to predict the same trend in three, say 4 years. In the interval of 4–10 years, we may expect that some of the styles which have already been a fashion will reoccur as such, but we do not know which ones and when. Even in the clothing industry, which obviously follows certain cycles of change, there are too many variables to account for. A shirt may have short or long sleeves, be tight or roomy, have any one of a large number of colors or a combination of these, have any of a larger number of patterns, and be of any of a large selection of fabrics, etc. The complexity of all these possibilities is difficult, sometimes impractical, to map down. The colors and the big, roomy size of the clothes from the sixties may come back, but the clothes will often never be just as they were then or have small alterations. Instead, there may come new fabrics and other combinations of clothes. Many investors who speculate on the stock market will try to look 6 months ahead, maximum of 1 year. They will not even attempt to try to guess anything further into the future. Alternatively, they may choose to remain in the market or hold stock in a company for the long term, provided no significant weaknesses emerge that would prompt them to reconsider and exit.

That which lies beyond, a time we may call Time + N, belongs to the field we call Future Studies, Futures Thinking, Foresight and Futurology. Although there are differences between them, as shown earlier in Chap. 2, rigorous analysis and systematic data gathering are often replaced by wide (and sometimes wild) speculations and, at worst, a good portion of fantasy, puffed up by more or less randomly chosen historical parallels. It does not mean that these futures studies cannot be right. Take the example of Alvin Toffler, his general prediction for the information age have been inspirational for a whole generation, but such exceptions are rare. The success of futurologists tends to depend more on their background and experience, their education, personalities, and interests than on the analysis of the subject matter. They will often be convincing because they are good public speakers. As with any young academic discipline focused on social predictions, the study of intelligence is full of futurologists, self-proclaimed management gurus, and experts trying to earn a living as consultants, and we cannot blame them. At best, these individuals are colorful speakers at company conferences, giving employees that much-needed pep talk for the new year or when a new product is launched. At worst, they deliver erroneous intelligence to top management who then not only believe them but act on their advice.

Historical data are always useful when we want to find patterns in some social developments. The argument, if one wills, is that because some things were so in the past, and one fact follows another, we should expect such occurrences in the future. In other words, the future is a function of the past. This is true, but not 100%, and it is that difference that causes the trouble. That it's not 100% true is also not a reason to disregard *the historical method.*

There is always an element of change, a certain percentage that will be different for all events. We evolve, society changes. It is enough to take a look at a photo of our grandparents to know that this is true: not only have the clothes changed, but many of the values, ways of living, not to mention the impact new technology continues to have on our lives, are different. Then there are events that we can be more certain of, like the occurrence of new wars. This is, of course, most unfortunate, but history has shown that it's true. After the end of the Cold War, many nations reduced their military drastically, even discarding many of their strategic positions, hoping to save money. The thinking was that the US or the West had won and that there would be no more major wars. That has changed drastically today, now recently with the war in Ukraine, a war in Gaza and increased conflicts between the US and China. What does change is the nature of wars. It may be that future wars are fought with swarms of drones. As the last pandemic showed us, we are also vulnerable to viruses, which can be fabricated in laboratories and used as weapons. This is probably the greatest risk to our survival right now, what is known as biological weapons. Then there is the ever-present nuclear threat, which carries the potential to wipe out the entire human race—not just through the devastation of the explosions themselves, but through the aftermath of a nuclear winter.

The largest problem with the historical method for use in Business and Public life is that it does not allow for *specific predictions* concerning detailed information like whether or not we should buy a certain property, reduce our prices, or hire a new employee. As it is these kinds of questions which are most relevant to the study and practice of Intelligence, and not the larger issues of human behavior used in *general predictions*, like the nature of man's sexual instincts, his need for friendship and proteins, the historical method will never play more than a supporting role in Intelligence analysis, especially on the micro level.

Another element that is changing the nature of intelligence in private companies is ever shorter product life cycles due to increased competition.

5.3 Efficient Intelligence Systems Leading to Shorter Product Life Cycles

As companies become more adept at handling information, they are able to bring new products to market faster. We may say that they are learning faster. This, in turn, increases competition and makes the management of information a competitive advantage in what may be illustrated as an *upward spiral of intelligence efficiency*. As more companies implement efficient intelligence systems, it becomes necessary for others to follow.

The concept of the product life cycle is often attributed to Raymond Vernon and his work from the 1960s.[1] Vernon introduced this concept as part of his international product life cycle theory, which was initially developed to explain certain trade patterns observed in the global market. His theory described how a product goes through various stages—introduction, growth, maturity, and decline—each of which could influence the manufacturing location, pricing strategies, competitive environment, and marketing tactics. The idea of product life cycles was derived from the concept of business cycles, which was first developed in the early twentieth century with significant contributions from economists like Joseph Schumpeter and researchers at the Kiel Institute for the World Economy (IfW) in Kiel, Germany. In 1926, the institute established a department for statistical economics and business-cycle research, significantly contributing to its profile in business cycle theory and policies. The new department was headed by Adolph Lowe and included researchers such as Gerhard Colm, Hans Neisser, Jacob Marschak, and Wassily Leontief, all of whom have made significant contributions to the study of economics and management.

Failing to plan for shorter business cycles and not being ready with a new product once the existing one experiences decreased sales can be catastrophic. This was evident in much of the British car industry. After the Second World War, many

[1] Vernon (1966).

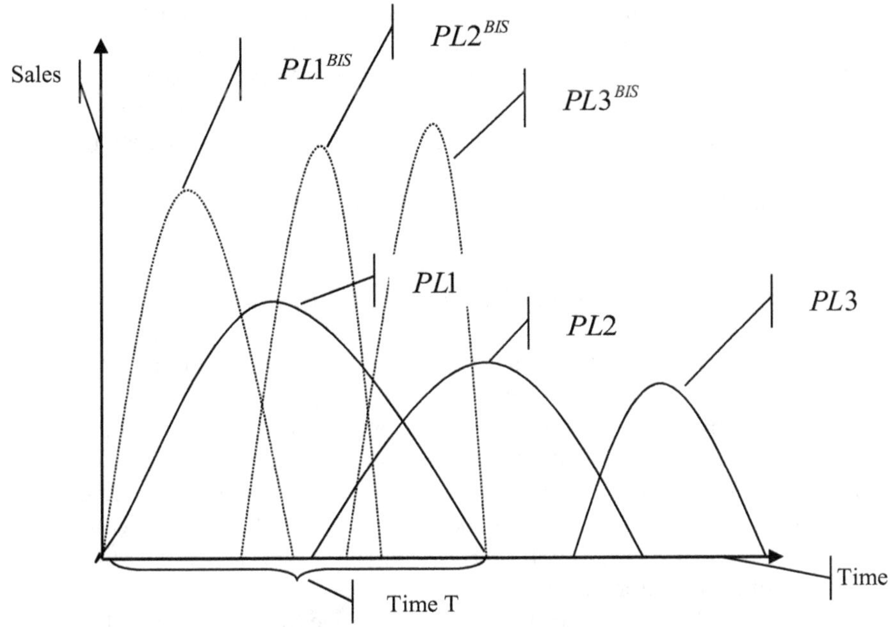

Fig. 5.2 Business intelligence systems and product life cycles

British car brands were merged into a conglomerate initially known as the British Motor Corporation (BMC). Formed in 1952, BMC combined several major British car manufacturers, including Austin and Morris. Over time, BMC also incorporated other well-known British car brands such as MG, Riley, and Wolseley. Later, in 1968, BMC merged with Leyland Motors (which included Rover, Standard, and Triumph) to form the British Leyland Motor Corporation (BLMC). This entity was nationalized in 1975 due to financial difficulties and rebranded as British Leyland Ltd. and mostly sold off to foreign buyers causing massive layoffs in the UK.

Instead of relying on one product over Time T, a company must launch multiple products to compensate for declines in sales, which must be done promptly. In the example below, a company launches three products in the same time interval and increases the total amount of sales when an efficient Intelligence System is implemented. The company is able to turn a negative spiral of sales for each new product into a positive trend when the market appreciates its speed of product development by purchasing its products. In the Fig. 5.2, we see two sets of product life cycles, one with and one without an implemented business intelligence system. Competition leads to ever shorter and steeper curves. This then seems to be the nature of global economic competition; itself pushed forward by ever faster exchange of information and new innovations.

Another good example is EV cars today. Battery technology is changing fast, and cars produced less than a year ago are by many standards considered unattractive due to short range and high prices. That you are a major EV car producer today is no guarantee that you will be around in a year's time. The competition is fierce.

The tendency in most industries is that the product life cycle is getting shorter as competition increases. This also means that it is becoming ever more important for the competitive advantage of firms that they implement a well-functioning intelligence system.

Most of the data in this system is going to be Open Source (OS).

5.4 Open Sources as a Policy and as a Philosophy

Open sources are information which is potentially available to everyone. Potentially because it assumes that you can read or have the money to buy it if it is not for free. As intelligence, by definition, is useful, Open Source information is seldom for free.

Open sources can be divided into *free sources* and *commercials sources*. A free source can be a document available on the Internet: a commercial source can be a report from say a consulting company like e.g. Frost & Sullivan. Many commercial reports are quite expensive, even for larger companies. This sets a clear limit to the availability of useful information.

The opposite of open sources is *secret sources*. Dedijer and Jequier distinguish between *Open information* (estimated to 90% of all information), *Gray information* (9%), *Secret information* (0.9%) and *Non-existent information* (0.1%).[2] Since the publication in 1987 The percentage of Open source have increased with the rise of the internet and digital communication technologies. But what has changed dramatically is the amount of information readily accessible to the public. The percentage of Grey information have also seen a relative increase due to the expansion of digital platforms that host semi-private data (such as databases requiring subscriptions or membership-based access). The business intelligence sector has grown, and professional networking platforms have made more of this type of information available to a broader audience, though it remains somewhat restricted. The percentage of Secret information have dropped, but the total amount has probably remained relatively stable or increased slightly in absolute terms due to more entities (corporations and governments) emphasizing data secrecy and security. Overall, though, their percentages of total information have not changed that much.

Gray information is defined as that which is time-consuming and difficult to locate. Non-existent information, on the other hand, may be defined as information you did not know you had.

Measuring non-existent information is obviously challenging, as it's hard to quantify what does not exist. However, with advances in technology and research, what was once non-existent (unknown or undiscovered) may now become known. Thus, this category might see a relative decrease as more of the unknown becomes discoverable.

[2] Dedijer and Jéquier (1987). Actual numbers have probably not changed that much.

Hidden sources refer to categories of information that are not publicly accessible or widely known to the general public. These sources are typically safeguarded due to their sensitivity, confidentiality, or strategic importance. Hidden sources include company information, state intelligence services, and what is held at embassies, to give some examples:

1. *Company Information*: This includes internal data that a company chooses to keep confidential for competitive, security, or proprietary reasons. Examples might include internal reports, unpublished research and development data, financial figures not disclosed to the public, strategic plans, and internal communications. Access to such information is typically restricted to company personnel, and it may sometimes be shared with selected stakeholders under non-disclosure agreements (NDAs).
2. *State Intelligence Services*: Information from state intelligence services encompasses classified data used for national security and diplomatic purposes. This can include information on national defense strategies, espionage activities, counterintelligence, and detailed assessments of foreign threats or political situations. Such information is tightly controlled and usually only accessible to government officials and authorized personnel. Disclosure of this information without authorization can lead to legal penalties, given its potential impact on national security.
3. *Embassies*: Embassies hold a variety of sensitive information related to diplomatic activities, bilateral relations, and assessments of the host country's political, economic, and social landscapes. This information can include internal communications between the embassy and its home government, reports on local developments, and strategic documents outlining diplomatic goals and tactics. Access to this information is generally limited to embassy staff and relevant government departments in the home country. These hidden sources are critical for various stakeholders, such as policymakers, strategic business leaders, and security officials, who rely on this type of information for making informed decisions. However, due to their sensitive nature, these sources are protected to prevent unauthorized access and the potential consequences that such exposure might entail.

Some of the most valuable assets a company holds are its patents. However, when a company files a patent application, the invention's details become publicly accessible through patent databases. This situation creates a problem known as the patent dilemma, where competitors can access and potentially utilize this information quickly, possibly even improving upon it. As a result, many companies choose not to pursue patents to avoid disclosing their innovations prematurely. Instead, they opt to protect their intellectual property through trade secrets, keeping their inventions confidential and securely stored to prevent unauthorized access. For the same reason, some applied research at universities is also kept secret from the world, for example when researchers work closely with state intelligence services. However, the basic science of this research is mostly open source.

5.4.1 The Intelligence Classification System

Secret sources may be divided by their degree of secrecy, often referred to as the classification system. Each time we conduct an analysis, we should have an idea as to its sensitivity. The degree of sensitivity of a report is often classified according to some scale. Information classification according to secrecy is a common practice within governments, military operations, and increasingly in private sector companies, especially those dealing with sensitive data or operations. The purpose of classifying information is to protect it from unauthorized disclosure, which could potentially lead to security risks or competitive disadvantages. Below is an illustrative example of how information is typically classified (Table 5.2):

Most of the rules on how to handle classification are found in the public sector, particularly within state organizations, and most stringently of all, in the military. In the private sector, handling, storing, and transmitting sensitive information involves a mix of legal requirements, industry standards, and best practices tailored to protect proprietary information, ensure privacy, and maintain a competitive advantage.

In all cases, the rationale for classification is to protect information that, if disclosed, could cause harm to national security, competitive posture, or operational integrity. As technology evolves and more information is digitized, managing access to classified and sensitive information continues to be a critical function for both government and business entities.

It's one question what information is classified according to what level of secrecy; it's a completely different question why. State intelligence services, at least historically, tended to classify almost anything as secret once it entered their organization, including newspaper articles. Hiding information is by itself costly and makes it more difficult for members of the organization to learn what is happening. In state organizations, this can be very frustrating because as an analyst there are many things you are not allowed to know, and this may even hinder you in your job.

It's often surprising how little people know about the companies for which they work. This is in part because companies are often secretive as to how they handle many operations inside of the organization, especially as far as money is concerned. One example is how profits are funneled from one subsidiary to the headquarters or to some account in a tax haven, or who really owns the company. Sometimes only a few in top management will know the details. It is as if there is also an unwritten system of classifying information.

5.4.2 The Philosophy of Open Source

There are many advantages to open sources. First of all, more and more information is today placed in open sources and made easily available through libraries, newspapers, books, and not to mention the Internet. The most important Open Sources are sources we do not think about, like the people we meet, for example at trade shows, our friends, and colleagues, but also customers and competitors (Table 5.3).

Table 5.2 The classification system matrix for public and private organizations

Organizational belonging	Type of intelligence	Specification of intelligence	Protocols for handling, storing
Government and Military Classification	Top Secret	The highest level of classification. Information is classified as Top Secret when its unauthorized disclosure could cause "exceptionally grave damage" to national security. Examples include details of critical national defense plans or covert operations (secret missions), or, with complete deniability: Black Ops	Must be logged and monitored access-controlled facilities often with multiple layers of security such as biometric access controls might include secure couriers for physical documents or encrypted electronic transmission methods such as secure VPNs or military-grade encryption standards.
	Secret	Information is classified as Secret when its disclosure could cause "serious damage" to national security. This might include details about military deployments, capabilities, or partnerships that are sensitive but not as critical as those classified as Top Secret.	Handling logs and access records are maintained. Digital information is encrypted and access is controlled through secure authentication methods. Encrypted emails, secure file transfer protocols, and controlled access to remote systems.
	Confidential	This classification is used when the unauthorized disclosure of information could cause "damage" to national security. It is the lowest level of classification used for national security information and might include less sensitive communications between diplomats or less critical military information.	Allow for a broader range of access within the organization or agency. Handling and access are logged controls might be less stringent
	Restricted (used less frequently)	Some systems include a level called Restricted, which is used for information that should not be public but whose disclosure is less likely to threaten national security significantly. It is more about controlling access than dealing with genuine security threats.	Limited to authorized personnel. May be stored in a locked drawer or on password-protected systems

(continued)

Table 5.2 (continued)

Organizational belonging	Type of intelligence	Specification of intelligence	Protocols for handling, storing
Private Sector Classification	Confidential	Used for information that, if disclosed, could adversely affect the company's operations, profitability, or competitive position. This includes trade secrets, new product specifications, or client information.	Strictly limited to personnel who need it to perform their job functions. This often involves signing non-disclosure agreements (NDAs) to legally bind employees to confidentiality stored in secure, access-controlled systems
	Restricted	This classification limits information to certain groups within the company who need to know this information to perform their jobs. It might include internal policy documents or certain financial data.	Accessible to a broader group within the company, Storage protocols for restricted information include password-protected documents and databases, Secure communication protocols such as TLS (Transport Layer Security) for emails and HTTPS for web-based transmissions are commonly used.
	Public or Non-classified	This includes information that can be shared with the general public without any risk to the company. It often includes press releases, product advertisements, or published financial data	Does not require stringent handling protocols, stored with minimal security, often transmitted using standard internet protocols

Table 5.3 Example of open sources

Internal environment	External environment
Business Periodicals Index	Macro analysis by the EIU[a]
Specialized Business magazines	Reports by environmental organizations (Greenpeace)
Commercial data (ex. Nielsen Company)	Information services (Esmerk, Reuters)
Standard and Poor's Industry	UN reports on technological development
Moody's Manuals	Dissertations in Sociology

[a]The Economist Intelligence Unit, same corporation which publishes the weekly journal the Economist

Another advantage of these sources, often neglected in the literature, is that they offer benefits that secret sources cannot match. Humans have an inclination to search for and find pleasure in obtaining true information, often taking pride in sharing it. This creates an upward spiral of information exchange and trust between analysts and decision makers. As professionals in a workplace, we want to show others how adept we are at our jobs, which includes collecting and analyzing information. Restricting this dampens enthusiasm for the job, making it less interesting, and spreading suspicion and animosities.

The opposite of Open Source or Knowledge Sharing is Knowledge Hiding. Knowledge Hiding means that employees intentionally withhold and conceal knowledge from others. This behavior impacts not only financial and task performance but also the organization's culture, as it damages relationships and can cause distrust among employees. Research suggests that you first need to develop an organizational culture of trust and fairness before you can hope to get employees to share information. Only then will leadership style and organizational design be able to come to terms with the problem of knowledge hiding in organizations.[3]

In much the same way, those who deal with secret sources can sometimes find themselves in an environment of plots, extortion, threats, hostility, and cheating, which, by definition, hinders the flow of information. Carriers of secret information are often afraid of disclosing too much, unsure how much to reveal, or even uncertain of whom they can talk to. This creates awkward social situations and can also degrade the quality of the intelligence. Thus, Open Source has much going for it.

We refer to this realization as a *philosophy of open sources*, believing that for use in private and public organizations, open sources will outperform their secret counterparts even in the short run because of the positive qualities associated with this kind of information and the effects it has on the organization's performance. Some organizations that subscribe to this belief are adopting open sources as a policy. While secrets are sometimes necessary, they often breed suspicion, and their importance is mostly exaggerated. This realization holds the potential to revolutionize even the secret intelligence services, understanding the potential efficiency of an intelligence organization built on transparency and the strategic use of open-source intelligence. In the information age intelligence is no longer an activity for a secretive elite but for all employees working in organizations that compete in one way or another, public or private.

Open-source organizations are challenging their secret-source equivalents, sometimes even within the realm of military intelligence. The American private intelligence company Stratfor, now Strategic Forecasting Inc., founded by a Texan professor of political science, collects military and economic intelligence based on open sources, specializing in geopolitics. The information gathered here has sometimes been known to be faster and more reliable than that produced by the CIA, and less expensive. Today, we have private companies—producers of software, hardware and data brokers specializing in Bulk Personal Data (BPD) that, in many cases, can outperform the data gathered by the NSA in their area of expertise.

Google Earth is another good example, and it has many user groups. Bellingcat is an example of a private organization that has achieved remarkable success in the field of intelligence, particularly in open-source intelligence (OSINT). In the realm of cybersecurity and network monitoring, companies like CrowdStrike and FireEye

[3] Oubrich et al. (2021).

have developed sophisticated tools and techniques for detecting and mitigating cyber threats. These companies often collaborate with or are contracted by government agencies to provide services that complement national capabilities.

Another open-source example that started in academia is the English company Oxford Analytica, which has been known to provide excellent political intelligence and strategic analysis of world events. Both of these open-source companies draw on a considerable network of outside experts. Thus, the quality of their intelligence depends much on the company's ability to build and maintain their network, primarily with academics and researchers.

The natural place to start a search with open sources is through a library database or any search engine for publications. Today, many switch between an AI application with different plug-ins for searches. This approach will provide some quality sources, which will lead to others and a dialogue is achieved between man and machine. Much of the newer academic research is available through Google Scholar and similar databases, especially with the help of the Sci-Hub plug-in, often referred to as the "Pirate Bay of Science." Created by Alexandra Elbakyan, Sci-Hub has been involved in numerous lawsuits and is considered illegal in many jurisdictions due to its unauthorized distribution of copyrighted material. While universities in wealthy countries can afford the subscription fees for academic journals, researchers in poorer countries and those unaffiliated with major institutions often cannot. For these researchers, Sci-Hub provides a vital means of access to academic literature.

As Westerners, we do not often search Chinese webpages that are translated into English. However, the Chinese search both. They have also made an inventory of all our sciences at most our universities, even many of the smaller ones. Thus, we may say that they know all about us, but we know very little about them. (Let that sink in for a moment) Our young generation in the West is not even curious about Asia. They have often not even heard about the city of Chongqing and do not care to listen. This gives the Chinese a tremendous competitive advantage. In the world of intelligence, the West thinks like a typical Wall Street CEO, running after quarterly results and betting on quick and fast operations. The Chinese, on their side, take time to lean and think strategically. Like the shallow-swimming fish that goes to the surface to eat, they bide their time. This is another tremendous competitive advantage of many Asian Cultures. We must rekindle our curiosity about the world and embrace the willingness to visit and live in uncomfortable conditions; without this mindset, we risk losing our competitive edge entirely.

There are almost three times as many internet users in China as in the US, with 1.092 billion compared to 312 million. Even when adding the 500 million users in the EU, the Chinese still lead in numbers. Additionally, their e-commerce platforms and interaction with services provided over the Internet are often more advanced than those in the West, including payment functions. This is significant as the Internet itself is by far the largest source of Open-Source Intelligence (OSINT).

Depending on what we search for on the Internet, this makes us smarter or less informed about the world around us. Today we are no longer bound by linear-TV, but can watch the best experts and researchers lecture, give interviews, or participate in pods online, much of it for free, and much of it in real-time. This is already revolutionizing learning but it is also turning the internet into a human rights issue. Everyone needs internet access today to have a chance to learn. It's also one of many reasons to be optimistic about the future, even though, as we have seen earlier, manipulation and e-piracy are growing problems, at least for now.[4]

Next, we ask, how do a company start with intelligence work. One way of answering can be given by explaining the nature of different reports needed within the company, starting with the business plan.

5.5 The Making of Reports: Comparing the Industry Analysis to the Company Analysis

Every employee in a private company needs to learn more about the industry they operate in. The single report which best describes this is often referred to as the company's *Industry Analysis*. The twin brother of the Industry Analysis is called the *Company Analysis*, which describes what is going on inside the company.

There are consulting companies offering ready-made Industry Analyses within most areas of interest: everything from Advanced Flat Glass to Biocides and Industrial Rubber. The advantage of purchasing reports from external consultants is, first of all, timesaving. When buying the report your organization receives expert help, but it also sacrifices some of the independent thinking that is important to maintain within the company. Furthermore, buying a report does not exclude the possibility of creating your own report, but in practice, it is difficult not to be influenced by the conclusions in the external reports. This is known as *anchoring bias*, where an individual relies too heavily on an initial piece of information to make subsequent judgments. Also consider this: The conclusions in the expert report have been distributed to a large number of your actual and potential competitors. If they are smart and received the intelligence before you, they may have acted on it already. Thus, if you are relying on the same Information Set for your strategic decisions, you should not expect to outperform your competitors, unless you can analyze the report you bought to gain what we call *analytical intelligence*.

The company analysis should help determine to what extent our organization is competitive. It includes key information concerning all relevant functions of the company: accounting, finance, marketing, production, and human resource management. This will cover marketing plans, cost analysis, and various financial models or financial projections. These tools are integral parts of a company's broader financial strategy and are used to forecast the financial outcomes of various business scenarios. Much of this will include budgets, supply chain analysis, profitability analyses, cash flow forecasts, and different kinds of strategic plans. It all contributes to answering the question of how the company is performing. Note that we do not yet know how competitive we are. We only know at this stage how we are

[4] Söilen (2016a).

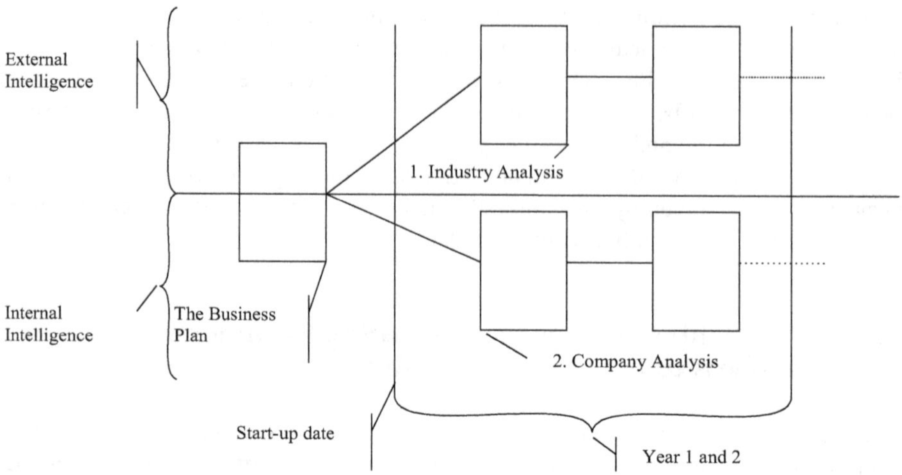

Fig. 5.3 The industry and company analysis as a continuation of the business plan

performing ourselves; not how other companies are doing. To do that, we need to combine the company analysis with the industry analysis.

Most businesses do not start with the company or industry analysis but with a *business plan*. A business plan is a combination of two plans, a marketing plan and a financial plan. As such, we could say it's a compressed industry and company analysis in one document. Business plans are what entrepreneurs or wannabe entrepreneurs like students create when they have a business idea. Normally, it is written only once and predominantly for one group of outside experts: investors. Once the company is up and running, the content of the plan is enlarged into the industry and company analyses. These analyses are then produced every year or so. They are often updated at the end of every year, either in a report or as slides for some management group presentation. Thus, the report landscape can look something like this for a company over time (Fig. 5.3):

There are many challenging aspects of a business plan, but the most significant is that the plan is essentially just predictions built on assumptions, as the company has not started yet and thus lacks historical data and benchmarks. This is, to say the least, problematic. We are making assumptions without really knowing much about the company or the industry. The person presenting the business plan must be able to provide credible answers for all the numbers presented. Most numbers in business plans are overly optimistic because, more often than not, it's more of a sales document to investors than a realistic document of facts. If you show in the plan that you don't make any money, you will not get the investment. However, on the other hand, if you show that you make money from the start, you will often not get any investment either, as your plan will be deemed unrealistic.

More 'realistic' business plans often depict the same narrative: a business struggling in the first few years but then quickly making money in years 3 or 4. Most business plans look 3–5 years ahead. Of course, this is not always realistic either, and most business ideas do not get off the ground, but this scenario is often thought of as a compromise for possible realities in the future. At the end, a business plan is more of a story where the key ingredients are not only the potential market—or need for the product—but where discussing assumptions is crucial to gaining confidence. In any case, we have to conduct a lot of market research, similar to the intelligence processes described throughout this book.

There are some notable exceptions to writing business plans, but they can convey the wrong impression. In Silicon Valley, sometimes it is enough to present a piece of paper with the names of the people who have committed to working full-time in a new company to secure financing from the local VC firm. The reason is that VCs know who the experts are in any field related to the digital world, so if you build a company and have persuaded the top five people in, let's say, semiconductors to join you, that in itself is a good indication that you will succeed. The same goes for other tech ideas. The story about Sam Bankman-Fried's pitch to the VC has become legendary. Supposedly, he just sat on a couch playing video games during much of his presentation.

Both the industry and company analysis are essential to the subjects called Strategy and Entrepreneurship. Both analyses are made available to top management and to the board of directors as a basis for strategic discussions regularly. Some companies combine the two reports into one, which may be called a 'Strategy Report' or just a 'Marketing Report.'

A strategy report hastily put together at the end of the year without thorough intelligence work risks falling victim to poor mental habits, preconceived notions, and reliance on secondary research in the form of expensive, often randomly chosen, and overly general consultant reports. It will come as no surprise that poor reports lead to poor decisions. However, most managers do not like to sit down and go through reports; they are men of action, not academics or nurds. Therefore, in organizations, there is a tendency to push the writing of reports forward and to delegate them to someone else, often ultimately to a manager in the marketing department or finance or to an external consultant.

So, how can we determine the optimal production levels that ensure a sustainable competitive advantage, given a specific set of costs and revenues? How do we compare the two documents, the company and industry analysis? This can be done in multiple ways, but let's try to illustrate how it can be done for one variable, the break-even analysis. When plotted on a Cartesian coordinate system, a break-even analysis curve will detect if and what the discrepancies are between what the market demands and what the company can offer in a competitive environment. Any activity beyond the competitive point may yield a profit, but only in the short term. It does not align with achieving a *sustainable competitive advantage*. (Fig. 5.4).

In the illustration, the industry achieves break-even at a significantly lower cost level than the company, implying that the company can only compete effectively at lower production levels. This disparity may arise from several factors. The industry at large likely benefits from economies of scale, spreading fixed costs over a larger output, thus reducing per-unit costs. Additionally, the industry might have access to advanced technology and efficient supply chains, lowering production expenses

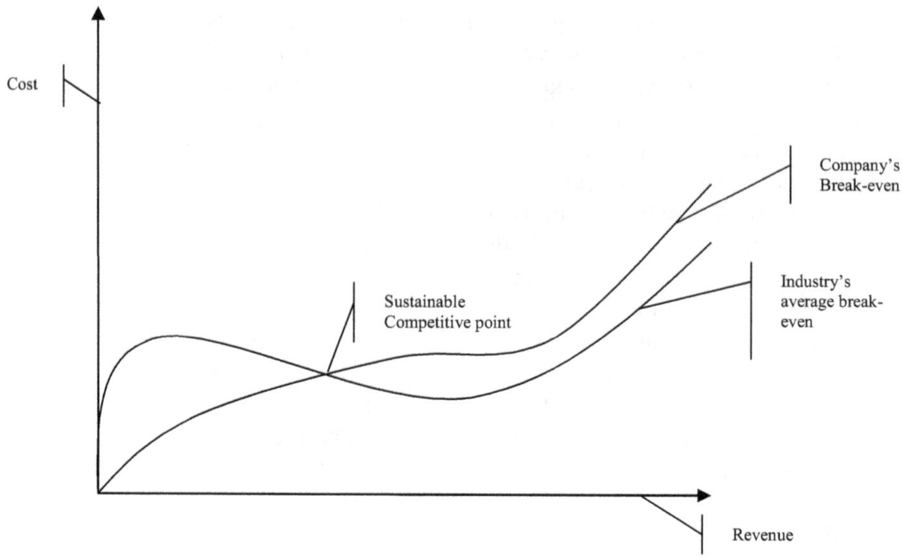

Fig. 5.4 Gap analysis for breakeven from industry and company analysis. (A version of Ansoff (1984, p. 16))

compared to the company. Furthermore, the industry may operate in regions with lower labor costs or have optimized labor use better than the company. Capital investment differences also play a role; the industry might have more resources to invest in cost-saving equipment and facilities. These elements collectively enable the industry to operate profitably at lower costs, whereas the company must focus on lower production levels to remain competitive.

We can express this gap as follows:

Let's define:

- $C(x)$ as the company's total cost function where x is the quantity of products sold.
- $R(x)$ as the company's revenue function.
- $CI(x)$ as the industry's average total cost function.
- $RI(x)$ as the industry's average revenue function.

The break-even point for the company and the industry occurs where the revenue equals the cost:

- For the company: $C(x) = R(x)$
- For the industry: $CI(x) = RI(x)$

To perform a gap analysis on the break-even points, we first need to solve for the break-even points:

- Company's break-even point: Solve $C(x) - R(x) = 0$ for x, let's denote this solution as xc

- Industry's break-even point: Solve $CI(x) - RI(x) = 0$ for x, let's denote this solution as xi

The gap in the break-even points between the company and the industry can be quantified as: Gap = $|xc - xi|$.

The gap tells us how far the company's performance (in terms of reaching a sustainable competitve advantage) deviates from the industry average. A larger gap before the competitive point indicates greater profit and a stronger competitive advantage, whereas a larger gap after the breaking point reflects a greater non-competitive advantage.

To visualize this, we can plot $C(x)$ and $R(x)$ on a Cartesian coordinate system, alongside $CI(x)$ and $RI(x)$. The point where each pair of curves intersect is the sustainble competitive point. The horizontal distance between these intersections (xc and xi) visually represents the gap.

To ensure accurate and unbiased insights, it is essential to approach the analysis systematically. By quantifying the gap and visualizing it on a Cartesian plane, we lay the groundwork for strategic decision-making, which can be further enhanced by delegating responsibilities to specialized teams. So, one piece of advice is to separate the work between two different teams: one handling the company analysis (perhaps someone from finance) and the other conducting the industry analysis (possibly within the marketing team). A strategic overseer should then compare the outcomes.

This separation helps prevent several cognitive and organizational biases that can skew data interpretation and decision-making. Here are some specific biases this approach can typically help mitigate:

- *Confirmation Bias*: The tendency to search for, interpret, favor, and recall information in ways that affirm one's preexisting beliefs or hypotheses.
- *Groupthink*: This occurs within teams that lack diversity or are too cohesive, leading to poor decision-making as the group prioritizes harmony and conformity over critical analysis. Separate teams are less likely to fall into uniform agreement without critique, especially if they operate in different departments with varied perspectives and goals.
- *Anchoring Bias*: This bias occurs when individuals rely too heavily on the first piece of information they receive (the "anchor") when making decisions.
- *Information Bias*: The tendency to seek information even when it does not affect action. Separate teams focusing on just the relevant data for their specific tasks (company performance vs. industry dynamics) can help ensure that only necessary information is gathered and analyzed, thus reducing unnecessary data collection and analysis.
- *Silos Effect*: Arises when separate divisions within an organization do not share information effectively, potentially leading to duplicated efforts or missed opportunities for synergy. Although the teams work separately, having a strategic overseer to compare and integrate the analyses helps bridge any informational gaps and ensures a holistic view.

Intelligence analysis, whether it pertains to industry or company specifics, does not discriminate between non-human variables (such as prices, tons of steel, environmental laws, political systems) and descriptions of specific people, including their degrees of competence and personal characteristics. Unlike in economics, we cannot disregard the human element, assuming all individuals, even those with similar education, are alike and that including people as a variable in analyses is irrelevant. The Silicon Valley examples mentioned underscore that specific individuals are often the most critical factor in intelligence analysis, sometimes even the sole focus of certain intelligence reports, such as the psychological profiles of decision-makers.

GDPR does not explicitly forbid creating reports about specific individuals as long as the data is processed lawfully, transparently, and securely. However, GDPR imposes strict rules on handling that information, and organizations must ensure compliance to avoid significant fines. For this reason, information about specific individuals in the organization and those in other organizations crucial for intelligence analysis often exists only orally, ultimately residing only in the memory of employees. As the reader will understand, this approach is not without its problems. For one thing, employees tend to change jobs.

Business plans, company and industry analysis are only one step in intelligence work within the organization. Once the company is operational, it will have many smaller requests for reports. We will deal more with these reports and how they may look later in Chap. 6. The focus in this chapter is on analysis. We have already alluded to the fact that intelligence reports are sometimes about persons. This is one dimension that sets these reports apart from most plans in the marketing or finance department. Most plans conducted by organizations can be said to be instrumental, but for intelligence analysis, the focus is not only on individuals but also on relationships, a topic which we will explore next.

5.6 The Mapping of Persons and Relationships: Instrumental Versus Relational Perspective on Organizations

It can be said that there are two leading paradigms in business theory: one relational and one instrumental. The relational perspective asserts that social behaviour is defined largely by the nature of the relationships between the parties involved. Conversely, the instrumental perspective posits that social behaviour is the result largely of changes in instrumental factors like price, unemployment rates, and interest rates and that therefore, personality traits can be discarded for all practical purposes, or assumed away. It certainly makes our models easier to understand and use. However, in some cases that assumption is more difficult to defend. There is nothing that says that you cannot use both perspective, mixing them, as to speak.

With a recent focus on information and knowledge as the primary sources of competitive advantage, the importance of understanding human relations has come to a new light. It has been recognized that an employee's competence—and not so much the office furniture or the buildings—accounts for most of the company's value, values which, incidentally, are nowhere reflected in the company's accounting figures. This is particularly true for high-competence industries like Information Technology, Biomedical, and Software companies. Many investors have experienced the painful reality that the whole value of a company can disappear when employees change jobs. This is leading to a renaissance of the relational perspective in business theory. The study of Intelligence means that more studies are done on employees, their background, knowledge, know-how, and motives for being with an organization.

The study of Marketing is an excellent example to illustrate this shift in focus. The Nordic School of Marketing, which emerged in the 1980s from the Nordic countries, notably Finland and Sweden, is characterized by an approach that emphasizes relationships, networks, and interaction between companies and their stakeholders, rather than just transactions.[5] This school of thought has significantly contributed to the development of relationship marketing and service marketing theories. For a long time, the subject was primarily instrumental, most famously finding the right mix of the four Ps: price, place, promotion, and product. This changed as marketers began defining and managing many different kinds of customer relationships to win more business. The relational perspective is particularly emphasized in Business-To-Business marketing, and in Customer Relationship Management, where IT is used to handle large quantities of information about customers' preferences. A similar shift occurred in what is known as Service Marketing.[6]

Unlike in business subjects, such as Marketing or even Human Resource Management (HRM), the description of individuals' character and relationships has always been a part of the subject of Intelligence, especially in the study of State Intelligence where the method of Human Intelligence (HUMINT) has a long tradition in observing and analyzing people's personalities. It's common for any head of state and minister to be briefed by its own intelligence services about the personalities of the people they meet in official meetings in other countries. This is a part of the reason for having these services in the first place.

The gathering of information through human sources and the description of relationships and personal character, what we call Personal and Relational Intelligence, is not only more sensitive but also includes a good portion of psychology as compared to other forms of intelligence analysis.

Other terms used for similar analyses, besides profiling, are psychographics. Psychographics refers to the study and classification of people according to their attitudes, aspirations, and other psychological criteria, especially in market research. It is a methodology used to describe a population based on psychological traits and characteristics. This method is often used in combination with demographic data to achieve a more complete understanding of a population or specific market segment (Table 5.4).

[5] A primary book here was Gummesson (1997). Later with Gummesson (2011).

[6] See for example Grönroos (1990).

Table 5.4 Key components of psychographics

#	Dimension of the personal	Explanation	Examples of applications
1	Personality Traits	This involves understanding the general attitude and personality characteristics of a person or group, such as whether they are introverted or extroverted, optimistic or pessimistic	Marketing and Advertising, Political Campaigning, State Visits, User Experience Design
2	Values and Beliefs	These are the core principles and standards that guide an individual's behavior. Values might include a person's views on religion, politics, education, and ethics.	Political Campaigning, User Experience Design
3	Interests and Lifestyles	This includes activities that individuals enjoy, their hobbies, and their general lifestyle choices, such as a preference for urban or rural living, active or sedentary activities, and cultural tastes.	Marketing and Advertising, Product Development
4	Motivations and Goals	Understanding what drives individuals, such as career ambitions, family, social status, health, or wealth, can offer insights into why they make certain decisions.	Marketing and Advertising, Political Campaigning, State Visits, User Experience Design

Psychographics provides a deeper understanding of the "why" behind consumer behaviors, helping businesses and organizations to effectively align their strategies with the intrinsic motivations of their target audiences. Unlike demographics, which may tell "who" a customer is in terms of age, gender, income, etc., psychographics explains "why" a person might prefer certain products, brands, or messages, making it a powerful tool in strategic planning and communication.

Similar terms used include Interpersonal Intelligence, which focuses solely on relationships; Behavioral Intelligence, Psychosocial Intelligence, and, more broadly, Human Behavioral Intelligence (HBI). More specifically, in a narrower sense, it is referred to as Character Intelligence.

It is easier and often more convenient to investigate a competitor or even one's own company from an instrumental perspective, looking at figures, ratios, and material facts. However, conducting an analysis of relationships between people is much more challenging because the information is harder to gather—it's not something you can buy off the shelf. Analysts are often uncertain about how to conduct relational analysis because it is sensitive and personal, but perhaps primarily because most businesses, and especially public organizations, do not have a tradition of seeking information by going outside and talking to people. So, they often outsource this work to people who have experience in state or military intelligence. But what may be overlooked in marketing is considered a cardinal sin in Intelligence Studies. People and relationships are key to understanding the competitive landscape. As a result, it is also very difficult to defend a private or public intelligence function as a desk job only.

Too many industry and company analyses falter because the analyst does not consider the human resource and relational facts in the organization. In a typical real-life situation, seen numerous times, a company lost its competitive advantage when a few key employees left. The factor, or risk, of losing key employees and its effects on the operations was not mentioned in the company analysis. The reason may be that there is some inherent reluctance on the part of many analysts to deal with human or 'personal' factors in the analysis due to the sensitivity of the material, or it may be a question of old habit or that the analysts have a certain theoretical approach to learning. In a second real-life example, a major weapons supplier lost a contract when there was a change of prime minister of India. The company doing the analysis had neglected the macro factor called "political". These are only too common examples. So, even though refraining from analyzing relationships may seem like a natural procedure at first, also from an ethical perspective, it often builds on the misconception that it is impossible to write objectively and guarantee employees' rights of integrity and confidentiality when key people among customers, suppliers, and competitors are analyzed. It's also a question of how you write these reports. Disrespect or humiliation should by no means be the content of such an analysis and can be eliminated through practice and feedback.

Any company should ideally know what knowledge (know-about) and skills (know-how) each employee possesses and to what extent the company is dependent or threatened—if it is a competitor—by it. Of course, such an analysis cannot be conducted for all employees in larger companies; it would take too much time, consume too many resources, and the data may change quickly. Regular employees are being hired and fired or simply leave the organization continuously. Instead, such an analysis should focus on key decision-makers and key competences.

When reading books on management, one often gets the impression that choosing between an instrumental and a relational perspective is necessary. That we either belong to one or the other camp, so to speak. Instead, it will be argued here that only the instrumental together with a relational perspective will give a complete analysis of the competitive advantage of the firm or organization. As the study of Intelligence depends as much on macro- as it does on micro-economic analysis, it is relevant to include both methods. For example, in the study of outside factors like demographic and legal dimensions, it may be advantageous to use a macro perspective and rely on more instrumental analysis. A micro perspective and relational analysis may be more appropriate for factors such as competitors and suppliers.

5.7 Developing the Intelligence Model and Conducting the Analysis

When we work with intelligence for an organization, we typically aim to use or build organizational models to gain a better perspective. In some cases, we can adopt a ready-made model, while in other cases, we want to adapt the model to fit our particular organization and environment.

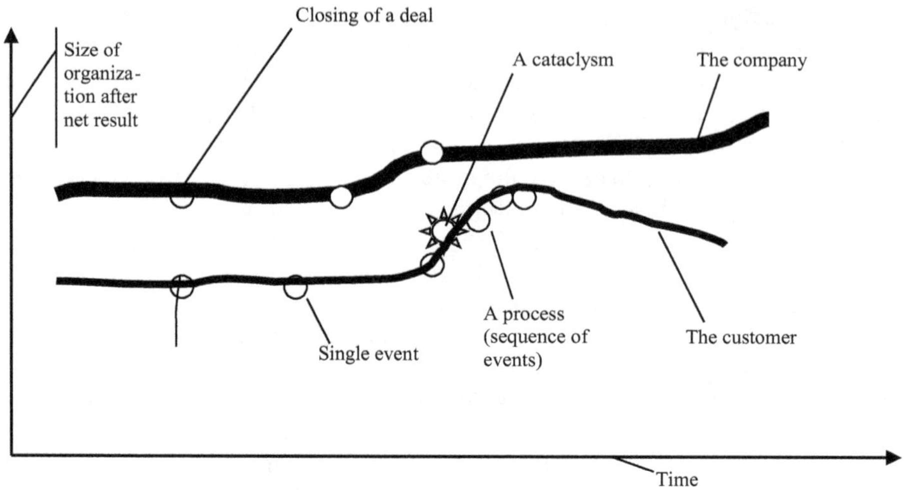

Fig. 5.5 A modified version of a factor X model

5.7.1 Models That Try to Catch Unexpected Events

The future always conceals surprises and unexpected events. What we thought was a non-issue may suddenly turn out to be a major problem. For instance, a company operating in Cameroon might suddenly discover that the delivery of electricity to a plant is problematic. Similarly, a company in Moldova might find that a nearby bridge is not constructed to handle their trailers' weight.

Part of the intelligence function is to try to detect the unexpected before it becomes an uncertainty, or worse, a risk not accounted for in the organization's operations. We are following Knight's definition here, where a risk is an event the company can insure against if detected, while uncertainty is an event the company cannot insure against, even if detected. Uncertainties are events the company has to live with.

Frankelius and Rosén call this Factor X, the unexpected factor.[7] To try to detect it, Frankelius suggests a model that builds on the logic of game-theoretical trees, or decision trees as they are also called, with different components describing various actions along a time horizon. In the adjusted version below, we have placed time on the x-axis and the size of the company or organization measured in net results on the y-axis. However, it could be any indicator that makes sense. The lines represent organizations, the circles or dots represent events, and the thickness of the line could indicate the number of employees in the organization, showing if it's a larger, medium, or small company by size (Fig. 5.5).

A cataclysm sets off a sudden and violent change or triggers a significant process. In theory, there is no limit to the different kinds of actions that we can define

[7] Frankelius (2001).

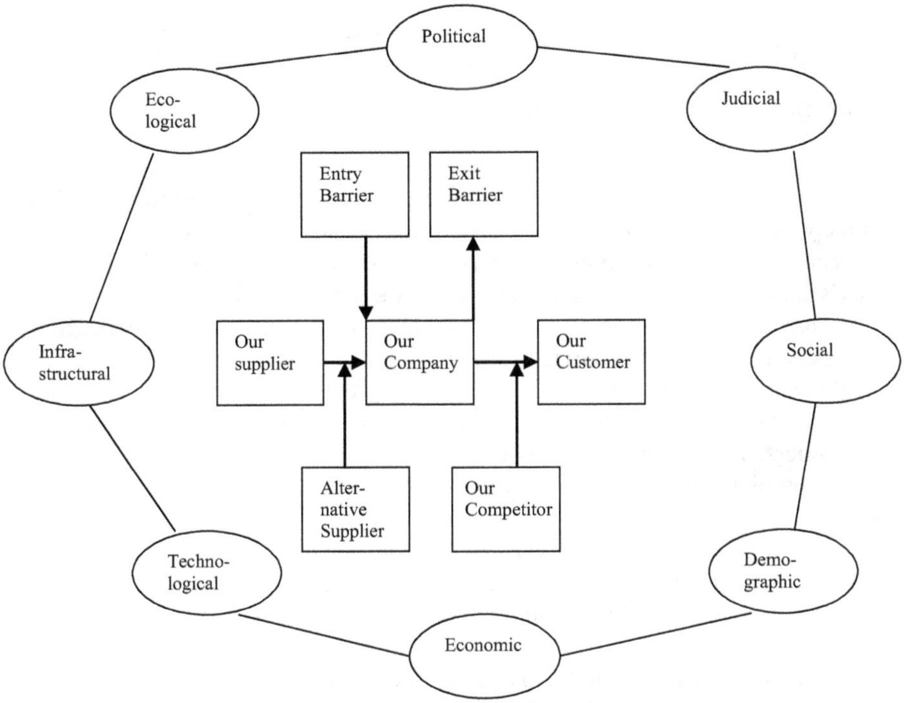

Fig. 5.6 Hussey and Jenster industry analysis model modified

and draw in the figure. Such a model should not be seen as a standard but more as a language for modeling, much like Lego pieces (but not a Lego set where every piece has fixed, correct place, if you get the difference). It offers a platform and pieces to define and document different actions between organizations.

The model does not offer strong predictive powers but is a way to lay out types of events to get a better overview. It can be useful for decisions with few parameters and predictions for the immediate future. One example can be following the change of prices in a market with few competitors and complete information.

5.7.2 Models That Catch the Micro and Macro Factors

Another way to create a model is to define a number of groups of individuals which, in one way or another, have influence on the organization. One such model has been suggested by Porter in his Five Forces. Since then, many researchers have presented their own interpretations and versions of Porter's model. An extended version of that model presented here in a modified version is made by Hussey and Jenster (Fig. 5.6):

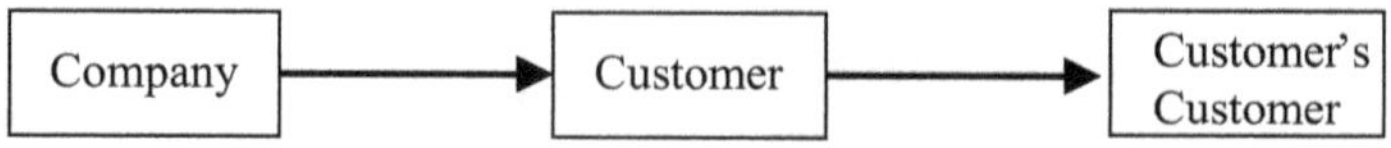

Fig. 5.7 Detail extended version industry analysis model

At the basis of the model is the value-creation process, from the supplier via the company to the customer. Such a process may consist of only two parties—company and customer—or it may list a large number of supplier's suppliers and customer's customers before the product is consumed. See Fig. 5.7:

A company delivering art to a cruise ship may see the cruise line as the customer and the end consumer, the tourist, as the customer's customer. It is not indifferent to how the customer's customer behaves or thinks. The tendency we see in business today is that the end consumer exerts a stronger influence on the decisions made by the suppliers. This means that suppliers are closely monitoring their end consumers to better predict what their direct buyers—our company in the model—are going to purchase.

Thus, in our example, if you want to find out whether you will sell more art to cruise lines, it will be important to scan media for articles on travelling. Another way of saying the same thing is that the company keeps its eyes on its customer's customers.

A company may also want to analyze its non-competitors, companies which are not direct competitors today but which have an influence on the business it is in and may become competitors in the future. Other versions of the above-mentioned model will include "influencers" as a special category, a common denomination for all other actors who, in one way or another, have or may have an influence on the performance of your company. An influencer may be a lobby organization or a single politician. Today we tend to think of influencers as younger people who run their own social media channels to attract large audiences and then try to monetize the platform, but this is only one part of its meaning.

The six categories which have an influence on the competitive advantage of our company are called Direct Categories. The eight categories placed as an octagon on the outside are called Indirect Categories because they only affect our business indirectly and belong to the company's macro environment.

To make the picture even more complicated, the eight external dimensions in the model have a relevant time horizon. As a company, we would like to know which dimensions have an influence on our company today, but also in the future, and sometimes it may be of use to know what the consequences were in the past.

Another model to help us understand the scope of intelligence work is the allegory of the Submarine. Subsoft was a project to put this model into software using the original model from Hussey and Jenster as a basis.

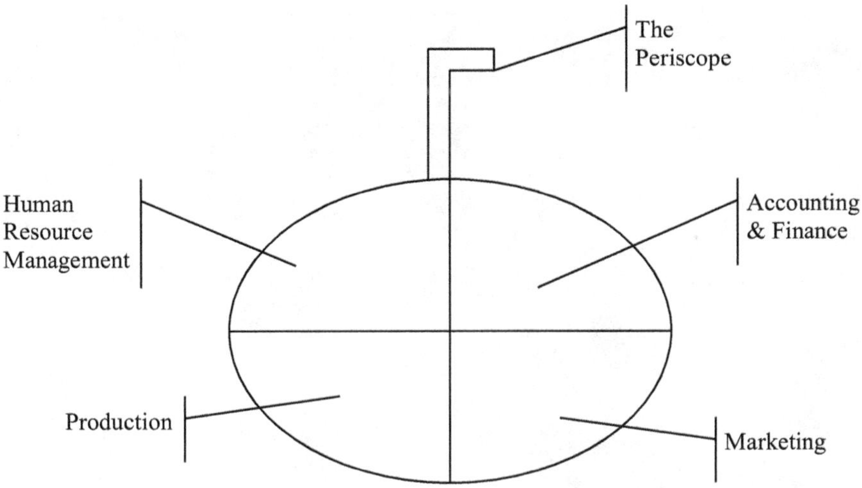

Fig. 5.8 The submarine allegory

5.7.3 Building the Model: The Subsoft Project Example

The first step for any company interested in developing a business intelligence system should be to ask: What does the world surrounding our organization look like? How can we simplify it to fit into a model that we can use? Let's consider the allegory of a submarine, where the periscope serves as the intelligence function (Fig. 5.8):

Every organization is akin to the trunk of a submarine, composed of several distinct functions such as production, HRM, accounting, finance, and marketing. This organization does not exist in isolation but operates within an environment filled with opportunities and threats—much like other submarines, the surrounding water and weather conditions, and ships on the surface. For optimal performance, it is not sufficient for internal operations to run smoothly; the submarine must also function effectively in response to external factors. Actually, it's very survival depends on it. Similarly, an organization must adapt and respond to its external environment. This is why it has a periscope.[8] The periscope of an organization is here equivalent to its Intelligence function.

Like the captain of a submarine, the CEO should be continuously informed about what is happening outside the submarine. Based on this information, she will then make decisions on how to navigate, whether to increase production, or decrease prices on certain products. The first thing she does when she wakes up in the morning is to look into the periscope or ask the person operating it if there is anything new happening. Similarly, the first thing the CEO does is to log onto the PC and check the Business Intelligence software, where some form of dashboard awaits.

[8] Modern subs check their environment with the help of Photonics Masts, Electronic Sensors, Satellite Communications (SATCOM) Systems and Drones and Unmanned Vehicles.

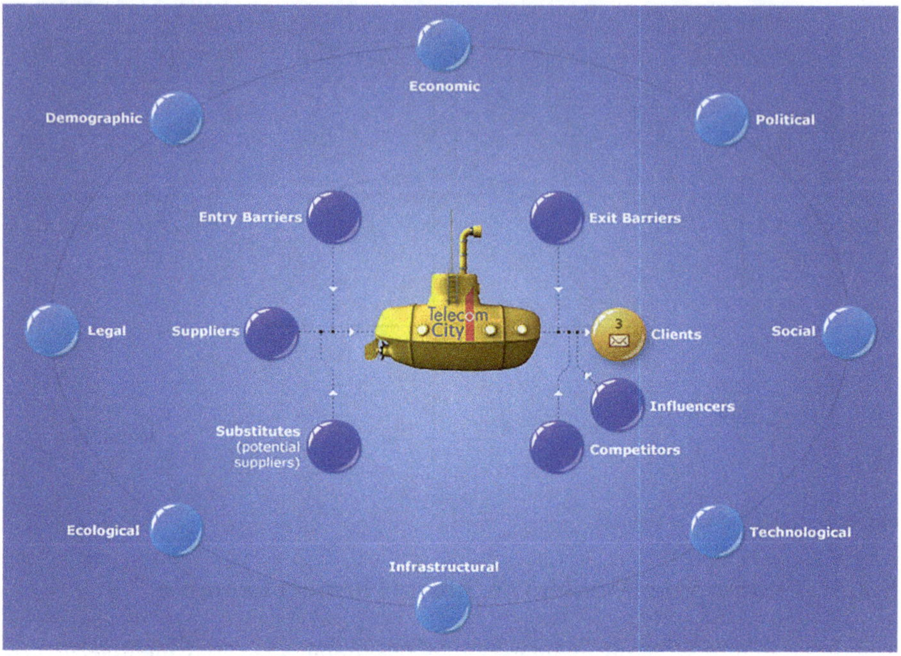

Fig. 5.9 TelecomCity business intelligence system overview

Based on this briefing, and the information she gathers throughout the day, she is now ready to start the day as a decision-maker.

Karlskrona in Sweden is not only a center for the production of some of the world's best submarines but also for telecommunications, with close cooperation with the Blekinge Institute of Technology (BTH), which was my employer for over 10 years. TelecomCity is a network consisting of 50 IT and Telecom companies with approximately 5000 employees. In the early 2000s, I led the development of Subsoft, a business intelligence system designed to work on the extranet of the organization. When employees log into the system, they are met with an image representing their surrounding world according to the model above. All new intelligence that has been placed in the system since the last time the manager checked shows in the form of an envelope and a number representing the number of new intelligence items added. The aim of the system is to present 'need to know' information and to cut out noise. To achieve this, specialists or experts are defined in each area. Only experts can add new intelligence (Fig. 5.9).

Internal factors are marked with a deeper blue because they typically (but not always) have a stronger effect on the companies' results. External factors are marked with a lighter blue and are positioned further away. Users can select and extract pieces of intelligence and transfer them to another module for analysis. A third module handles the printing format for the completed report. The idea is quite simple.

The challenge lies in getting users to use the system. This is achieved gradually, much like a company that starts by securing a few satisfied customers. If employees like it, they will come back to it. It was the same with the Subsoft system, as it is with any major intelligence system developed in MNEs today. You have to try to win over users, one by one, by showing what value the systems have.

5.7.4 Tailormade Models for Private and Public Intelligence

Any organization is faced with three environments: (1) Its own internal environment, which consists of all the different departments and functions within the organization, (2) the microenvironment, which includes other organizations that our organization interacts with, and (3) the macro environment, which consists of forces over which the organization has little or no influence. Environmental scanning focuses only on the last two environments—the micro and the macro. The task of gathering information from the internal environment falls within the purview of the established disciplines. For example, finding accounting information within one's own organization is the responsibility of the accounting department, etc.

The surrounding world for any organization consists of a micro and a macro environment. In many cases, the macro environment will be the same for all organizations within a certain culture, whether private or public, as they are affected by a similar set of macroeconomic, judicial, and political factors. For instance, if the price of oil increases, it will not only affect your own company but all of our competitors as well. Macroeconomic factors are considered a cross-cultural dimension because they affect companies regardless of their location, whereas judicial factors are mostly cultural. An example of the former could be a currency, like the euro, and an example of the latter could be a new law passed in a specific country.

It is helpful to start by creating a model of the microenvironment for the organization. For a private company, it might look like this (Fig. 5.10):

The model is created using the same circles, squares, and arrows or lines that we have previously utilized. The squares represent organizations, while the lines indicate the existence of a direct commercial relationship between them. In this instance, our customer has a customer who sells to the consumer. Each customer also has its competitors. It's important to understand that these models are not standard; they are more akin to a language that should be tailored to fit a specific reality.

For a public organization such as a region, the model may look like this (Fig. 5.11):

We observe that public models are more complex. The number of taxpayers is significantly smaller than that of citizens, yet there are some taxpayers who are not citizens, possibly because they live abroad. Most individuals who are both taxpayers and citizens are also voters, that is, direct influencers. The number of voters is fewer than that of citizens and encompasses most of the taxpayers.

A taxpayer may choose to locate her business in another region. Consequently, other regions become competitors to our own. There are entry and exit barriers for a region, but not in the sense we typically see in private organizations since there are

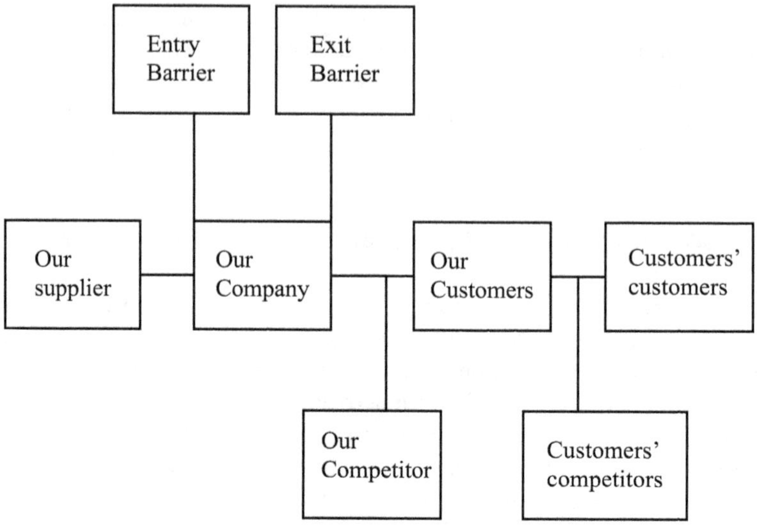

Fig. 5.10 Example of ES Model for a private company

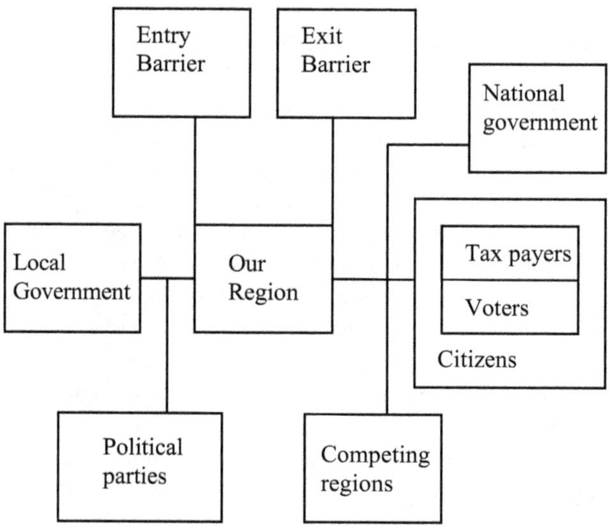

Fig. 5.11 ES Model for public intelligence

no competing regional governments within the same region. However, there are certain costs associated with starting and ending a regional activity, where the most obvious entry cost may be infrastructure expenses, such as building a new school. Exit costs may be related to the loss of income from office rent, and employee benefits paid by the regional or local government.

This is why we argue that public organizations can be modeled much like private organizations despite their differences. Both types of organizations consume resources and are rewarded by some definition of output, which corresponds to their usefulness. A private company is rewarded with higher sales. A public organization typically receives more funds when there is higher demand for its services among the public; for example, a library may get higher allocations next year if they can demonstrate that their patrons ordered more books.

Customers make little distinction between private and public organizations; only their needs differ. One day they may ask for a new toaster, another day they ask for better social security.

As long as we live in a market economy, a regional government cannot ignore the income-expenses perspective in their activities. Practically all political parties rely on economic growth to fulfill their political objectives.

Local and regional governments receive funding partly from local taxpayers and indirectly via national governments. The method varies significantly by country. This means that within a country—and even within a union of nation-states like the EU—taxpayers in one region may be funding activities in another region.

Political parties and interest groups may also be seen as influencers in our model. At the same time, selected representatives from these political parties make up the category of local and national government. The mix of different political parties within these governments will largely determine the guidelines or policies under which the regional government operates.

The form of the model will depend on the political system of the country we are analyzing. For example, the proportion of a region's income that comes from the central government versus what is raised locally varies from one country to another.

Once we have created a model for our organization, whether private or public, we can proceed to select the types of analyses for each group of actors. This is the next step in the Intelligence Process.

5.8 How to Do Intelligence Analysis

We often have an almost magical relation to the word 'analysis', expecting it to reveal surprising results, much like in statistics when we suddenly see the mean for a large set of data. The name of an analysis—like the PEST Analysis (Political Economic Social and Technological Analysis) or the BCG Matrix (Boston Consulting Group)[9]—can take on the proportion like that of a black box in our imagination. It's important, therefore, to know what analysis does, and for that, we need to start with what an analysis is.

We need to understand not only how to perform an analysis but also the logic behind it well enough to choose the right analysis and, if needed, make useful alterations in existing analyses to adapt them to the needs we have. In other words, we need to learn the language of analysis.

[9] BCG.

5.8.1 The Language of Analysis in the Social Sciences

An Analysis is simply the procedure of taking data apart (analysis) and putting them together again in a new and different manner (synthesis), hoping that the exercise will bring us to see the problem clearer. This clearness can be seen as the extra or *additional value* of the exercise or as *new knowledge*. We can illustrate this by using small and capital letters:

- Analysis (a): take apart
- Synthesis (s): put together
- Analysis (A) = a + s + additional value

One way to analyze analyses is by Function (Strategic, Financial, Marketing, Operational, HR, etc.), Purpose (Descriptive, Diagnostic, Predictive, Prescriptive), or Methodology: Qualitative (e.g., content analysis), Quantitative (e.g., statistical analysis), or Mixed Methods.

In business, analysis techniques are incredibly diverse, each suited to specific objectives and data types. These methods can be broadly categorized into a few main types, based on the nature of the analysis and the decision-making process it supports. Here is one approach that predominantly builds on function (Table 5.5):

Many of these analyses simply involve mean calculations from a basic Excel sheet, such as turnover analysis. Others are straightforward surveys, like Employee Satisfaction Surveys, which are often a staple in marketing analysis. In statistics, we mostly examine relationships between data. In finance, we analyze ratios and study budgets and accounting figures. None of this is very difficult to learn or to execute.

5.8.2 The Adaptation of Different Analyses Used to Fit a Problem

Another perspective on analysis is to consider how we can adapt them to any necessary situation. Let's take a few examples. The SWOT analysis, for instance, instructs us on how to deconstruct data but not on how to reassemble it. The synthesis depends on how we handle the data—statistically or otherwise—and is influenced by any external facts and opinions we incorporate into the process. To conduct a truly verifiable analysis, we need to utilize pieces of intelligence that have not been sorted into any predefined boxes. This can be challenging. What is even more challenging is keeping opinions from influencing the analytical process. We aim to be as objective as possible, knowing that eliminating all biases is unrealistic.

The value added by an analysis is not always apparent. It depends on factors such as our ability to choose the right kind of analysis for the problem at hand and whether we have sufficient amounts of valid data. To ensure effectiveness, we want the analysis to be accurate, objective, timely, comprehensive, and clear. If we simply reintegrate the information in the same way it was initially organized before deconstruction, the additional value will be nil, and the exercise futile.

Table 5.5 The language of analysis in business studies by function

#	Type of analysis	Analysis	What is does
1	Strategic Analysis (These analyses help in understanding the strategic position of the business within its industry and against competitors).	SWOT Analysis (Strengths, Weaknesses, Opportunities, Threats)	Assesses internal and external factors affecting the business.
		PESTEL Analysis (Political, Economic, Social, Technological, Environmental, Legal).	Evaluates external factors that might impact the business.
		Porter's Five Forces.	Analyzes industry competitiveness and market profitability.
2	Financial Analysis (This involves the assessment of financial data to understand current financial health and project future performance).	Ratio Analysis.	Uses ratios like debt-to-equity, return on investment (ROI), and others to gauge financial health.
		Break-even Analysis.	Determines at what point the business will be able to cover all its expenses.
		Budget Analysis:	Compares budgeted financials to actual figures to manage financial planning.
3	Operational Analysis (Focuses on improving the internal processes and efficiencies within a business)	Process Mapping	Identifies and documents the specific steps in a business process.
		Capacity Analysis:	Assesses the maximum output levels and efficiency of production or service operations.
		Supply Chain Analysis	Examines the logistics of the supply chain to optimize cost and efficiency.
4	Marketing Analysis (Helps in understanding market dynamics, customer behavior, and positioning strategies. Common methods include)	Market Segmentation	Identifies different groups within a market to target them more effectively.
		Competitive Analysis	Evaluates the strengths and weaknesses of competitors within the market.
		Marketing Mix Analysis	Studies the effectiveness of the business's marketing strategies across different channels.
5	Statistical Analysis (Involves quantitative models to infer patterns and relationships from data)	Regression Analysis	Determines relationships among variables to forecast outcomes.

(continued)

Table 5.5 (continued)

#	Type of analysis	Analysis	What is does
		Cluster Analysis	Groups a set of objects in such a way that objects in the same group are more similar to each other than to those in other groups.
		Time Series Analysis	Analyzes data points collected or indexed in time order.
6	Data Analysis (Employs data mining and data visualization tools to make data-driven decisions).	Predictive Analytics	Uses historical data to predict future outcomes.
		Descriptive Analytics	Provides insight into past performance by using historical data.
		Prescriptive Analytics	Suggests decisions based on both predictive and descriptive analyses.
7	Human Resources Analysis	Workforce Analytics	Uses statistical methods to analyze employee data and optimize HR strategies.
		Employee Satisfaction Surveys	Gathers insights on employee engagement and satisfaction.
		Turnover Analysis	Studies patterns and reasons behind employee turnover.

In analysis, we categorize information into specific boxes much like a mailman sorts letters based on their destinations. In a SWOT analysis, there are four such categories: Strengths, Weaknesses, Opportunities, and Threats. Choosing these four categories means we are excluding others we deem less important. The more categories we include in an analysis, the more complex it becomes. The SWOT analysis is widely used because it effectively captures both positive and negative effects in a manageable framework. We could consider adding a neutral category (N), but then we must consider what qualifies as neither positive nor negative and why it would be significant enough to include.

Looking at the Opportunities (O) and Threats (T), they are often regarded as future-oriented positives and negatives, respectively. Adding these categories introduces a time axis to the analysis. We could enhance this by incorporating a historical dimension, denoting past positives and negatives as Past Strengths (PS) and Past Weaknesses (PW). However, for practical purposes, these might be less valuable than the existing four categories. Thus, if we were to expand, we could reformat the SWOT into a 3 × 3 matrix instead of a 2 × 2, but this would require careful consideration of the value each new category brings. Our job is also to not overcomplicate the job for the mailman (Table 5.6).

We couldn't name the model by its initial letters due to the excessive number, but we could call it a Comprehensive SWOT Timeline Analysis. However, would this

Table 5.6 Adjusted SWOT

Past Strengths	Neutral events in the past	Past weaknesses
Strengths	Neutral events today	Weaknesses
Opportunities	Neutral events in future	Threats

model be more useful than the SWOT? Some may argue that it's too complex and question the necessity of adding a neutral dimension. In some cases, perhaps a 3 × 2 version might be more appropriate. The purpose of using SWOT as an example is not to dissuade the reader from using SWOT altogether but to demonstrate what an analysis entails, the components it includes, and, by extension, the aspects it omits.

Another suggestion is to combine different analyses. One example of a Combined Analysis is VRIO. VRIO stands for Value, Rarity, Imitability, and Organization.[10]

- Value: Does the resource or capability allow the firm to exploit opportunities or defend against threats?
- Rarity: Is the resource or capability currently controlled by a relatively small number of competing firms?
- Imitability: Is the resource or capability costly for other firms to imitate?
- Organization: Is the firm organized to capture the value of the resources and capabilities?

Adding a VRIO analysis to the SWOT framework provides more depth to the analysis by assessing the sustainability of the identified strengths and opportunities. This integration allows for a more detailed understanding of how specific resources and capabilities contribute to competitive advantage.

To take another example, consider a power analysis, which involves just one category: the power dimension. Within this category, we could use a nominal scale, an ordinal scale, or interval and ratio scales to measure power. This doesn't mean it is a poor analysis; it is only inadequate if the category is irrelevant. To arrive at the one-box figure or ratio we could follow a procedure like this:

Step 1: Identify Power Factors

List all the factors that contribute to each party's power. Common factors include:

- Resource Control: Access to critical resources.
- Information Asymmetry: Superior knowledge or information.
- Negotiation Skill: Experience and skill in negotiation.
- Alternatives: Availability of alternatives (e.g., Best Alternative to a Negotiated Agreement, or BATNA).
- Stake: Importance of the outcome to each party.
- Support: External support or backing.
- Legal or Institutional Power: Powers derived from legal or official authority.

Step 2: Assign Weights to Each Factor

[10] Bensoussan and Fleisher (2013).

Each factor may not contribute equally to the overall power. Assign weights to each factor based on their perceived importance in the specific context of the negotiation. The total of all weights should sum to 1 (or 100%).

Example:

- Resource Control: 20%
- Information Asymmetry: 15%
- Negotiation Skill: 10%
- Alternatives: 25%
- Stake: 10%
- Support: 10%
- Legal Power: 10%

Step 3: Score Each Party on Each Factor

Rate each party on a scale (e.g., 1–10) for each factor. The scale represents how strongly each party possesses that particular factor.

Step 4: Calculate Weighted Scores

Multiply each party's score by the corresponding factor weight and sum them to get a total score that represents each party's power level.

Example Calculation for Party A:

- Resource Control: 8 (score) × 0.20 (weight) = 1.6
- Information Asymmetry: 6 × 0.15 = 0.9
- Negotiation Skill: 7 × 0.10 = 0.7
- Alternatives: 5 × 0.25 = 1.25
- Stake: 7 × 0.10 = 0.7
- Support: 4 × 0.10 = 0.4
- Legal Power: 9 × 0.10 = 0.9
- Total Power Score for Party A = 6.45

Repeat the same calculation for Party B.

Step 5: Normalize the Scores (Optional)

To compare the power levels more intuitively, you can normalize the scores so they sum to 100%. This step gives you the percentage of power each party holds.

Example:

- Total Power Score for Party A = 6.45
- Total Power Score for Party B = 5.55
- Total Power = 6.45 + 5.55 = 12

Percentage of Power for Party A = (6.45/12) × 100% = <u>53.75%</u> Percentage of Power for Party B = (5.55/12) × 100% = <u>46.25%</u>

This approach quantifies the power each party holds before a meeting, helping negotiators understand their own strengths and weaknesses relative to the other

53.75/46.25%

Fig. 5.12 One-box presentation of power analysis for two parties

party. The analysis can guide strategy development, including identifying areas where one might need to bolster one's position or leverage one's strengths effectively.

For a negotiation between a company and its supplier, it may be the most crucial analysis to perform, especially considering the conclusion that when we enter that room, 53.75% of the power lies with the opponent, 46.25% with the other, so the difference is not big (Fig. 5.12).

Knowing how power is distributed has consequences for both parties. If we are the weaker party we must prepare more thoroughly, establish our must-haves, try to build leverage by focusing on the additional value we can bring, be prepared to make concessions, and aim for mutual gains or win-wins. If we are the stronger party, we will clearly identify our primary goals and deal-breakers from the outset, assert our position, and make clear what we expect and what we are willing to offer. It's a take-it-or-leave-it situation. However, in our example, both parties were almost equally strong, so these positions should not be exaggerated. Instead, we could focus more on identifying win-win solutions and enlarging the pie.

5.8.3 How to Make Decisions Based on Results in Analyses

How do we make or suggest a decision based on the values in our boxes? Take, for example, the SWOT analysis: if we have more elements under Threats and Weaknesses, our conclusion might state, 'There are more threats than opportunities in this business idea.' If we want to be quantitative and more specific, we could say, 'There are 30% more threats than opportunities,' or using probability, 'the possibility of threats is 0.7'. This is the second step in the analysis—counting. We examine each box and count the contents. In other cases, we make a qualitative evaluation of the content. In the example of the power analysis, counting has already been done. Of course, this assumes that all threats have the same weight, which is not the case, so each threat has to be assigned a fraction for the counting to work.

The third step is to make a conclusion based on these findings. A conclusion for a SWOT might simply state, 'There are more negative factors than positive ones with the new business idea.' The fourth step is to describe the consequences of these conclusions. This step follows a cause-and-effect logic, where the cause is the conclusion, and the possible effects are the consequences. This might be articulated as 'We should not proceed with the new business idea.'

The fifth step involves implications, often the most important yet frequently overlooked step. The questions to answer include, 'What are the implications if we decide not to start the business?' For instance, it could mean that we might have to look for other work. Alternatively, it could mean deciding to travel for a year instead, taking a year off. It is the implications that we really aim to understand because they help us discern the best choices.

The five steps in the analytical process are:

1. Choosing the appropriate type of boxes/analysis.
2. Counting/evaluating the content of each box (more/less than next year/last year, percentage increase, etc.).
3. Drawing conclusions from the counting/evaluation.
4. Outlining the consequences of the conclusions.
5. Considering the implications.

This procedure—while not always guaranteeing new knowledge—is useful and can be considered part of the study of scientific method and logic.

5.8.4 How to Pick the Right Analysis

We will suggest some further steps in the analysis of analyses. Firstly, analysis may be proactive or reactive. If it is proactive, the analyst can shape the information gathered by choosing a specific analysis method, such as selecting a focus group, which will produce results that do not yet exist and are shaped by the process itself. On the other hand, when individuals fill out a questionnaire, they usually have an idea of what is to be answered, making the method reactive.

Secondly, the number of boxes may vary significantly. For practical reasons, they seldom surpass 8–12, but this number may also be left open, as in the case of benchmarking, a method by which the performance of similar products is compared. There is no preset number of products/variables or companies to be compared in benchmarking before we start the analytical process. We call this an open-ended analysis. A similar situation occurs when we list Key Success Factors (KSF); it often makes sense to include a comprehensive list for the entire company, encompassing all its departments and functions. Thus, we have two versions: one with fixed boxes, like a SWOT, and one with open boxes, like an analysis of KSFs. We do not know how many boxes there will be until we finish. However, the second time we use the analysis, we should use the same format to enable comparisons and maintain consistency—then we know in advance how many boxes there are, unless it makes sense to add new boxes since last year, as there may be new KSFs. The first type is called a structured analysis.

Key Success Factors (KSFs) vs. Driving Forces Analysis (DFA).

Key Success Factors are the critical elements or areas that are essential for an organization to achieve its objectives and maintain competitive advantage in its industry. KSFs are often industry-specific and can include factors such as technology, customer service, product quality, or operational efficiency. Driving Forces Analysis is a strategic tool used to identify and understand the forces that drive change within an industry. DFA focuses on external factors that influence industry dynamics, such as technological advancements, regulatory changes, economic shifts, and social trends. KSFs focus on internal elements crucial for an organization's success within its current industry context. DFA focuses on external forces that drive industry change and affect all competitors within the industry. KSFs are often controllable by the organization (e.g., improving product quality, enhancing customer service). By understanding both KSFs and DFA, organizations can effectively balance their internal priorities with external realities, ensuring they remain competitive and adaptable in a dynamic business environment.

It's important to choose the right and optimal analysis. The analysis should fit the problem. By a complete analysis, we mean that there are no major categories in the actual problem that do not have their box. Thus, we may say that the PEST analysis has a fixed number of boxes—namely four: Political, Economic, Social, and Technological—but is not complete for a problem where the Judicial dimension is of major importance. So, another version is the STEEP (social, technological, economic, ecological, and political/legal), but this one is missing Demography and Infrastructure, unless you group them together under one of the other labels. The models that are missing important dimensions we call non-complete analysis. That is why the Industry Analysis is such a useful model for most organizations. It can be adapted to fit all organizations, whether private or public, e.g., the Industry Analysis includes all the relevant categories of our environment, while the PEST analysis is more of a 'best-of' analysis and the STEEP more inclusive.

A third way to analyze an analysis is by assessing the amount of dynamics it offers. By 'dynamics,' we refer to the adaptability of the analysis to reality. For instance, a questionnaire has a low degree of dynamics built into it when the respondents cannot express their opinions through the given alternatives. This can partly be solved by leaving space for 'comments,' but this solution is not ideal as it compromises our ability to compare and further analyze. However, a 'comments' field is often vital to understand the 'why' of the survey, so even though it complicates statistics, its value is often indispensable. Thus, we can talk of dynamic vs. non-dynamic analysis.

A fourth way to understand an analysis is by placing it on a time axis: some analyses like trend analysis focus on the future, while others, like benchmarking, focus more on the present. Thus, we have a time-dimension of analyses.

We may also differentiate analyses based on whether they register human opinions or material facts. For example, in a PEST analysis, we may choose whether we want to register technological facts or people's opinions of the technology. If we decide to accommodate both variables, we could call it an extended PEST with a normative and a non-normative part. What we are doing is essentially playing with the language of modeling to find ways they may fit. The rules are determined by logic. The limitations are our individual understanding of logic and its practical use.

When we understand what each analysis does, we can choose the one that best serves our purpose. We will then be less impressed by the name of a new analysis when we encounter one the next time and instead try to understand its qualities. This is what distinguishes a skilled analyst from a beginner: he has understood the nature of analysis. Choosing and adapting the right analysis is key to the art of analysis, which is essential for intelligence studies. The rest is mostly form and procedure.

Another important question is the amount of confidence we should place in the result of our analysis. In many assignments, it may be advisable to employ

Redundancy in Method, that is, using several different analyses for the same problem. This allows us to compare one result with another to determine how robust the conclusion is. If the results from using two different analyses differ, we may want to consider conducting a third analysis. If the conclusions from the two analyses are the same, we may place more confidence in our findings.

An analysis does not have to be anything more than a spreadsheet. In fact, a spreadsheet—characterized by having two dimensions, at least two categories under each dimension, and several data points under each category which must be true for both corresponding categories—is one of the more useful types of analysis. Many students opt for more advanced analyses believing that there is a correlation between the difficulty or complexity of the analysis and the quality of the conclusions. This is not true; in fact, often the more complicated the analysis, the greater the chances of committing analytical errors.

The surrounding world has many dimensions of intelligence: political, judicial, etc. We have divided the environment into micro and macro dimensions. In the microenvironment, the company studies its suppliers, customers, and competitors. In the macro environment, the company studies factors classified as political, judicial, etc. As we have seen, it is a common mistake to think that the micro dimensions are all-important. Many companies will develop excellent micro analyses of their competitors and customers but ignore or underestimate the dimensions in the macro environment.

In one example, a company wanted to sell arms to the Brazilian government. Then a new president was elected, and the whole deal was called off. All the conclusions of the microanalysis pointed in the direction that the company was going to be favoured with the contract because it had the better price and the better product. But it did not anticipate that there could be a shift in governmental power, which was unforgivable because it was so obvious. If you asked any Brazilian who was voting, he would probably know. When we exclude a dimension, as in this case, the macro dimension labelled 'political', it means that we assume it is of no importance. In our case, the analyst did not see the assumption, and the result was a lost contract to the company worth billions of USD. The Industry Analysis model may help us to remember all the major relevant dimensions.

At the end of our analysis of analyses, it can sometimes be made clear which dimensions are important and which are less important by using different colours for each category, e.g., red for important categories, yellow for less important ones, etc. This will help us to gain a quicker view of what is important by a quick glance at the model.

In the Table 5.7, we see the different variables in the micro and macro environments of the Industry Analysis, their corresponding subjects or functions, and some examples of analyses to be used:

The label 'Subject/Function' indicates where the problem is studied academically and the corresponding department within the organization. The analysis suggests which type of analysis is appropriate for that particular problem. All the subjects studied under the internal environment fall within the domain of business studies. In the study of macro-level problems, only one of the subjects is directly

Table 5.7 Choosing the most appropriate analysis

Variable:	*Subject/function:*	*Analysis:*
Micro environment:		
Customers	***Marketing***	***Focus groups*** ***Questionnaires*** ***Trend analysis*** ***Forecasting***
Competitors	***Marketing***	***Benchmarking*** ***SWOT*** ***Game theoretical approaches*** ***Simulations***
	Finance	***Ratio analysis*** ***Cost analysis***
Suppliers	***Industrial management***	***Benchmarking*** ***Game theoretical approaches***
	Finance	***Cost analysis***
	Marketing	***Simulations***
Entry barriers	***Finance***	***Spread sheets*** ***Cost analysis***
Exit barriers	***Finance***	***Spread sheets*** ***Cost analysis***
Substitutes to suppliers	***Industrial management***	***Devil's advocate*** ***Spread sheets***
Marketing	***Simulations***	
Substitutes to customers	***Marketing***	***Devil's advocate*** ***Spread sheets*** ***Simulations***
Macro environment:		
Economic	***Economics, Macro***	***PEST analysis*** (Economic, Political, Social, Technological)
Political	***Political Science***	
Social	***Sociology***	
Technological	***Technology-Sociology***	
Infrastructural	***Technology-Sociology***	***State-of-art reporting***
Ecological	***Ecology***	***Power analysis*** (Infrastructural, Ecological, Legal)
Legal	***Law***	
Demographic	***Political geography***	***Statistical analysis***

related to business studies, namely macroeconomics. This highlights the interdisciplinary nature of Intelligence Studies. It also implies that unless the Intelligence Team (IT) itself possesses expertise outside of the business curriculum, it will need to rely on external expertise for assistance. Most companies address this issue by hiring expertise from consultants. Having a full-time expert for a peripheral subject can be very costly. For example, few companies, apart from those in, let's say, the oil industry, can afford to employ a full-time ecological analyst within their IT. Resources, but also the level of competition will often decide the efforts made by an organization to organize its intelligence efforts. Performing good intelligence analysis, on the other hand, is not so much a question of resources as of competence and can be learned.

5.9 A Short Presentation of Analyses Used in Intelligence Studies

Some readers may want to go straight to this part of the book to read about how to actually use each analysis, especially maybe the second time when using this book. The selection made here is not complete but based on which types of analyses are most used in Intelligence. The description has been kept as short as possible.

We have excluded analyses which are typical for the study of strategy matrixes like the BCG, Ansoff and GE/McKinsey, as these are well covered in other books. Nor will we treat Porter's Diamond on National Advantage, his Value chain analysis, or generic strategies. These methods are more applicable to the study of other subjects, like strategy.

5.9.1 Focus Groups

A focus group is a form of organized discussion and a well-established methodology in social research. Typically, a group consisting of five to ten individuals is selected by the analyst—often referred to as the moderator—to discuss and comment on specific issues or questions based on their personal experiences. Unlike group interviews, where participants directly respond to the analyst's questions, focus group participants interact with each other, enriching the discussion with their diverse perspectives.

Key Characteristics and Benefits of Focus Groups:

- Interactive Dynamics: Focus groups capitalize on the interaction between participants, which can reveal deeper insights into their feelings, attitudes, and reactions. These dynamics are often obscured in other data collection methods such as surveys or telephone interviews.
- Moderator's Role: The moderator facilitates the discussion without controlling it, ensuring that the conversation remains on topic but allowing the natural social dynamics of the group to steer the process. The moderator's primary role is to observe and subtly guide the discussion to prevent significant deviations from the subject matter.

To quantitatively enhance the analysis of focus group data, consider the following steps:

1. Coding Responses: Assign numerical codes to specific types of responses or themes that emerge during the discussion. For example, if a recurring theme is "customer satisfaction," you might assign it a code of 01.
2. Frequency Analysis: Tally the number of times each theme is mentioned across all sessions. This can provide a quantitative measure of the importance or prevalence of each theme.
3. Sentiment Scoring: Apply a simple sentiment score to the responses, such as +1 for positive, 0 for neutral, and −1 for negative. This scoring can help quantify the overall sentiment of the discussion regarding specific issues.
4. Inter-rater Reliability: If more than one moderator or observer is involved, calculate the inter-rater reliability to ensure consistency in the observation and coding process. A common statistical measure for this is Cohen's Kappa.
5. Graphical Representation: Use bar charts or pie charts to visually represent the frequency and sentiment of the discussed themes. This can be particularly effective in presenting your findings to stakeholders who may prefer a quick, visual interpretation of data.

In conclusion, the focus groups offer a unique opportunity to observe and analyze complex social interactions and the nuanced opinions of participants. By integrating simple quantitative methods into the analysis of focus group data, analysts can provide a more robust and objective interpretation of the data collected, enhancing the overall value of the findings. This approach not only supports qualitative insights with quantitative data but also facilitates a clearer communication of results to decision-makers.

5.9.2 Questionnaires

A questionnaire is fundamentally a set of questions designed to elicit specific information from respondents. It serves as a structured method for identifying and gathering data from a target group that can provide the necessary answers for analysis.

Characteristics and Challenges of Questionnaires:

- Sensitivity and Bias: Respondents may not always provide honest answers, particularly to questions that are sensitive or perceived as intrusive. To mitigate this, it is advisable to avoid questions that might prompt respondents to give socially desirable answers rather than truthful ones.
- Structural Design: A questionnaire typically begins with straightforward, non-sensitive questions (e.g., demographic information like age, sex, years of experience) to ease the respondent into the survey. This is followed by more targeted questions related to the research objectives.
- Comprehensive Response Options: It is crucial to design answer choices that cover all possible opinions to ensure that the data collected is representative of the true views of the respondents. This involves careful question formulation and the inclusion of a diverse range of response options.

To quantitatively enhance the analysis of questionnaire data, consider these steps:

1. Likert Scale Implementation: Utilize a Likert scale (commonly a 5-point or 7-point scale) for questions to quantify the intensity of respondents' feelings or agreement with statements. Odd-numbered scales include a neutral middle point, allowing for a midpoint in responses.
2. Quantitative Analysis:
   - Average Score Calculation: Compute the mean score for each question to get a general sense of respondents' attitudes.
   - Standard Deviation: Calculate the standard deviation to understand the variability or dispersion of the responses, indicating how much consensus there is among them.
3. Correlation Analysis: Apply statistical methods to analyze the relationships between different questions or between questionnaire responses and external data. This can help identify patterns or predictive factors in the responses.
4. Regression Analysis: For more advanced analysis, use regression techniques to see how predictor variables (demographic factors, for instance) affect responses to key questions.
5. Graphical Representation: Create histograms, pie charts, or bar graphs to visually represent the distribution of responses and to highlight key trends and outliers.

In conclusion, questionnaires are a vital tool in gathering structured data, but their effectiveness hinges on careful design and analysis. By incorporating quantitative measures such as Likert scales and employing statistical techniques to analyze the results, researchers can provide a more nuanced and scientifically robust interpretation of the data. This approach not only supports the reliability of the findings but also enhances the actionable insights derived from the questionnaire data.

5.9.3 Trend Analysis

Trend analysis, closely related to scenario analysis, emphasizes descriptive over predictive elements, focusing less on quantifying outcomes and more on depicting comprehensive visions of future scenarios and their potential implications for consumer behavior. This method is particularly vital not only in industries sensitive to design or fashion trends but also in understanding broader social trends such as shifts in political opinions, hobbies, and even preferences for certain types of education and professions.

The time frame for trend analysis often extends longer than that of scenario analysis, typically spanning 5–10 years, depending on the industry. This method is frequently described as industry forecasting when applied specifically within a certain sector.

For example, consider the automotive industry, where trend analysis might examine the shift towards electric vehicles (EVs). Analysts would gather data on sales trends, regulatory changes, technological advancements, and consumer sentiment towards green technology over the past decade. They might use statistical tools like linear regression to project future growth rates of EV adoption based on this historical data. The analysis would also consider potential disruptors, such as advancements in battery technology or changes in oil prices, to paint a more nuanced picture of future developments.

However, questions about what the world might look like in 20 years or more typically fall under the purview of futurologists, whose studies, though broader and more speculative, are harder to substantiate and verify. Trend analyses are more grounded, often subjected to stringent tests of causality to ensure their reliability. Analysts must establish clear cause-and-effect relationships and support their conclusions with empirical evidence to ensure their analyses hold up under scrutiny.

A practical application of trend analysis involves employing statistical methods to detect patterns or directional trends in data over time. Techniques such as moving averages or exponential smoothing might be used to identify trends by dampening random "noise" in the data. These methods help in clarifying the direction in which market factors, consumer behaviors, or technological advancements are moving.

In summary, while trend analysis provides valuable foresight into future developments, it is crucial to approach this analysis with critical thinking and robust methodology. Analysts need to ensure that their predictions are based on reliable data and logical projections that accurately reflect the trends and the dynamics driving these trends. This thoughtful approach helps businesses and policymakers make informed decisions that are strategically aligned with future market conditions and societal shifts.

5.9.4 Forecasting

In the realm of business, forecasting serves as a more narrowly defined and parameter-driven analysis compared to the expansive scopes of trend and scenario analyses. It is often termed business or strategic forecasting to differentiate it from other forecasting techniques, such as weather forecasting, which have different focuses and methodologies.

This analytical practice is typically situated within financial or accounting departments that emphasize quantitative analysis over qualitative insights. The central focus of forecasting in business contexts often revolves around predicting financial performance or market demand. These forecasts are directly integrated into the company's strategic planning, incorporating specific, measurable targets.

Forecasting frequently involves sophisticated statistical analysis of historical data to project future conditions. One of the most common methods employed is regression analysis, which enables analysts to explore relationships between multiple variables and use these relationships to predict future outcomes. For example, a company may use linear regression to forecast sales based on historical sales data:

Example of a Simple Linear Regression for Sales Forecasting Suppose historical data from the past 5 years shows the following annual sales figures (in thousands of units): 100, 120, 140, 160, 180. To forecast sales for the upcoming year, an analyst might establish a linear relationship between time (year) and sales volume as follows:

1. Assign time as the independent variable (X): X = [1, 2, 3, 4, 5]
2. Assign sales figures as the dependent variable (Y): Y = [100, 120, 140, 160, 180]

The analyst would then apply linear regression to find the best-fit line that models this relationship. The equation for a linear regression line is typically expressed as Y = a + bX, where:

- Y is the predicted sales,
- X is the time variable,
- a is the y-intercept,
- b is the slope of the line.

Using statistical software or a calculator, the analyst calculates the slope (b) and y-intercept (a) based on the least squares method, which minimizes the sum of the squared differences between observed values and values predicted by the model.

Upon calculating these coefficients, suppose the equation of the line is found to be Y = 20X + 80. With this model, predicting sales for the sixth year involves plugging 6 into the equation:

$$\text{Predicted Sales for Year } 6 = 20(6) + 80 = 200 \text{ thousand units.}$$

To enhance the accuracy of these forecasts, adjustments for inflation, population growth, or other economic factors might also be considered. Additionally, techniques such as time series analysis, Theil's U-statistic, and calculation of forecast errors could further refine the predictive power of the model.

Forecasting errors, which are crucial in assessing the reliability of predictions, are computed as the difference between the actual values and the forecasted values. These errors help in understanding the effectiveness of the forecasting model and in making necessary adjustments.

Overall, the application of forecasting in business facilitates informed decision-making by predicting future trends and helping strategize accordingly. Through mathematical rigor and strategic integration, forecasting not only prepares companies for future challenges but also guides them towards achieving their strategic goals.

5.9.5 Benchmarking

Benchmarking is a strategic approach used to evaluate various aspects of performance by comparing key success factors (KSFs) between an organization and its competitors. Traditionally, companies engage in benchmarking within their own industry to ensure their products or services meet or exceed the standards set by their competitors. However, significant insights can also be gleaned by comparing operations across different industries, particularly in areas like customer service, outsourcing practices, and employee incentives.

A classic example of benchmarking is when Boeing released its 707 model in 1958, and Air France purchased a plane only to disassemble it in Toulouse. This act was aimed at understanding Boeing's design and manufacturing practices, thereby using this information to enhance their own aerospace solutions.

Benchmarking is particularly prevalent in technology-driven industries such as the automotive sector, where companies continually strive to ensure their products reflect the state of the art. The process can be conducted secretly, in collaboration with competitors, or through an independent third party, depending on the strategic goals and ethical considerations of the benchmarking entity.

As an example, consider an automobile manufacturer looking to enhance the fuel efficiency of its vehicles. The company decides to benchmark its cars against a leading competitor known for its fuel-efficient models. The benchmarking process involves several steps:

Identification of Key Success Factors: The company identifies fuel efficiency as a key success factor for benchmarking.

- Data Collection: Historical data on fuel efficiency from both the company and the competitor are collected. Suppose the last five models from each company have the following miles per gallon (MPG) ratings:
- Own Company: 20, 22, 23, 24, 25 MPG Competitor: 24, 26, 27, 28, 30 MPG Statistical Analysis: The company uses statistical methods to compare these ratings. A simple analysis might involve calculating the average MPG for each company and comparing these figures:
- Average MPG Own Company: (20 + 22 + 23 + 24 + 25)/5 = 22.8 MPG Average MPG Competitor: (24 + 26 + 27 + 28 + 30)/5 = 27 MPG Gap Analysis: The gap in fuel efficiency between the two companies is then calculated to determine the target improvement:
- Gap: 27 − 22.8 = 4.2 MPG Strategy Development: Based on this gap, the company develops specific strategies aimed at improving the fuel efficiency of their next model to close or even surpass this gap.

To further refine their analysis, companies might employ more sophisticated mathematical tools such as variance analysis to understand the consistency of performance across different models or regression analysis to predict future improvements based on historical trends.

Table 5.8 SWOT and Devils' advocate

Positives	Negatives
Strengths Our Perspective	Weakness Our Perspective
Strengths Their Perspective	Weakness Their Perspective
Opportunities Our Perspective	Threats Our Perspective
Opportunities Their Perspective	Threats Their Perspective

In conclusion, benchmarking serves as a critical tool for companies aiming to maintain competitive advantage by systematically comparing and measuring their performance against the industry best. By quantitatively analyzing how their products or processes stack up against those of their peers, companies can identify areas for improvement and innovate more effectively. In doing so, they not only meet the industry standards but also push the boundaries of what is considered state of the art in their sector.

5.9.6 SWOT (Strengths, Weaknesses, Opportunities and Threats)

The SWOT analysis is, as we saw earlier, an evolved version of the traditional pros and cons analysis. It enhances the basic model by integrating two additional dimensions: opportunities and threats, which can be regarded as potential future strengths and weaknesses. The significant contribution of SWOT is its ability to facilitate future-oriented thinking by exploring potential opportunities and identifying possible threats.

We showed earlier one way in which the SWOT could be altered. Here is another suggestion: It's conceivable to expand the SWOT model to incorporate historical analysis—comparing past and present strengths, weaknesses, and potential future challenges—but the value of including such historical dimensions often yields limited additional insight.

A more dynamic adaptation of SWOT involves viewing issues from multiple perspectives, not just the organization's internal viewpoint but also through the lens of competitors. This approach effectively combines SWOT with a Devil's advocate analysis, enriching the analysis by considering various angles and perspectives.

Here is how such an extended SWOT analysis might be structured (Table 5.8):

The aim of presenting this extended version of SWOT is to demonstrate yet again that analytical frameworks are not rigid; they can be modified and adapted to meet specific needs and situations. What matters most is the utility of the model in fostering comprehensive strategic thinking.

The integration of SWOT with Devil's Advocate encourages a thorough evaluation by ensuring that all possible factors are considered, including those that might remain obscured when viewed solely from one's own organizational perspective. This method not only broadens the scope of analysis but also deepens the strategic insights that can be gleaned, making it an effective tool for enhancing decision-making processes.

5.9.7 Game Theoretical Approaches

Game theoretical approaches offer a structured framework for analyzing strategic interactions between different players, where the actions of one player directly affect the outcomes of others. The most commonly utilized structures in game theory within a business context are simple decision trees and 2 × 2 decision matrices.[11] These models help in mapping out possible actions and their consequences, providing a clear visualization of strategic choices.

For more sophisticated analyses, each action in a decision tree can be augmented with probability calculations or associated values using a principal-agent model. In this model, each actor is characterized as either a principal, who initiates and drives the strategic decisions, or an agent, who executes these decisions and whose interests may not fully align with those of the principal.

A classic example of a game theoretical model is the Entry Deterrence I game, which involves two firms: an entrant considering whether to enter a market and an incumbent deciding how to respond. The game can be diagrammed as follows:

• Entrant's Decision:	
– Enter:	The entrant decides to enter the market.
– Stay Out:	The entrant decides against entering the market.
• Incumbent's Response:	
– Collude:	The incumbent decides to cooperate with the entrant, leading to shared market profits.
– Fight:	The incumbent decides to aggressively compete against the entrant, potentially leading to reduced profits for both.

The payoffs are structured around the idea that a monopoly allows the incumbent to earn significant profits (e.g., 300 units), but these profits are threatened if the entrant decides to enter the market. The cost of entry for the entrant is considered (e.g., 10 units), and the revenue in a duopoly scenario might drop to 100 units for each due to increased competition (Fig. 5.13).

In the context of business intelligence, understanding and applying game theoretical concepts goes beyond memorizing classical games and their standard solutions. The real value lies in applying these principles to actual strategic decisions within an organization. Analysts should be adept at identifying relevant game structures, anticipating potential moves by competitors, and calculating possible outcomes to guide strategic planning and competitive positioning.

This approach not only enriches strategic analysis but also equips decision-makers with a robust toolkit for anticipating and responding to competitors' actions in a calculated and informed manner.

[11] To learn more, see, e.g. Rasmusen (1989).

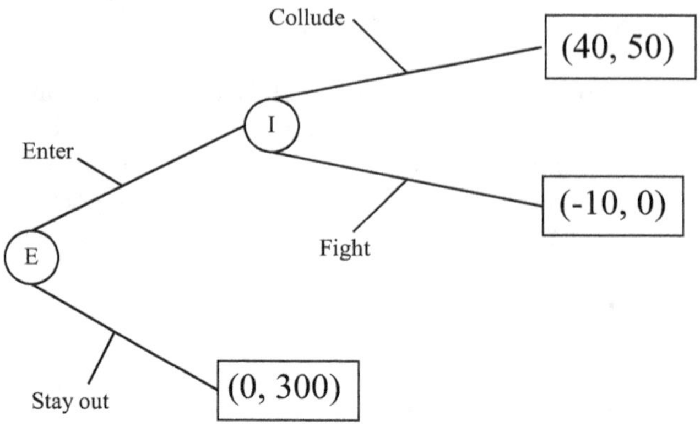

Fig. 5.13 A Game theoretical example: Entry Deterrence I (Rasmusen, 1989, pp. 96–98)

For use in Intelligence Studies, it is less important to learn all the well-known games and their solutions by heart and more important to know how Game Theory works. We should then start to apply simple concepts to actual problems.

5.9.8 Simulations

The advent of computer software has significantly broadened the possibilities for business simulations. Companies can now simulate potential revenue and profit scenarios for the upcoming years based on a set of predefined assumptions. This capability is invaluable for strategic planning and risk management.

In a typical business simulation, a company might project itself into hypothetical future scenarios to assess how it would respond to various changes in its operating environment. For example, a company might simulate the impact of a dramatic increase in sales—say, a 150% rise—or consider the ramifications of having to lay off half of its workforce. Such simulations enable companies to prepare for potential future events by playing out their consequences in a controlled, risk-free setting.

Example of a Revenue and Profit Simulation:
Suppose a company wants to simulate its potential revenue and profit for the next 5 years under varying market conditions. Here's how a simple mathematical model might be structured:

1. Assumptions:
   - Current annual revenue: $100 million
   - Annual growth rate scenarios: 5%, 10%, 15%
   - Cost as a percentage of revenue: 80%
   - Initial profit margin: 20% (which is 100% – 80% cost)
2. Simulation Model:
   - The revenue for each subsequent year can be calculated using the formula:

$$\text{Revenue}_{\text{year}} = \text{Revenue}_{\text{previous year}} \times (1 + \text{growth rate})$$

- Profit can be calculated as:

$$\text{Profit}_{\text{year}} = \text{Revenue}_{\text{year}} \times \text{profit margin}$$

3. Running the Simulation:
   - For a 10% annual growth rate, the revenue and profit calculations over 5 years might look like this:
   - Year 1: Revenue = $110 million, Profit = $22 million
   - Year 2: Revenue = $121 million, Profit = $24.2 million
   - Year 3: Revenue = $133.1 million, Profit = $26.62 million
   - Year 4: Revenue = $146.41 million, Profit = $29.282 million
   - Year 5: Revenue = $161.05 million, Profit = $32.21 million

This type of simulation not only helps in financial forecasting but also in contingency planning. Contingency plans often use simulations to prepare for potential crises, allowing businesses to develop strategies in response to hypothetical disasters or market shifts.

Simulations are also prevalent in fields such as military strategy and politics, where they are used to model potential real-world scenarios and their outcomes. For instance, a business or political simulation might explore the consequences of a merger between two major competitors and analyze the strategic responses available to the company.

Historically, figures like Napoleon utilized what can be considered early forms of simulation, gathering extensive information about potential adversaries and mentally simulating various campaign strategies. This approach, while rudimentary compared to today's software-driven simulations, underscores the timeless value of preparative strategizing.

Simulations in business provide a dynamic platform for decision-makers to visualize the impact of their decisions and refine their strategies accordingly. They allow organizations to test different scenarios and develop robust responses to a range of potential future events, enhancing their preparedness and strategic agility.

5.9.9 Ratio Analysis

Ratio analysis is a powerful tool utilized extensively in finance and managerial accounting to derive meaningful insights from relationships between quantifiable data. This analytical method involves comparing different financial metrics to assess various aspects of a company's operational efficiency, liquidity, profitability, and solvency. The fundamental requirement for ratio analysis is that the figures compared must be directly related and logically comparable.

Example of Profitability Ratio: Return on Capital (ROC)
One of the fundamental ratios in financial analysis is the Return on Capital (ROC), which measures the efficiency with which a company utilizes its capital to generate profits. This ratio is a critical indicator of a company's profitability and operational efficiency.

Equation 5.1 Return on Capital (ROC).

$$\text{ROC} = \frac{\text{Net Operating Profit}}{\text{Total Captial Employed}}$$

Calculation Example:
Suppose a company has a net operating profit of $200,000 and the total capital employed is $1,000,000. The ROC can be calculated as follows:

$$\text{ROC} = \frac{200{,}000}{1{,}000{,}000} = 0.2 \text{ or } 20\%$$

This result indicates that for every dollar of capital employed, the company generates 20 cents in profit, reflecting its capital efficiency.

While traditionally used within financial contexts, ratio analysis can also be applied to other domains such as marketing and human resources to derive insights about operational efficiencies:

- Marketing: Analyzing the cost efficiency of in-house versus outsourced marketing activities. For instance, if a company spends $100,000 on in-house marketing and $150,000 on outsourced efforts, a ratio can be calculated to determine cost efficiency.
- Human Resources: As we mentioned earlier we can measure employee productivity by calculating the turnover per employee. If a company has a turnover of $5 million and employs 50 workers, the turnover per employee would be:

$$\text{Turnover per Employee} = \frac{5{,}000{,}000}{50} = 100{,}000$$

- This figure suggests each employee contributes $100,000 to turnover.

Ratio analysis can also be effectively combined with other analytical methods such as benchmarking. For instance, comparing the ROC of one company against industry averages or specific competitors can provide a deeper insight into relative performance. This synergistic use of ratio analysis with benchmarking not only enhances the depth of analytical outcomes but also bolsters strategic decision-making by providing a clearer comparative perspective across industry standards.

5.9.10 Cost Analysis

Cost analysis is a crucial function within the financial management of a company, aimed at dissecting and understanding the costs associated with various aspects of the operation. This analysis helps in identifying the actual expenses of producing a specific unit or offering a service, which can be particularly challenging in the service industries where outputs are not as tangibly quantifiable as in manufacturing.

The goal of cost analysis is to provide detailed insights into the costs incurred during the production or service delivery process, enabling management to make informed decisions aimed at enhancing operational efficiency and profitability. This involves not only pinpointing direct costs associated with production but also allocating indirect costs accurately.

Example of Cost Analysis in Production
Consider a manufacturing company that produces widgets. To conduct a cost analysis, the company needs to aggregate and assess both direct and indirect costs associated with the production of widgets:

1. Direct Costs: These are costs that can be directly attributed to the production of widgets, such as raw materials and labor. Suppose the raw materials cost $5 per widget and direct labor costs $3 per widget.
2. Indirect Costs: These costs are not directly tied to production but are necessary for the operation, such as maintenance and utilities. Assume indirect costs allocated to each widget based on production volume amount to $2 per widget.

Calculation:

$$\text{Total Cost per Widget} = \text{Direct Materials Cost} + \text{Direct Labor Cost} + \text{Indirect Costs}$$
$$\text{Total Cost per Widget} = \$5 + \$3 + \$2 = \$10$$

Cost-Effectiveness and Cost-Benefit Analysis:
Beyond determining the cost of production, cost analysis evaluates the cost-effectiveness of different production methods and strategies. For instance, if an alternative method reduces the direct labor cost per widget from $3 to $2 without compromising quality, the cost-effectiveness of this method would be evident.

Additionally, cost-benefit analysis plays a vital role in strategic decision-making:

- Cost-Benefit Analysis**:** This analysis involves comparing the total costs of a production method against the total value of the benefits it provides. The net rate of return is calculated by subtracting total costs from total benefits.

Example of Cost-Benefit Analysis:
Suppose the company invests in automated machinery that reduces direct labor costs but increases maintenance costs. If the investment leads to a reduction in total production costs and increases production capacity, the net benefit might look like this:

- Initial Investment: $100,000 on new machinery
- Annual Savings: $20,000 in labor costs
- Additional Annual Maintenance Cost: $5000

Net Rate of Return Calculation:

$$\text{Net Rate of Return} = \text{Annual Savings} - \text{Additional Costs}$$

$$\text{Net Rate of Return} = \$20,000 - \$5000 = \$15,000 \text{ per year}$$

In conclusion, cost analysis is integral to understanding and managing the financial dynamics of a company. It provides a granular view of where money is spent and where efficiencies can be gained. In service industries, despite the challenges of quantifying outputs, cost analysis remains essential for gauging the profitability and sustainability of service offerings. The insights derived from detailed cost analysis are crucial for strategic planning and operational adjustments in any business, ensuring resources are used most effectively to enhance financial performance and competitive positioning.

5.9.11 Spreadsheets

Spreadsheets are ubiquitous in the realm of data analysis and often serve as the backbone for various analytical tasks. Their simplicity, coupled with powerful data manipulation capabilities, makes them one of the most widely used and effective analytical tools available. Spreadsheets provide an instant overview of data and can be an excellent predictive tool when the dimensions and categories are thoughtfully selected.

The fundamental concept of a spreadsheet is its ability to organize data across two dimensions: the x-axis and the y-axis. For instance, a company's critical success criteria could be listed on the y-axis, while the different departments of the company might be aligned along the x-axis. These axes represent the categories and dimensions within the spreadsheet.

A well-organized spreadsheet is inherently easy to read, and its readability can be further enhanced by placing the most extensive variables on the y-axis, allowing for vertical rather than horizontal review. This layout leverages the natural way most people scan information, thereby improving the user's ability to quickly assimilate the data presented.

The evolution of information technology has significantly simplified the use of spreadsheets. Programs like Excel, Quattro Pro, Lotus 1-2-3, and Microsoft Works have long facilitated complex data analysis. However, as technology advances, these programs are continually updated or replaced by even more efficient tools, reflecting the dynamic nature of IT development.

In practice, spreadsheets are not only used in conjunction with other analytical methods but can also stand alone as powerful tools. Their ability to aggregate and compare data makes them indispensable for tasks ranging from financial modeling and budgeting to more complex predictive analytics. The flexibility of spreadsheets allows users to tailor analyses to specific needs by adjusting variables and parameters directly within the tool.

Moreover, the widespread familiarity with spreadsheet software enhances its utility as a tool for collaborative analysis. Team members can contribute to, edit, and review spreadsheets in real-time, making it a valuable tool for projects that require collective input and rapid decision-making.

In conclusion, spreadsheets remain a fundamental tool in the analyst's toolkit due to their versatility, ease of use, and the profound impact they can have on the decision-making process. Whether used for simple data entry or complex predictive analytics, the role of spreadsheets in business intelligence and data analysis cannot be overstated.

5.9.12 Devil's Advocate

The Devil's Advocate Analysis involves adopting the perspective of an external party, such as a competitor, customer, or supplier, to critically evaluate one's own strategies and decisions. This analytical approach aims to understand how an opposing party might perceive and react to the same challenges faced by your organization.

By stepping into the shoes of an adversary or a stakeholder with potentially conflicting interests, a company can better predict and counter potential objections and strategies. This method is particularly useful in strategic planning, where anticipating the moves of competitors can provide a significant competitive edge.

Implementation of Devil's Advocate Analysis:
Typically, a company may appoint a designated troubleshooter or a devil's advocate for this role. This individual's task is to critically assess the company's plans and approaches from an adversary's viewpoint, challenging assumptions and testing the strength of the company's arguments and strategies. It is crucial that the person assigned to this role does not hold any other responsibilities within the project to ensure an unbiased perspective. Often, selecting an individual from outside the project team or even from a different department—or in some cases an external consultant—can be beneficial.

Application in Business Scenarios:
An effective way to utilize Devil's Advocate Analysis is through interactive case studies within learning laboratories or simulated environments. These simulations are designed to mimic potential real-world interactions, allowing the organization to rehearse responses to various scenarios. For instance, before entering a critical negotiation, a company might conduct a session where team members role-play both their own and the opponent's parts. This exercise helps in refining strategies, identifying weak points in arguments, and developing more robust counter-strategies.

Example Scenario:
Consider a company planning to launch a new product. The Devil's Advocate might raise potential objections that could be posed by competitors or consumers, such as concerns over product safety, pricing strategies, or the effectiveness of the product compared to existing alternatives. The company can adjust its strategies to mitigate these risks by addressing these points during the planning phase.

Advantages of Devil's Advocate Analysis:

1. Enhanced Strategic Insights: Provides a broader perspective on potential challenges and competitive dynamics.
2. Risk Mitigation: Helps identify and address potential flaws or weaknesses in strategies and operational plans.
3. Improved Decision-Making: By considering diverse viewpoints and potential criticisms, decisions are more well-rounded and robust.

Overall, the Devil's Advocate Analysis is an invaluable strategy for testing the resilience of company strategies against potential external challenges. It fosters a culture of critical thinking and proactive problem-solving, ensuring that strategies are not only well conceived but also resilient to external pressures and competitive dynamics.

5.9.13 PEST (Political, Economic, Socio-cultural and Technological Analysis)

PEST analysis is a strategic tool used to evaluate the macro-environmental factors that might impact an organization. It categorizes external influences into four types: Political, Economic, Socio-cultural, and Technological factors. Each of these categories can significantly affect a company's operation and performance.

Political Analysis
Political analysis within the PEST framework focuses on assessing the stability and implications of government policies on a company's operations. Analysts typically explore variables such as political stability, tax policies, employment laws,

environmental regulations, and trade restrictions. Mapping these factors into a simplified world model helps in visualizing the impact across different regions. For instance, a company operating internationally may use a stylized map to identify and categorize regions based on political stability and government attitudes towards business.

Consider a company evaluating potential expansion regions:

- Zone of Destabilization: Areas marked by political unrest which may impact business operations.
- Security Zone 1: Regions where the company can provide adequate security and stable operations.
- Security Zone 2: Areas where security concerns are significant, and the company might opt for local partnerships instead of direct involvement.

First, we must learn to draw a map of the world to illustrate our ideas. This part of the exercise should not take more than a minute, so practice something like this (Fig. 5.14):

The degree of details on the map will depend on its use, e.g. in the map we have drawn above the whole of Europe is presented as a cube, not accounting for areas such as the Baltic Sea or the British Isles.

Then we draw in the actual zones (Fig. 5.15):

In the analysis above (an old slide written in Norwegian), we have focused on one dimension of political analysis: security for Europe. Traditionally, it has been said that for Europe to be stable, we need to create peace and security in Zone 1. The truth of this observation has been confirmed by popular revolts or revolutions in

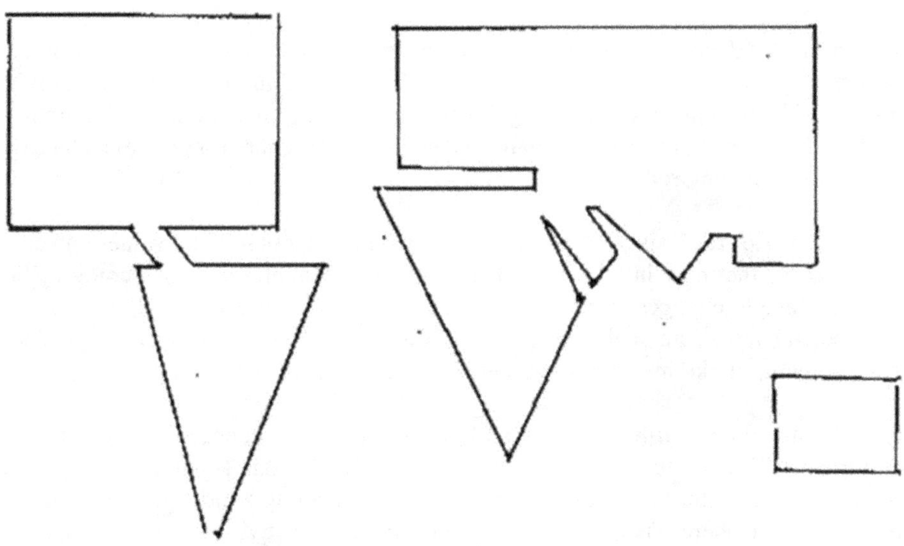

Fig. 5.14 Quick draw of map of the world

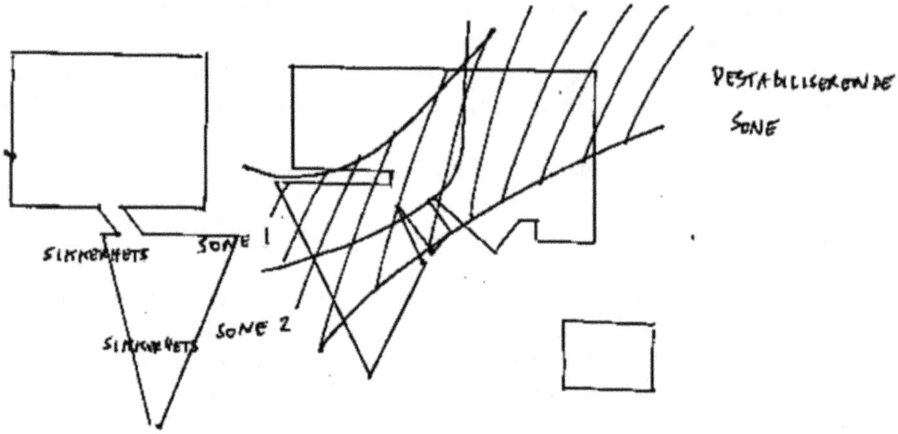

Fig. 5.15 Example of political analysis for the PEST using quick draw map

Libya, Egypt, and Tunisia. We also see it in numerous conflicts between Israelis and Palestinians in the Middle East. What happens here spills over to Europe and becomes a European problem as well. Because of this, it is important for Europe to keep this zone stable. However, if we look at Zone 2, what happens there does not affect us in the same way. That does not mean that the suffering there is any less severe, just that the effects on European countries are smaller. We see the same logic in the mass media: what happens in Zone 2 seldom becomes news, while the smallest incident in Zone 1 attracts everyone's attention.

We can use maps to analyze other dimensions too, like economic factors or socio-cultural ones. For example, on a general level:

Economic Analysis This aspect examines economic conditions that directly affect business operations. Key variables include interest rates, inflation rates, economic growth (GDP), consumer spending levels, and unemployment rates. Economic analysis helps predict shifts in demand and supply and prepare for potential changes in the operating environment.

Socio-cultural Analysis Socio-cultural factors encompass societal values and cultural aspects that may influence market dynamics. Variables such as demographic trends, lifestyle changes, consumer behaviors, educational levels, cultural norms, and societal values are analyzed. Understanding these factors is crucial for product development, marketing strategies, and customer engagement.

Climate and Geography Climate and geography also influence cultural aspects. High economic activity on the planet is concentrated in certain geographical regions, partly due to weather conditions, known as the temperate zones, primarily in the northern hemisphere. There are no significant economic activities in the polar zones, except that the Arctic Circle is poised to become a major transportation route for

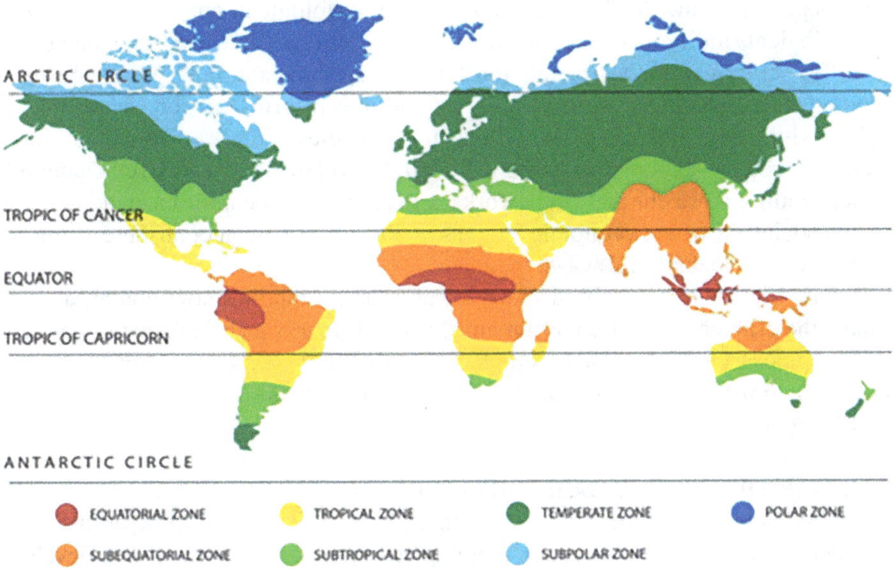

Fig. 5.16 The world map with temperature zones

goods passing from Asia to the Western world as much of the ice melts. Similarly, there are few competitive nations around the equator, that is, between the Tropic of Cancer and the Tropic of Capricorn, as it is simply too hot for most purposes (Fig. 5.16).

It is no coincidence that the most productive cultures are found in the temperate zone, where conditions such as agricultural productivity, industrial development, and a lower disease burden promote economic success. However, temperature alone does not guarantee prosperity. Colder climates often foster a strong work ethic, distinguishing 'do' cultures, which typically have economic advantages, from 'be' cultures, which excel in social and familial domains.

While "be" cultures might not excel in economic terms, they play a crucial role in human value beyond economics, excelling in family and social cohesion. It's essential to recognize that human existence transcends mere economic output, emphasizing that economic metrics do not determine the intrinsic value of human lives. These cultures enrich human experience through strong social networks, community support, and emotional well-being, highlighting the multifaceted nature of societal contributions. Understanding this broadens our perspective on what constitutes a valuable and fulfilling life, reminding us that economic success is just one aspect of a prosperous society.

Historically, geography and climate have shaped human behavior, once a respected study known as 'Geographische Physiognomik' in Germany. Though it later fell into disrepute due to its dogmatic approach, the importance of climate in human activity cannot be overstated, and the relationship between culture and climate remains important for analyzing economic performance. More recently, the concepts of "be" and "do" cultures come from sociological, anthropological, and psychological studies that examine differences in cultural values and societal priorities. "Be" cultures emphasize relationships, social cohesion, and presence, often aligning with collectivist values, while "do" cultures prioritize action, achievement, and productivity, reflecting individualist tendencies. These distinctions have been explored by scholars like Edward T. Hall, Geert Hofstede, and Jared Diamond. Understanding these cultural frameworks helps highlight the multifaceted nature of human societies, where economic success and social cohesion contribute in different but equally meaningful ways.

Today, the focus has shifted more towards understanding how human actions impact the climate and our environment. This shift marks a critical area of concern in contemporary social sciences, emphasizing the urgent need to address our environmental impact, though detailed strategies for such initiatives are beyond this book's scope.

Technological Analysis is the last dimension covered in the PEST:
The focus here is on technology trends that could affect industry operations. This includes innovations in production techniques, automation, research and development levels, technological adoption rates, and IT infrastructure. For businesses, staying updated with technological advancements is vital to maintain competitiveness.

Integrated Example:
A global tech company uses PEST analysis to gauge potential markets for its new smartphone line:

- Political**:** Evaluates countries based on government support for tech products and intellectual property protections.
- Economic: Looks at consumer income levels and mobile penetration rates to assess market potential.
- Socio-cultural: Studies population demographics and smartphone usage patterns.
- Technological**:** Analyzes local tech infrastructure and the prevalence of digital payment systems.

Using this comprehensive approach allows the company to identify optimal markets and tailor strategies accordingly. This process highlights the interplay of various external factors and their combined impact on strategic decision-making.

In conclusion, PEST analysis provides a broad framework that helps businesses understand the broader macro-environmental contexts affecting their operations. By systematically evaluating political, economic, socio-cultural, and technological environments, companies can better anticipate external changes and adapt their strategies to meet evolving conditions.

5.9.14 Power Analysis

We've previously discussed how to conduct a power analysis, but let's revisit some general aspects. A power analysis specifically examines the distribution of economic or political force, which often overlap, among individuals and organizations.

In private organizations, power is more directly linked to economic size, whereas in public organizations, it's tied to political influence, the strength of support, and relationships with key figures. Assessing power in public sectors is more complex than in private sectors. Economic size can typically be quantified using public data, such as in annual reports, making it relatively straightforward to measure. In contrast, mapping and quantifying the political influence of each manager, based on their contacts and the strength of these relationships, is considerably more challenging.

In practical applications like negotiations, understanding the Power Ratio can be crucial. For example, if the Power Distribution in a negotiation is 40–60, our organization would have a power ratio of 0.4, and our opponent 0.6. This indicates that the opponent enters the negotiation with a stronger position and could leverage this advantage in case of conflicts.

For a more detailed analysis, we might need to consider various dimensions of power within an organization. For instance, a competitor may be more powerful due to having a robust financial structure, superior human capital, an extensive distribution network, a high level of entrepreneurial spirit, or a stronger company identity. In conducting a power analysis, it's essential to identify and quantify these different dimensions of power.

An example of Power Analysis:
Consider the economic size and political influence as variables in a power calculation:

$$\text{Economic Power Index}\left(\text{EPI}\right) = \frac{\text{Annual Revenue}}{\text{Total Revenue of Industry}}$$

$$\text{Political Influence Index}\left(\text{PII}\right) = \frac{\text{Number of Key Contacts} \times \text{Influence Score}}{\text{Maximum Possible Score}}$$

The overall Power Index (PI) might then be calculated by weighing these indices based on their relevance to the situation:

Equation 5.2 The overall Power Index (PI).

$$\text{Power Index}\left(\text{PI}\right) = w_1 \times \text{EPI} + w_2 \times \text{PII}$$

where $w1$ and $w2$ are weights reflecting the importance of economic size and political influence, respectively.

This formula allows for a quantifiable approach to power analysis, combining various factors into a single, comprehensive metric.

What this means is that in a negotiation between a small supplier with $10 million annual revenue and limited industry connections (Supplier A) and a large retail chain with $1 billion annual revenue and strong political influence (Retailer B), the Power Index (PI) heavily favors the retailer. Assuming economic size is weighted at 0.7 and political influence at 0.3, Supplier A's PI is 0.067, while Retailer B's PI is 0.97. This indicates that Retailer B has a significantly stronger position in the negotiation.

5.9.15 Statistical Analysis

Statistical analysis encompasses a suite of techniques aimed at organizing, summarizing, and interpreting data to uncover patterns and relationships. This domain of analysis is foundational in many fields, providing insights through quantitative methods.

The process begins with descriptive statistics, which include measures like mean (average), median (middle value), and mode (most frequent value). These statistics help in understanding the central tendencies and distribution spread of data. For instance, calculating the mean of a dataset involves summing all numerical values and dividing by the number of observations:

Equation 5.3 Mean calculation.

$$\text{Mean} = \frac{\Sigma(\text{all values})}{\text{number of values}}$$

Beyond summarizing data, statistical analysis investigates relationships through inferential statistics, utilizing methods such as variance analysis and regression modeling. Variance measures how widely the data points in a set are spread about the mean, indicating the distribution's dispersion:

Equation 5.4 Variance calculation.

$$\text{Variance} = \frac{\Sigma(\text{each value} - \text{mean})^2}{\text{number of values} - 1}$$

Regression analysis further explores the relationships between variables, helping to predict the outcome variable based on the influence of one or more predictor variables. The simplest form of regression, linear regression, can be depicted as:

Equation 5.5 Linear regression.

$$y = \beta_0 + \beta_1 x + \epsilon$$

where y is the dependent variable, x is the independent variable, $\beta 0$ the y-intercept, $\beta 1$ the slope of the line, and ϵ the error term.

Statistical analysis has evolved from basic population counting for administrative purposes such as tax collection into a comprehensive tool used across both natural and social sciences. It assists in making informed decisions based on data-driven insights. However, it's crucial to apply these techniques judiciously—ensuring data integrity and selecting appropriate methods are paramount to avoid misinterpretations.

Moreover, understanding the limitations of statistical tools is essential. Every statistical method has conditions and assumptions that must be met to yield reliable results. For example, regression analysis requires that the data meet assumptions about normality, linearity, and homoscedasticity.

In summary, while statistical analysis is a powerful tool for data examination, it demands careful application and consideration of underlying assumptions to effectively inform decision-making processes.

5.9.16 Scenario Analysis

Scenario analysis, a primarily qualitative method, involves constructing detailed narratives about possible future states of the world. Typically, this analysis involves crafting 2–5 potential scenarios, with three being most common: a worst-case scenario, a best-case scenario, and a moderate-case scenario.

In scenario analysis, the focus is on exploring the potential consequences of each scenario unfolding. This approach is less reliant on mathematical calculations compared to decision tree analysis, and it does not focus primarily on economic data like forecasting. It also allows for a broader range of potential events than trend analysis, making it particularly useful in strategic planning where multiple futures are possible.

For example, let's consider a company assessing the impact of an emerging technology on its operations across three scenarios:

1. Best-case scenario: The technology leads to significant market expansion.
2. Moderate-case scenario: The technology gradually integrates without major disruptions.
3. Worst-case scenario: The technology causes significant market disruption and loss of revenue.

Quantitatively, the company might assign probabilities to each scenario based on expert input and market research, such as 20% for the best-case, 50% for the moderate-case, and 30% for the worst-case. The financial impact for each scenario could also be estimated, allowing the company to weigh the potential financial outcomes based on the probability of each scenario occurring.

Equation 5.6 Probability calculations of scenarios.

$$\text{Expected Financial Outcome} = \left(0.20 \times \text{Best} - \text{case Impact}\right) + (0.50 \times \text{Moderate} - \text{case Impact}) + \left(0.30 \times \text{Worst} - \text{case Impact}\right)$$

This integration of qualitative descriptions with quantitative assessments enhances the decision-making process, providing a richer, more nuanced view of the future.

In the Foresight discipline, multiple plausible scenarios are common, considering a wide range of factors and uncertainties. For instance, when analyzing the future market for electric vehicles (EVs), we might create:

1. Tech Breakthrough Scenario: A significant technological advancement drastically reduces EV costs and increases range.
2. Regulatory Shift Scenario: New international regulations mandate EV adoption faster than anticipated.
3. Consumer Preference Shift Scenario: A major shift in consumer preferences towards eco-friendly products accelerates EV market growth.
4. Economic Downturn Scenario: A global recession slows down overall market growth, impacting EV sales differently across regions.
5. Supply Chain Disruption Scenario: Critical material shortages disrupt production, delaying market expansion.

We can express this as:

- Multiple Scenarios (S1, S2, …, S10):
  - $P(S_1) = 0.15$
  - $P(S_2) = 0.1$
  - $P(S_3) = 0.05$
  - $P(S_4) = 0.2$
  - $P(S_5) = 0.1$
  - $P(S_6) = 0.1$
  - $P(S_7) = 0.1$
  - $P(S_8) = 0.05$
  - $P(S_9) = 0.05$
  - $P(S_{10}) = 0.1$

And the probability sum as:

Equation 5.7 Probability Sum in Advanced Scenario Analysis.

$$\sum_{10}^{i=1} P\left(S_i\right) = 1$$

By considering these varied and detailed scenarios, Foresight provides a more comprehensive analysis of potential futures, allowing them to better prepare and strategize for a wider range of possibilities. This approach enables them to anticipate and adapt to changes more effectively than our limited three-scenario method.

It is crucial, however, to understand that unlike more rigid mathematical formulas, scenario analysis depends on the flexibility and creativity of the analyst to adapt the scenarios to the specific needs and realities of the organization. While statistics and other analytical tools can complement scenario analysis by adding depth to the scenarios, they should be applied carefully to avoid skewing the narrative framework. This balanced approach ensures that strategic planning remains both imaginative and grounded.

5.9.17 Signal Analysis

Signal analysis plays a crucial role in environmental scanning, for example where analysts actively monitor various media and information sources to detect useful intelligence signals. The effectiveness of signal analysis is fundamentally linked to the specific objectives of the information gathering process.

Subscribing to a set of sources is easily done, but finding the right sources to subscribe to takes time and experience. It's important to get a good balance of sources, from different cultures and languages, and from different spectra of the political line. Take the example of news channels. Consumers have moved from linear channels to on-demand channels, like subscriptions on YouTube for news. The younger generation gets it from TikTok, which has a much shorter format and is even more explicitly visual. The Internet provides greater opportunities for quality and diversity of sources, but it also locks people into dangerous "bubbles."

There are Social Bubbles where we are often lured into being part of a close-knit community that avoids interaction with others who have different lifestyles or beliefs. Then there are Information Bubbles when we consume news and media from a limited range of sources that align with our preexisting views, thereby reinforcing those views without challenge.

We talk of Confirmation Bias, the tendency to search for, interpret, favor, and recall information in a way that confirms or supports one's preexisting beliefs or values. And Availability Bias, the tendency to overestimate the importance of information that is readily available to them. But also, Echo Chamber Effect, which occurs when beliefs are amplified or reinforced by communication and repetition inside a closed system, often leading to the homogenization of opinions and the exclusion of outside perspectives. Groupthink, like when members of an internet forum or social media group may prioritize harmony and consensus over critical analysis, leading to poor decision-making and the marginalization of dissenting views. The biggest risk still may be Selective Exposure: where we tend to preferentially expose ourselves to information that aligns with our beliefs and avoid information that challenges them.

We are already seeing the consequences of this play out on a global scale: increased polarization, misconceptions, and maybe the worst of all, reduced critical thinking. At least in major linear TV stations, there was someone trying to be critical. So even before we start collecting the signals, the most difficult part is to select the sources.

In signal analysis, each piece of information is evaluated based on its relevance and potential impact on strategic decisions. For instance, analysts might employ a scoring system ranging from 1 to 10 to assess the importance of each article or piece of information they encounter. A score of 6 or 7 might indicate that the information is relatively important, while a score of 10 signifies extreme importance, and a score of 1 indicates minimal importance.

To quantify the process, consider an analyst who reviews 10 articles in a day and rates them according to their relevance to a specific strategic question, assuming here that each source has the same value:

- Article 1: 7
- Article 2: 3
- Article 3: 6
- Article 4: 10
- Article 5: 5
- Article 6: 2
- Article 7: 8
- Article 8: 4
- Article 9: 1
- Article 10: 9

The average score of these ratings can be calculated to gauge the overall importance of the day's findings:

$$\text{Average Score} = \frac{7+3+6+10+5+2+8+4+1+9}{10} = 5.5$$

This average score helps to contextualize the day's information scanning efforts and assess whether the sources scanned are yielding sufficiently relevant data.

Signal analysis demands not just the identification but also the justification of why certain information is considered a strong signal. Analysts must articulate the significance of a signal relative to others, backing their evaluations with clear, objective reasoning. This approach ensures that priority is given to the most impactful information, thereby enhancing the strategic decision-making process.

5.9.18 Early Warning Analysis

Early Warning Analysis is pivotal in identifying potential future trends or threats based on current, often subtle, signals. This analysis involves monitoring for signals that might seem insignificant at present but could gain importance under certain conditions in the future.

Consider an analyst tracking the ice cream industry for a client. They read an article indicating consumer satisfaction with new ice cream products launched just as the summer season approaches. The analyst constructs a predictive syllogism based on two premises and a conclusion:

- P1: The average temperature in June and July remains high.
- P2: Competitors do not replicate our new products.
- C: Significant increase in ice cream sales this year.

This setup allows the analyst to categorize the information as an early warning signal. By framing it as a syllogism, it becomes simpler to revisit and assess the accuracy of these predictions later.

To systematize the analysis, each piece of information can be scored with a dual time perspective scale from 0 to 10. For example, an article rated as "3/8" suggests that while the current importance is moderate (3), its future relevance could be high (8). This dual-rating system effectively merges Signal and Early Warning Analysis, enhancing the strategic foresight of the analysis.

Although these analytical techniques are universal and not confined to any specific field, they hold particular significance in the realms of intelligence. Tools like SWOT are universally applicable, whereas PEST, Signal, and Early Warning Analyses are more specific to intelligence studies.

Understanding the language of analysis, rather than merely memorizing various analytical methods, is crucial. This foundational knowledge enables analysts to appropriately classify and apply different analyses based on the specific requirements of each scenario. The forthcoming sections will delve deeper into these classifications and the application of analytical rigour to various problems.

5.9.19 Win Loss Analysis

Win-Loss Analysis is a technique used to understand the reasons behind winning or losing a business opportunity. This analysis not only provides insights into customer preferences and competitor strategies but also helps refine future business approaches by learning from past outcomes.

The process involves examining specific cases where a company won or lost a contract and then quantifying the factors that contributed to the outcome. For example, consider a company that participated in 100 bids over a year. By analyzing each case, they determine that:

- 60 bids were won due to superior product quality.
- 30 bids were lost due to higher pricing compared to competitors.
- 10 bids were lost due to inadequate customer support.

From this, we can calculate the win-loss ratio and identify areas for improvement. The win-loss ratio is calculated as follows:

Equation 5.8 Win-loss ratio.

$$\text{Win}-\text{Loss Ratio}=\frac{\text{Number of Wins}}{\text{Number of Losses}}$$

If the company won 60 bids and lost 40, the win-loss ratio would be:

$$\text{Win}-\text{Loss Ratio}=\frac{60}{40}=1.5$$

This ratio indicates that for every loss, there are 1.5 wins. Higher ratios signify greater success rates, prompting a review of successful strategies for further reinforcement. Conversely, lower ratios highlight areas needing strategic adjustments.

In conducting a Win-Loss Analysis, it is crucial to categorize the reasons for wins and losses to establish actionable insights. For instance, if price is a recurrent factor in losses, the company might consider revising its pricing strategy or enhancing the value proposition of its offerings to align more closely with market expectations.

This analytical approach is not just about tallying wins and losses but involves a deeper dive into the qualitative aspects of each engagement to ensure continuous improvement. This method allows companies to adapt more dynamically to market demands and to refine their competitive strategies effectively. At the end it less about ratio and more about what you learn about the reason you won and the reason you lost.[12]

5.9.20 Battle Cards

Battle cards are a strategic tool used to equip sales teams with concise, comparative insights on competitors' products versus their own offerings. They draw from a variety of sources, including win-loss analyses, to form a comprehensive view that aids in competitive selling situations. A well-designed battle card will summarize:

- key selling points,
- potential objections from customers, and
- effective rebuttals.

For instance, it may highlight specific features of a product that outperform those of a competitor, based on feedback from customer reviews or performance metrics.

[12] For more on this see Naylor (2016).

An example of the application of mathematics in battle card development could involve calculating the percentage of features where a product outperforms its competition. For example, if SAP's software has 20 key features and outperforms Oracle in 16 out of these 20 features, SAP's competitive advantage can be quantitatively expressed as 80%.

By presenting data in a structured and easy-to-digest format, battle cards empower sales representatives to deliver targeted and persuasive arguments that effectively communicate the value of their products over competitors. This approach not only supports direct sales efforts but also aligns with broader marketing strategies by reinforcing the brand's competitive strengths.

In practice, creating an effective battle card involves gathering and synthesizing information from various internal and external sources, ensuring that the data is accurate, relevant, and up-to-date. The integration of data-driven insights into battle cards leverages both quantitative metrics and qualitative feedback to provide a robust tool for sales enablement.

5.9.21 Defining the KPIs

Key Performance Indicators (KPIs) are vital metrics used to evaluate the success of an organization in achieving its operational and strategic goals. Effective KPIs are relevant, quantifiable, and aligned with the company's objectives, providing clear targets and benchmarks that drive performance and strategic decision-making.

The process of defining KPIs involves a detailed analysis of business objectives, operational processes, and strategic priorities. For example, a company might decide to focus on customer satisfaction as a key objective. The KPI in this scenario could be the Customer Satisfaction Score (CSS), which is calculated based on survey responses. Mathematically, this might involve averaging the scores given by customers on various aspects of service or product satisfaction, providing a numerical value that reflects overall customer sentiment.

In setting up KPIs, it is important to ensure that they are SMART: Specific, Measurable, Achievable, Relevant, and Time-bound. For instance, if a company aims to improve its customer support, a relevant KPI might be the average response time to customer queries. Here, reducing the response time from 24 to 12 hours over 6 months would provide a clear, measurable, and time-bound target for the customer support team (Fig. 5.17).

Implementing KPIs typically requires gathering data from various sources, such as financial systems, customer relationship management (CRM) software, and employee performance tracking tools. This data must then be accurately analyzed to ensure that the KPIs reflect true performance against goals. Additionally, KPIs should be regularly reviewed and updated to adapt to changing business needs or market conditions.

KPIs not only guide operational improvements and strategic shifts but also foster a culture of performance and accountability within the organization. By clearly

- Market position
- Competence
- Commercial desirability
- Technological feasibility
- Product application
- Creativity
- Product knowledge
- Investigative skills
- Company-wide commitment
- Wide involvement in innovation activities
- Ability to respond
- Continual investments
- Quality
- Training
- Pollution and environmental control
- Engineering expertise
- Energy of management
- Flexibility
- Speed of response
- Market knowledge
- Courage of our convictions
- Staying very close to the customer
- Operating in teams with freedom of expression
- Senior management commitment
- Removing fear in the organization
- TQM program
- Small size/ability to make rapid decisions
- Simple technology
- Idea generation
- Category focus
- Freedom to act
- Collaboration
- Senior management support
- Flair of development team
- Synergistic benefits with existing processes
- Customer consultation and support
- Corporate culture responsive to innovation
- Dedicated innovative resources

Fig. 5.17 Example of KPI's for a company

defining and communicating these indicators, organizations can align their teams and resources towards common goals, ensuring a cohesive and directed effort towards achieving key business outcomes.

5.9.22 War Gaming

War gaming is a simulation technique used in strategic planning that allows organizations to test strategies in a risk-free environment. This method involves role-playing a series of competitive scenarios that could occur in the marketplace. It helps companies anticipate potential moves by competitors, understand possible outcomes, and evaluate the effectiveness of their strategies.

Process of War Gaming:

1. Scenario Development: War gaming begins with the creation of detailed scenarios that might unfold in the business environment. These scenarios are based on potential actions of competitors, changes in market conditions, or shifts in consumer behavior. For example, a scenario might simulate the entry of a new

competitor into the market or a sudden change in regulatory policies affecting the industry.

2. Role Assignment: Participants are assigned roles representing different stakeholders such as competitors, customers, or regulatory bodies. Each participant or team is given specific objectives and resources aligned with their role's strategic interests.
3. Decision Making and Simulation: The game progresses through a series of decision points where participants make strategic choices based on their role's objectives. Each decision influences the next phase of the scenario. For example, if a company chooses to lower prices, competitors might react by improving their product features, influencing consumer preferences and market share.
4. Mathematical Modeling: To quantify outcomes, simple mathematical models are often employed. For instance, market share shifts might be modeled using basic algebraic equations to represent changes based on strategic decisions:

Equation 5.9 War gaming example with New Market Share.

$$\text{New Market Share} = \text{Old Market Share} + \left(\text{Increase from Price Cut}\right) \\ -\left(\text{Loss to Competitor's Response}\right)$$

5. Analysis: After running through the scenarios, the results are analyzed to evaluate the effectiveness of strategies and their potential impacts on the organization. This analysis helps identify strengths and weaknesses in the strategic plan and guides future strategy development.
6. Feedback and Iteration: Insights gained from each session are used to refine strategies and improve decision-making processes. Multiple rounds of war gaming may be conducted to explore different scenarios and strategies, enhancing strategic agility and preparedness.

The benefits of War Gaming are many:

- Risk Mitigation: Allows companies to test strategies and anticipate potential challenges without real-world consequences.
- Strategic Insight: Provides valuable insights into how competitors might react to changes in business strategy or market conditions.
- Decision Making: Improves decision-making skills under pressure and fosters a deeper understanding of strategic dynamics within the industry.

War gaming, with its structured yet flexible approach, equips leaders with the tools to make informed decisions and adapt strategies dynamically, ensuring robust strategic planning and execution.

There are many more analyses, but these are some of the more well used in Intelligence Analysis. Note that none of these are specific to Intelligence Studies but are used in a wide selection of management disciplines.

5.9.23 Supply Chain Analysis and KPIs

Conducting a supply chain analysis involves several steps designed to understand the flow of goods, information, and finances within a supply chain (Table 5.9).

In step 4 in the process, we can use a number of analyses. This then becomes a situation where we have analyses within the analysis. The Supply Chain Analysis then become a Meta-analysis. In the example above, except for the SWOT we can use Value Stream Mapping, identifying and eliminating waste, and improving overall efficiency, Root Cause Analysis, using tools like fishbone diagrams to find the root causes of problems and Benchmarking, comparing performance metrics against industry standards or competitors. We can also use Vertical Linkage Analysis examining the relationships and dependencies between different stages of production within an industry, from raw materials to finished products to identifies how changes or disruptions in one stage can affect subsequent stages and overall industry performance.[13]

Textbook models of Supply Chain Analysis often appear straightforward. However, in practice, they quickly become intricate and challenging to document comprehensively without producing a confusing mosaic. This complexity is particularly evident in production and large tech companies (Fig. 5.18).[14]

EMP no longer exists as a company, nor does the mobile phone part of Ericsson, of which it was the brain, one could say. Much of it boils down to one poor decision: The company was convinced it had the best technology, ignoring the rise of the touchscreen phone introduced by Apple.

5.10 What Kind of Intelligence Analyses Organizations Use

According to an older survey by SCIP, conducted in 1998 by The Pine Ridge Group, Inc. and the T.W. Powell Company, the most used analyses are:

1. Competitor profiles: 88.9%
2. Financial analysis: 72.1%
3. SWOT analysis: 55.2%
4. Scenario development: 53.8%
5. Win/loss analysis: 40.4%

[13] Bensoussan and Fleisher (2013).

[14] Solberg Söilen et al. (2012).

Table 5.9 Supply chain analysis procedure for identifying KPIs[a]

#	Steps	Objectives	Action
1	Define the Scope and Objectives	Determine what you aim to achieve with the supply chain analysis.	Objectives could include identifying inefficiencies, reducing costs, improving quality, or increasing responsiveness.
2	Map the Supply Chain	Create a detailed map of the supply chain, including all entities involved from raw material suppliers to end customers.	To get an overview of Suppliers, Manufacturing, Distribution and Retailers/ Customers
3	Collect Data	Gather data on various aspects of the supply chain.	Lead Times: Time taken for products to move from one stage to another. Costs: Detailed cost information at each stage. Inventory Levels: Data on stock levels across the supply chain. Quality Metrics: Information on defect rates, returns, and other quality indicators. Service Levels: Customer service metrics like delivery times and order accuracy.
4	Analyze the Data	Perform quantitative and qualitative analyses to identify trends, bottlenecks, and areas for improvement.	Examples include SWOT Analysis, Value Stream Mapping, Root Cause Analysis, Benchmarking and Vertical Linkage Analysis
5	Identify Key Performance Indicators (KPIs)	Establish metrics to measure the performance of the supply chain.	Identifying variable such as Cycle Time (Time taken from order to delivery), Fill Rate (Percentage of customer demand met without stockouts), Order Accuracy (Percentage of orders delivered correctly) and Total Supply Chain Cost (Overall cost of running the supply chain).
6	Implement Changes	Put the improvement strategies into action. This may involve process changes, new technologies, or re-negotiating supplier contracts.	Use Pilot Programs to test changes on a small scale before full implementation. Change Management to ensure all stakeholders are on board with the changes and provide training if necessary.
7	Monitor and Review	Continuously monitor the performance of the supply chain against the established KPIs.	Do Regular Audits: Conduct regular audits to ensure processes are followed. Engage with Feedback Loops: Establish mechanisms for continuous feedback and improvement.

[a]Based on Hugos (2018) and Chopra and Meindl (2016)

6. War gaming: 27.5%
7. Conjoint analysis: 25.5%
8. Simulation/modeling: 25%

Competitors present the single biggest direct threat to most companies and are, as a consequence, continuously analyzed. Financial analysis, an analysis based on the

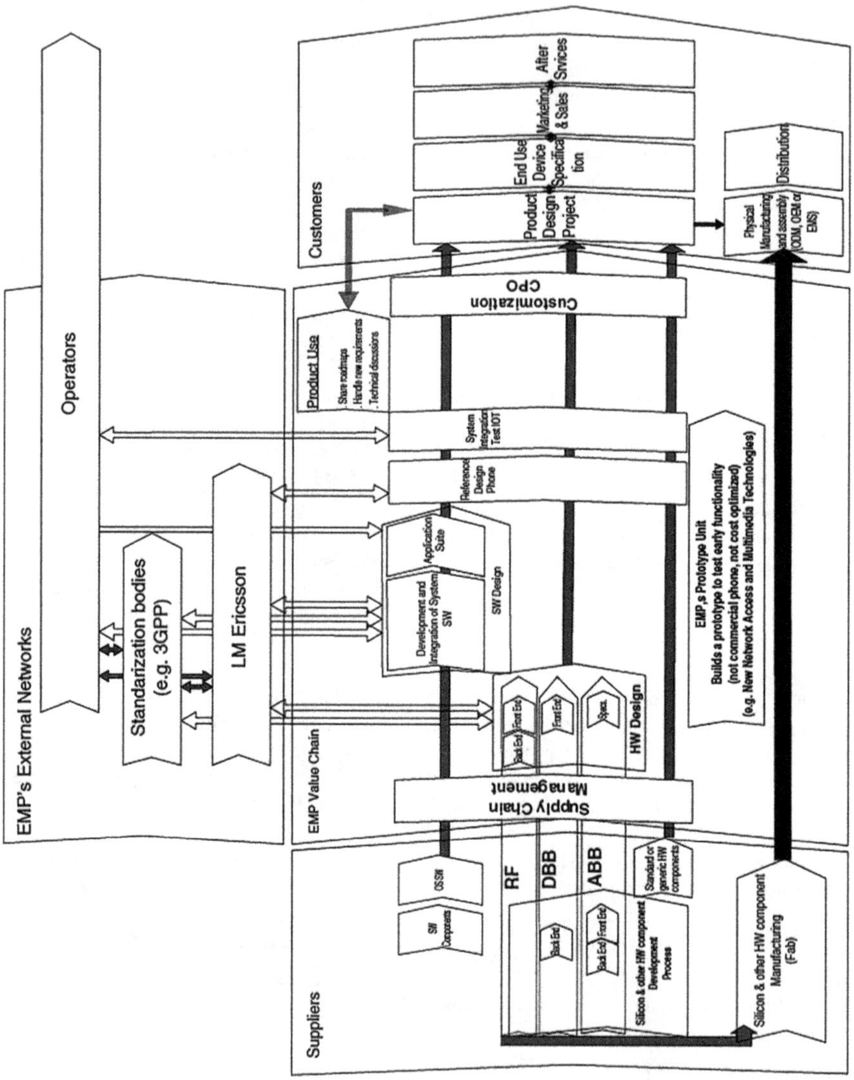

Fig. 5.18 Supply chain analysis example for Ericsson Mobile Platforms (EMP)

accounting figures of an organization, is performed the whole time by our own as well as other organizations, e.g. investment companies and banks. The financial sector probably has the strongest or most established culture for the development of analysis in any single area of business. SWOT analyses are popular because they can be used practically in every department for any problem. They are also a good way to start a larger analytical process because they help us list the major issues of any problem in a simple way.

Conjoint analysis is a statistical technique used in market research to determine how people value different attributes that make up an individual product or service. The core idea is to break down a product into its individual components and understand what combination of these elements is most influential on consumer decision-making.

A useful analysis that is similar to conjoint analysis is the KANO Model. The KANO model is not a type of conjoint analysis, but both are used to understand consumer preferences and influence product development, they approach this goal from different perspectives. It categorizes product features based on how they relate to customer satisfaction and loyalty but does not inherently quantify the trade-offs between different levels of those features. The KANO model divides feature into:

- Must-be Features: Basic features that, if not present, lead to dissatisfaction.
- Performance Features: Features that increase satisfaction linearly with their functionality or performance.
- Delighters: Features that are not expected but can significantly increase satisfaction if present.[15]

Competitor profile is simply a listing of competitors' characteristics. War gaming is, as we saw, a form of game theoretical approach to a power analysis, trying to figure out alternative responses to the opponents' actions in advance, much according to the formula IF-THEN: If company B raises prices by n% then company A is likely to choose another supplier.

The critical reader may have noticed that the analyses presented in the list above with the most popular analyses are not directly comparable. Unlike the SWOT, financial analysis is not one specific analysis but defines a number of analyses, first of all different ratio analyses,[16] but also Net Present Value, opportunity cost of capital, and the market capitalization rate (the return that is expected by an investor) of a given stock.

A way to avoid mixing apples and pears is to classify analyses by some relevant criteria, e.g. by a business function:

- Strategic, ex. Critical Success Factors (CSF)

[15] For more on the KANO model, see Tontini et al. (2013, 2017).

[16] Like the Leverage ratios which include the debt ratio, the debt-equity ratio and times interest earned. Other groups of ratios include profitability ratios and market-value ratios. See e.g. Brealey and Myers (1981/2000, pp. 824–836).

- Product oriented, ex. Benchmarking
- Environment oriented, ex. SWOT analysis
- Customer oriented, ex. Price performance
- Financial oriented, ex. Ratios
- Technology oriented, ex. Reengineering
- Behavioral, ex. Analysis of culture, psychological dimensions.

New types of analyses are presented continuously in the business literature on the market of management theory production, we may say. Most of them are adaptations from earlier analyses, e.g. a PEST analysis is a selection of macro factors (Political, Economical, Social and Technological) which could have been treated separately. Hussey's industry analysis model is an extended Porter Five Forces + an extended PEST. The industry analysis presented in this book is an adjusted version of the model of Hussey and Jenster. There are no other rules to the adjustments and extension of analysis besides the fact that they should fit the reality which they are trying to describe and supply answers which can then be used.

Some analyses are used more often for continuous intelligence tasks, like Sales forecasting, Competitor analysis and Customer satisfaction surveys. Other types of analysis are used more for problem related intelligence tasks, like the SWOT analysis, ratio analysis and focus groups.

5.11 Scope and Logic of the Language for Analysis

Analyses are articulated using numbers, words, figures, or drawings. Two dominant "languages" in management are often described as "the language of lines and circles", or alternatively, "the language of arrows and circles". Management seeks to address specific, practical business problems, and visual representations aid in this process. This geometrical language, distinct from the language of equations and Cartesian curves found in Economic Theory or algebra on Econometrics, is favored in management for its practicality in translating data and words into visual forms. These visualizations are preferred because they are more intuitive and accessible than dense textual descriptions or complex equations. By simply observing a table or diagram, numerous relationships between data points become immediately clear—this is "the language of management".

Words in analysis are commonly organized into lists. These lists are typically ordered by numerical value, where a lower figure represents a higher priority, or marked by bullet points, suggesting equal importance despite the order of presentation. It is rare to find lists organized alphabetically. The next time you encounter a list of factors, consider why it contains seven or eight points instead of five or ten. Challenge yourself to identify additional relevant factors (testing for completeness) and examine whether the listed points overlap (testing for exclusiveness). This concept of exclusiveness can be visually represented using a Venn diagram (Fig. 5.19).

What the figure illustrates, as the reader will remember from Set Theory, is that the area BC belongs to both B and C, indicating it is not exclusive. Many lists are

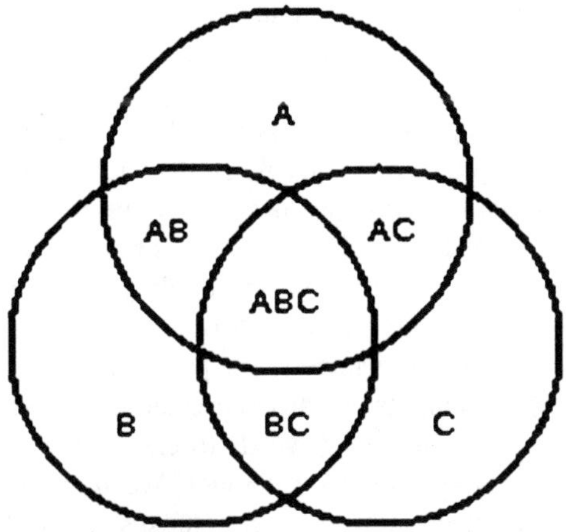

Fig. 5.19 Test of exclusiveness in analysis by the use of a Venn diagram

compiled arbitrarily yet are presented as though they were complete—if not, the list would be longer. As an intelligence analyst, you should treat lists as rigorously as you do the rest of your analysis. This means indicating whether some factors on a list are exclusive (A, B, or C) and questioning their order of appearance. You should also strive to list them according to specific criteria, as this division will provide additional information that may be useful. Do not arrange them according to some ranking (1, 2, 3 or a, b, c) if you cannot justify their positions on the list. The analyses used in intelligence studies seldom take the simple form of A, B, and C but are shared by business theories and many social sciences. SWOT is as close as we can get to an ABC-style analysis.

Each analysis presented can be categorized broadly into three types: mathematical analysis, primarily statistical, what we shall call linguistic analysis, and then geometric language analysis using lines and circles. We have demonstrated the geometric language through various examples. Here, we explore the relationship between mathematical and linguistic data for intelligence analysis. Of these two, the latter is by far the more complicated but also the more utilized. Linguistics, or the science of language, involves the study of language history and scientific investigation. An analyst will be aware of the social aspects of language, or what is called social linguistics, as the meaning of what is said often depends on who is saying it. From an international perspective, we are interested in the socio-cultural aspects of language.

It is always advantageous when we can transform linguistic data into mathematical data because numbers are easier to compare than words. This ease of comparison allows us to include more data without losing control of each part. The more data we have, often the more unexpected results we obtain because we cannot see the answer right away, that is, before we perform the analysis. For example, it is easy to see that the average of 3 and 6 is 4.5, but it is more challenging to see that 4.5 is the average of 3, 6, 7, 2, 5, 7, 1, 5.

For these kinds of analyses, transforming data to numbers is preferable. However, it is impermissible to transform sentences into numbers if the original meaning of the data is lost in the transformation, as this will yield incorrect conclusions. Knowing when to transform data into numbers and when not to is an important skill for any analyst. The rule is, if you are uncertain, then do not proceed with the transformation. You may also want to undertake the time-consuming exercise of comparing the results of several different analyses. If the results are significantly different, the transformation has probably gone wrong. However, the more data you have, the more difficult it is to perform the comparison. By using math, we gain simplicity but often lose relevance in the process.

As analysts, we are interested in the syntax of linguistic data, that is, we consider the relationship of words to each other as expressions of the conveyance of ideas from a speaker to a listener. We then study the principles of their grouping into thought units (sentences, clauses, etc.). The sentence, a word or group of words expressing a mental concept, is the unit of speech. The relationship of its words is largely determined by psychological and social factors. We listen for and analyze sentences, so-called thought units, not words. The fact that one thought unit can be expressed in many ways, giving rise to misunderstandings, makes numbers preferable to work with, but as stated earlier, only if a conversion to numbers can be justified without losing the meaning of the linguistic data.

To take an example, if 350 out of 1000 eligible voters in a multiparty system, asked before an election, say they will vote for a certain political party, we may conclude that the likelihood of that party being elected is 35%. In the example, we do not lose any meaningful data because the voters gave a direct answer to a clear question about a specific political party. If the voters also gave political comments in addition to stating their voting preference and we disregarded these comments, or if the questionnaire was structured to allow for less clear answers, we would risk losing meaningful data. If some of the voters were unclear about which political party, they would vote for but left it to the analyst to interpret their statement, we would even obtain erroneous data.

As Bertrand Russell illustrated in his book 'Principles of Mathematics,' mathematics and language are rooted in the same logic.[17] What this means is that what we call mathematics consists of deductions from logical premises. The same applies to our geometrical analyses: they are deductions from the same premises and can, to the extent that we have symbols for them, be translated into either of the other two languages. At the introductory level of Intelligence Studies, where we are, it is only required that we understand that all three languages stem from the same source of logic. We may choose one for performing an analysis and substitute it with one of the other two as needed.[18]

[17] Russell (1903).

[18] There are a number of excellent books on the foundation of language and the logic of language and mathematics. For the reader who wants to go deeper into the subject matter than what is required for our level. See e.g. Gray (1939). For an introductory book in logic e.g. Williams (1919). For more advanced books on Logic, e.g. van Dalen (1980/1997). Or on mathematical logic, e.g. Ebbinghaus et al. (1978/1996).

Table 5.10 Types of analysis divided into Linguistic and Mathematical analysis

Linguistic analysis	Mathematical analysis
SWOT	Ratio
Devil's advocate	
Benchmarking	
Critical Success Factors	
	Cost analysis
Scenario	
Trend	
Game theoretical approaches	
	Statistical analysis
Market research	

Some analyses, as products or outcomes, are a combination of numbers and letters, or mathematics and linguistics. As illustrated in the Table 5.10, we could classify the different analyses accordingly. We have not done so here, but it would be more accurate to place them on a scale ranging from numbers to letters, or to plot any analysis on a three-dimensional scale where the geometric dimension is placed on the depth axis. However, this introduces more complexity. Complexity is key to predicting human behavior and events, but traditionally our cognitive abilities have not allowed us to handle it meaningfully—until now, with the advent of supercomputers and AI.

It is worth noting that many preferred analyses are valued for being simple, easy to use, and involving a combination of mathematical, linguistic, and geometric languages. For example, a spreadsheet utilizes sums and averages; each piece of data is described using words, its values presented in numbers, which are processed using statistical methods, and everything is displayed in a two-dimensional table. This simply reflects our cognitive limitations.

We can categorize analyses by identifying the main aspects they encompass. Understanding these aspects makes it easier to construct our own analysis from scratch or to modify an existing one (Table 5.11).

1. The time aspect is accounted for in all analyses by necessity; you either focus on the present, the past, or the future. Most analyses concentrate more on the present, others on the future, and very few on the past. This has been a significant weakness in the study of business throughout most of the twentieth century, going back to the methodological quarrel known as 'die Methodenstreit'. The outcome of that dispute was that historians lost out, and the future study of business and economics was built more on the natural sciences, specifically physics, moving away from its roots in biology and history. This shift led to an overly instrumental science.[19]

1. Perspective is another aspect that differentiates analyses. Most analyses focus on the perspective of one's own organization, but the perspective of other parties can be integrated into almost any analysis. This could be the perspective of a

[19] For more on this, and maybe for another course, see Söilen (2010b, 2015, 2016a, 2017b).

Table 5.11 Aspects in analyses: time, perspective and pro and con

Aspects in analysis	Aspect possibilities	The analysis
Time	Past	Historical facts
	Present	Factor X
	Future	Trend
Perspective	Own	Most kinds
	Other (multiples)	Devil's advocate
Pro and con	Pro/+	SWOT
	Con/–	

competitor, a supplier, or an influencer, such as a local politician or a YouTuber. To the extent that they influence your company, it is worthwhile to understand how they think and what their arguments are. Such an analysis will also help you better plan your responses to their actions.

2. A third aspect is the pros and cons, or the positive and negative sides, which we find in analyses like the SWOT (note that a SWOT analysis combines the Pro and Con aspect (S + W) with the Time aspect of present and future (O + T)).

We have discussed the scientific language of analysis and demonstrated how the study of Intelligence is built upon—and is inseparable from—the discussion of scientific method and epistemology, which is concerned with the limits of what we can know.

While on the topic of method, we should also address the trade-off between the value of analysis versus the value of spending time finding new data, as this is a dilemma faced by all organizations that work with analysis.

5.12 Gathering Relevant Facts Versus Doing Analysis

We return to the initial question posed in this analysis: Is conducting analysis truly valuable? Contrary to what many readers might expect me to think, especially after having read the chapter on analysis, analysis is often an overrated method for acquiring new knowledge. The primary reason is that obtaining new knowledge or value-added information through analysis is inherently challenging. We often end up no wiser than when we started the exercise. Analysis excels at clarifying existing intelligence but not necessarily at generating new insights.

A common misconception is that thorough analysis can compensate for a lack of data. However, the reality is that acquiring the right data often renders further analysis unnecessary, as the conclusions become self-evident. This can be likened to finding DNA evidence on a murder weapon: with such definitive proof, additional interviews or analyses are redundant. Conversely, without critical data, no amount of analysis can compensate.

This argument does not intend to diminish the role of analysis in intelligence work. Analysis remains crucial, but it often confirms what is already known rather than uncovering new information. Therefore, given that organizations work with very limited resources, allocating efforts towards data collection may be more effective rather than expanding analytical capacities. Intelligence organizations frequently face opposite challenges. For instance, the NSA and other national intelligence agencies amass vast amounts of data without fully understanding or even knowing what they possess. Similarly, private organizations might own valuable reports without recognizing their significance. The key issue in both cases is ensuring that existing information reaches the right people at the right time. For this, it can be enough to sort the data so that it can be found in a data search.

Accurate data is often more valuable than extensive analysis. Simple statistics, such as GDP growth rates, inflation rates, or unemployment figures, can be highly informative on their own and do not require further analysis. Comparative data from other countries or historical periods can further enhance understanding without necessitating complex analysis. Much of this information is readily available through national statistics bureaus, research institutes, or international organizations like the UN, and is often cited in various publications. It may be false too, of course—itself the victim of false analysis—so to the extent that we can, we should contact the people who produced it to ask how they arrived at the figures. That many use the GDP figures does not mean that they are correct. Countries like Italy are also known to have altered the calculation of how they measure GPD to get better, or positive, figures. This can easily be done by including new groups of production.

The challenge with analytical reports lies in their reliance on the accuracy of the input data. If the data is flawed, the analysis will be too, a principle known as "garbage in, garbage out" (GIGO). It's crucial to assess the confidence level of all sources and intelligence used, but this is often overlooked in favor of analytical methods that will just assume good data quality. This approach may work in other fields but is inadequate for intelligence work, which, by its very definition, demands the highest standards of information accuracy.

State intelligence organizations sometimes struggle to convey accurate information to decision-makers, sometimes knowing that the intelligence is false. This topic extends beyond the scope of this book, but it's noteworthy that intelligence agencies occasionally prioritize political considerations over factual reporting. It's also not uncommon for heads of state to have a strained relationship with the heads of their intelligence services, or at least some lack of trust. For example, it is said that American President Bill Clinton preferred to get his intelligence from reading newspapers, exaggerated no doubt but probably true. In a previously used example, the CIA and other western intelligence agencies believed Iraq possessed WMDs based on various sources, many of which were later discredited, raising questions about whether the CIA was meddling in politics. This is not unique; in many countries, heads of intelligence are among the most powerful politicians. Some states, like today's Russia, are even run by intelligence services, merely pretending to be democracies through staged elections. These examples highlight that even the most sophisticated intelligence services can fail at fundamental tasks, such as ensuring data accuracy. Intelligence agencies worldwide operate in environments where mistakes are often concealed by secrecy. This error is not possible to the same degree in the realm of private intelligence, which is not only subject to audits but also relies solely on providing useful information for its mere existence, revised annually. Because of this control, it is also not uncommon for entire departments or positions in competitive or market intelligence to be shut down if they fail to deliver value or gain trust.

The effectiveness of an intelligence function and its ability to avoid mistakes and deliver actionable insights to decision-makers largely depends on its organizational structure as we shall see in Chap. 7, but also on how the intelligence product is conveyed or presented, discussed in Chap. 6.

The Intelligence Report 6

The intelligence report is the written output of intelligence work. The output does not have to be a written document but can be any kind of advice reported or transmitted in any way, including, as we have seen—for reasons of sensitivity—orally.

There are no best formats, but there are a number of useful requirements for an intelligence report, which sets it apart from other types of papers, reports and analyses. This special format addresses questions like, "How do we know that this is true?", "Where did you find it?", and "Is it important?". Not only do we want to know the answers to these questions, but we also want to measure each variable.

6.1 Types of Intelligence Reports

To start with the more known example, on the state level, there are the famous President's Daily Brief (PDB) in the US, a document typically between 1 and 20 pages which contains intelligence analyses on key national security issues and developments. The PDB can vary but typically includes brief, summarized intelligence reports and analyses, often accompanied by maps, charts, and other graphical elements to aid in understanding. Heads of other states receive similar reports. In the UK, the Prime Minister receives a daily intelligence briefing provided by the Joint Intelligence Committee (JIC). This briefing includes assessments and reports from the UK's intelligence agencies on domestic and international matters. The German Chancellor and other top officials receive intelligence briefings from the Federal Intelligence Service (BND), which include analyses of global political, economic, and military issues.

In the private sector, the equivalent of the President's Daily Brief (PDB) would be executive briefs or electronic dashboards tailored to the needs of top corporate leaders, such as CEOs or board members. These documents and tools serve a similar purpose: to quickly inform decision-makers about critical issues that affect the organization, enabling swift and informed decision-making. Here's how they compare:

K. Solberg Söilen, *Intelligence Studies in Business*, Management for Professionals,
https://doi.org/10.1007/978-3-031-76491-2_6

- Executive Briefs: Like the PDB, executive briefs in corporations summarize key business intelligence, competitive insights, and strategic metrics. These briefs are concise, often prioritizing information based on its immediacy and impact on the business.
- Dashboards: Many companies use digital dashboards that provide real-time data across various metrics important to the business. These can include financial performance indicators, market trends, operational efficiencies, and more. Dashboards allow executives to monitor the company's performance at a glance, often in real time, which is crucial for dynamic decision-making.
- Strategic Reports: These are periodic (daily, weekly, or monthly) reports that analyze trends, forecast performance, and review ongoing strategies. They are similar to the PDB in that they aim to prepare and inform leaders about significant changes or updates in the business environment. These tools are crafted to ensure that busy executives can quickly absorb the necessary information and are prepared to make informed decisions without needing to delve into the underlying details unless needed.

Then there are the reports from the different departments of the company, like in the marketing department. They are seldom known as intelligence reports, but more often as marketing reports and are more specific and operational, less strategic (Table 6.1).

These reports can vary widely depending on the industry, the specific goals of the marketing department, and the available data sources. Each of these reports provides critical insights that help marketing teams make data-driven decisions, tailor their strategies, and optimize their campaigns to better meet the needs of the market and the objectives of the business.

6.2 Sensitive Information

Much sensitive information does not exist in reports, and this is intentional. Intelligence about people, sensitive issues, and ideas that have not yet materialized into analytical work typically only exists in oral form.

As everyone know by now, "knowledge is power". This implies that when powerful individuals meet, they often start with niceties and trivial questions but typically and quickly "get down to business", where intelligence is exchanged like assets of knowledge, sometimes even like a form of competition to see who has the best information, who is best informed. We want to do business with people who are well informed, and for partnerships, it's an advantage to cooperate with organizations and people who are better informed than we are, smarter, more knowledgeable. This is the game of wise and powerful men.

People of power gain and keep their power in large part through valuable information that they gain by reading and talking to people. Every meeting is a chance to portray this power, especially if you are part of the state intelligence services, but on

Table 6.1 Example of reports produced in the marketing department and their function

#	*Report*	*What the report does*
1	Market Analysis Reports	provide an overview of the current market conditions, including size, growth trends, and potential opportunities. They might analyze customer demographics, behavior patterns, and market needs.
2	Competitive Analysis Reports	detail the competitive landscape, highlighting the strengths and weaknesses of competitors, their market share, marketing strategies, and recent market moves. This helps the company position itself more effectively.
3	Customer Segmentation Reports	divide the company's customer base into groups (or segments) based on various criteria like demographics, psychographics, purchasing behavior, or product usage. This enables targeted marketing strategies.
4	Consumer Insight Reports	delve into customer preferences, buying behaviors, and trends. They often use data from market research, social media monitoring, and customer feedback to build a deeper understanding of what drives customer decisions.
5	Campaign Performance Reports	assess the effectiveness of marketing campaigns against their objectives. Metrics such as ROI, engagement rates, and conversion rates are typically analyzed
6	Brand Health Reports	monitor brand perception, reputation, and visibility over time. They may include metrics from brand awareness studies, brand equity measurements, and public sentiment analysis
7	Product Performance Reports	focus on the sales performance of products, providing insights into sales trends, product lifecycle status, customer feedback, and inventory levels.
8	Digital Marketing Reports	analyze the performance of the company's digital marketing efforts, including website traffic, search engine rankings, social media engagement, and email marketing metrics.

a more general scale, also if you are a manager. Higher positions in the organizational hierarchy comes with more and better information. Never assume you are the most knowledgeable person until you have gotten to know your fellow conversationalist. It will take you half an hour, maybe an hour, so be patient and enjoy everything you learn along the way as you draw your conclusions.

6.2.1 Kompromat

"Kompromat" is a type of sensitive intelligence used primarily in political contexts, but it is as used in the private as well as the public sector. The term "kompromat" is derived from the Russian words "komprometiruyushchiy material," which translates to "compromising material." It refers to information collected with the intent of damaging or discrediting an individual, typically a public figure or political opponent. But it can also be some damaging documents about any person in an organization locked in some drawer, or more likely today, in some folder on a PC or USB. The point is it must be in the form of evidence, so it cannot be something heard, a mere rumor, but something that is proven, that can be used. It often contains information that can be damaging to a person's career. This type of intelligence can include evidence of illegal activities, immoral behaviour, or any other information that could be used to blackmail, coerce, or manipulate the target.

The idea with kompromat is not to use it right away but when you need it, when it has the most value for you. So, it can sit in that folder for years. In Russia, the example goes that kompromat are used in the Duma before elections or major voting. It is so common and the use of it so systemic that there is even a market for kompromat, where secrets are traded or exchanged. During the Cold War, the KGB was known for using kompromat to manipulate politicians and other influential figures. Most hotels used for official visits were bugged, even embassies, and the foreign dignitaries knew about it or suspected it beforehand, so they took precautions and behaved accordingly.

Characteristics of Kompromat:

1. Compromising Nature: The core feature of kompromat is its potential to embarrass or discredit the target. This can include personal scandals, financial irregularities, criminal activities, or socially unacceptable behavior.
2. Blackmail and Coercion: Kompromat is often used as a tool for blackmail or coercion, forcing the target to comply with the demands of those who possess the information.
3. Political Manipulation: It is frequently used in political warfare to undermine opponents, sway public opinion, or influence elections and policy decisions.
4. Psychological Operations: Kompromat can be part of psychological operations (psyops), aiming to create distrust, fear, or confusion among the target's supporters or the general public.
5. Media Leaks: The information is often leaked to the media to maximize its damaging impact. In modern times, this can include the use of social media and online platforms to disseminate the compromising material quickly and widely.

6.2.2 Types of Information Used in Kompromat

Kompromat can be classified into the following types: Personal Scandals: Affairs, drug use, or other morally compromising activities.

- Financial Misconduct: Tax evasion, money laundering, or embezzlement.
- Legal Issues: Evidence of crimes, whether proven or alleged.
- Socially Unacceptable Behavior: Actions or behaviors that, while not necessarily illegal, would be frowned upon by society and could damage a person's reputation.

The use of kompromat raises significant ethical and legal issues. Collecting and disseminating compromising material often involves an invasion of privacy, and the act of blackmail or coercion is illegal in many jurisdictions. Despite this, it remains a potent tool in the arsenal of political operatives and intelligence agencies and is by no means typical for Russia or the former Soviet Union but is practiced worldwide and all the time, even among academics and researchers, who, it should be noted, do not have any higher ethical standards than most other people and who may also end up working for an organization that becomes, at times, overly political like we see today.

6.3 Structuring the Intelligence Report

Some intelligence will be noted in an intelligence report. An intelligence report can look very different, but the one I prefer include the following variables (Table 6.2):

Each piece of intelligence can here be identified with a number or reference. The intel is distinct from other parts of the text and often expressed in a sentence. The source of the intel is clearly shown. This initial part is done by those gathering the intel, marked in blue. The subsequent analysis, marked in red, involves assessing the value of the intel, the confidence in the sources, and the confidence in the intel itself. For instance, a valuable piece of intel might score a 10, but if it's unreliable, it might score a 0 in confidence.

Whatever format is used, the intelligence should be presented so that the reader is led straight to the point and he can get all the important data about the source and its importance. Producing intelligence is a structured process, quite different from writing a poem or a novel. While it may seem boring, if the intelligence is useful, it will be interesting to read. In fact, that is the litmus test.

6.3.1 Establishing Formal Communication Channels

A company serious about intelligence should start by establishing formal communication channels. The agent must respond to every request, and the manager should communicate:

1. What she wants to know,
2. Why (purpose),
3. When she needs the answer, and
4. The sensitivity (classification) of the information.

Most companies do not have the time or resources to write large reports themselves and rely on external information services. However, as companies develop their own intelligence systems, they must address standardization early in the process.

Table 6.2 The headings on the intelligence template

Intel #	*The Intel (RI/AI)*	*Source (APA style)*	*Value of intel (1–10)*	*Confidence in Source (1–10)*	*Confidence in intel (1–10)*

6.3.2 Standardization in Intelligence Processes

Using standardized formats helps in sorting and finding information in archives and aids readers in absorbing information quickly. New IT solutions allow for making documents searchable through databases.

In organizations with structured intelligence processes, findings are presented in standard forms to make reading and understanding easier. The intelligence function needs to develop a full set of standards or templates for all types of products and procedures. These templates are best collected in a manual and distributed to all personnel working with intelligence. This standardization is not unique to intelligence functions; similar procedures are found in other organizational departments, such as accounting and auditing. An auditor is, very much like an intelligence officer, concerned with the data that is important—representing the larger picture—and verifications, or proof of the information recorded.

There are many ways to present written material, and while there is no one right way, certain standards have been tested for efficiency, but they are also culturally dependent. A parallel here is how different cultures have their own academic writing standards. For instance, the APA Manual in the US and Gerhard Gerhards' book for German-speaking nations provide guidance on writing papers and dissertations. None of them is clearly best, they both have their advantages. Academic reports typically have an executive summary, followed by recommendations and implications, with empirical data summaries and analyses.

Intelligence reports differ from academic reports in their focus on action. A summary of an effective intelligence template may look like this (Table 6.3):

The template includes a short title covering the report's content. Relevant information is presented without comments (light grey area), allowing for later re-analysis if needed. The analysis follows, with conclusions drawn using relevant methods (darker grey area). Next are the implications, followed by suggested actions. All of this must logically follow from the previous step, ensuring that there is no hesitation about whether the actions naturally stem from the implications, if any actions are omitted or forgotten, or if the analyst has drawn incorrect conclusions from their analysis. If there are errors, the entire structure falters, causing the whole framework to crumble.

An executive summary can present this information concisely, with additional details in appendices. This helps ensure that busy executives can quickly absorb essential information and make informed decisions without delving into details.

Table 6.3 Main components of the intelligence report

Classes of Information
Title, Date
Information
Analysis
Implications
Actions

Table 6.4 Example of dimensions and indicators in a comparative country analysis

Dimensions	*Indicators*	*Country N*	*CL*	*Country N+1*	*CL*
Demographic	Population				
	Inhabitants per km2				
	Annual Birth Growth				
	Annual Mortality Rate				
	Life Expectancy				
	% of Population in Cities				
Sociocultural	Development Indicator				
	Doctors per % of Inhabitants				
	% Illiteracy (Men)				
	% Illiteracy (Women)				
Economic	GDP (Total)				
	GDP (per Capita)				
	Yearly Growth Rate				
	Investment Rates (% of GDP)				
	Inflation Rate				
	% of GDP on Education				
	% of GDP on Military				
	External/National Debt				
	Annual Payment % of Debt				

An analysis of a country may involve various dimensions and indicators, compared across nations. However, figures can be difficult to compare due to differing collection methods. Evaluating data involves defining confidence levels, typically using a scale from 1 to 10 (Table 6.4).

Given the ease of publishing online, it's crucial to critically analyze sources. Information found in large newspapers can be false due to misunderstandings or unverified sources. AI results must be marked as such, and AI prompts must be verified by the author's experience and knowledge.

Most business students write in a prosaic style when turning in their papers, influenced by reading magazines and newspapers. Writing clearly in an analytical style as for the purpose of intelligence is very different and comes with practice.

Knowing how to gather information and analyze it using a good format is only one step. To succeed in the intelligence function, the organization also needs to be effectively organized for that purpose. This means that the intelligence function must have enough room and legitimacy to operate, it must have resources, and it must encourage and ensure that the intelligence work is seen by employees inside of the organization. Much of this depends on how the intelligence function is organized.

7 Organizational Models for Information Gathering

In this chapter, we list and describe the various possibilities for where the intelligence function can be placed within the organization. Suggestions are made as to optimal locations under different circumstances, all based on research. We will also examine the types and levels of competence needed in the different parts of the intelligence cycle and discuss the interdisciplinary nature of intelligence work in organizations.

Understanding where the intelligence function should be placed within an organization is crucial for optimizing its effectiveness and integration with other functions. This chapter explores various possibilities and provides research-based suggestions for optimal locations under different circumstances. Additionally, it addresses the interdisciplinary nature of intelligence work, ensuring that organizations can strategically position their intelligence functions to enhance decision-making and maintain a competitive edge.

7.1 Required Qualifications at Different Stages of the Intelligence Cycle

Different competencies are required at various stages of the intelligence cycle, and involvement varies across management levels. This problem can for example be illustrated according to the degree of analysis required in each stage.

In this version of the intelligence cycle, which focuses more on knowledge, we have chosen to divide it into five stages, combining collection and processing while treating dissemination and feedback as separate steps. The process begins with Planning and Direction (1), where the problem is defined, priorities are set, and tasks are assigned to align with organizational goals. Next, Collection and Processing (2) ensures that relevant data is gathered from various sources, then organized and formatted into usable information for further analysis. This leads to Analysis and Production (3), where the processed information is interpreted to generate

K. Solberg Söilen, *Intelligence Studies in Business*, Management for Professionals,
https://doi.org/10.1007/978-3-031-76491-2_7

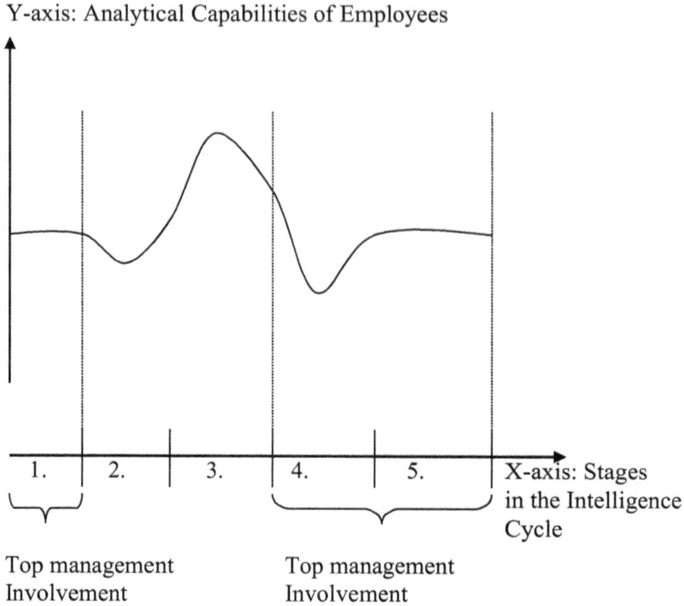

Fig. 7.1 Level of competencies related to the five stages of the intelligence cycle

actionable insights, identifying patterns and synthesizing findings to support decision-making. The refined intelligence is then presented during Dissemination (4), ensuring that decision-makers receive the information in a format tailored to their needs, such as detailed reports or visual summaries. Finally, Feedback (5) closes the cycle by evaluating the relevance and accuracy of the delivered intelligence, providing insights that refine and enhance future processes. This approach underscores the importance of efficiency and continuous improvement within the intelligence workflow. The analysis stage demands the highest formal analytical competence and should, therefore, be entrusted to those who possess such competence and have the time to fulfil the task. While executives and top managers may have the analytical experience, their contribution is more impactful at the initial stage of forming questions and at the final stage of assessing results. Typically, they possess the longest experience in matters of intelligence and decision-making (Fig. 7.1).

Analytical Capabilities of Employees across the Five Stages of the Intelligence Cycle: The initial and final stages involve top management heavily, while the intermediate stages require varying levels of higher degree analytical skills.

The gathering stage requires understanding the process without needing to control it; similar competency levels apply to those tasked with distributing or making intelligence accessible. Primary competence in this stage is relational; the ability to connect effectively with decision-makers. Effective delivery is key, as even the best analysis is worth little if it is never read. The nature of these roles does not demand the same depth of analytical skills but rather focuses on operational efficiency and communication.

Many organizations have experienced challenges in timely and accurate intelligence, leading in some cases to a pull strategy's adoption. The intelligence functions have simply forfeited on its push abilities. The pull approach allows recipients to seek out intelligence themselves, reducing the risks associated with push strategies, which, in worst cases, become associated with spam or propaganda if not tailored to specific information requests.

To address time constraints faced by executives, some companies are experimenting with advisor models. These models combine push and pull strategies, where a trusted advisor maintains a direct line to top management and coordinates an Intelligence Team. This structure allows for quick exchanges of intelligence and decision-making inputs, which is crucial when management cannot delve into extensive research due to time constraints.[1]

The advisors and intelligence officers manage specialized teams, with each team member's role clearly defined by their specific analytical or field expertise. This setup helps in maintaining a streamlined flow of intelligence and ensures that efforts are not duplicated.

The Intelligence working process, Business Intelligence (BI) or simply Intelligence Cycle (IC), is analogous to the scientific process as taught in academic settings, involving hypothesis formulation, method selection, data gathering, analysis, and reporting. However, it adapts to the dynamic and often urgent nature of specific intelligence needs. This involves rapid iterations across the stages and a pragmatic approach to fieldwork, eschewing lengthy theoretical discussions for hands-on, practical research.

Top management, particularly CEOs and board members, play a crucial role by ensuring the intelligence questions posed are critical for strategic decision-making. Constantly shifting focus or frequently redefining questions can demoralize intelligence teams. Demonstrating how intelligence impacts decisions can significantly motivate teams and validate their efforts.

Overall, the Intelligence cycle doesn't just mirror scientific processes but adapts them to the high-pressure, fast-paced demands of the business environment. Coordination across different intelligence units within the organization is vital to harness synergies and avoid overlapping efforts.

7.1.1 Checking Competence Levels

Understanding what people know is an essential part of Intelligence Studies, and the core objective of the field we call Knowledge Management. This used to be tricky, for example in the world of research. However, today, with extensive bibliometrics—measures of research output and relevance—this has become easier, for example, with the use of Google Scholar. Google Scholar ranks academic

[1] One may think of this model as depicted in the book 'The Prince', where the Agent is Machiavelli, and the Principal is Lorenzo II de' Medici, even though in reality that relationship turned out to be complex and ultimately unfulfilling for Machiavelli.

Fig. 7.2 Using Google Scholar to check competence levels of researchers

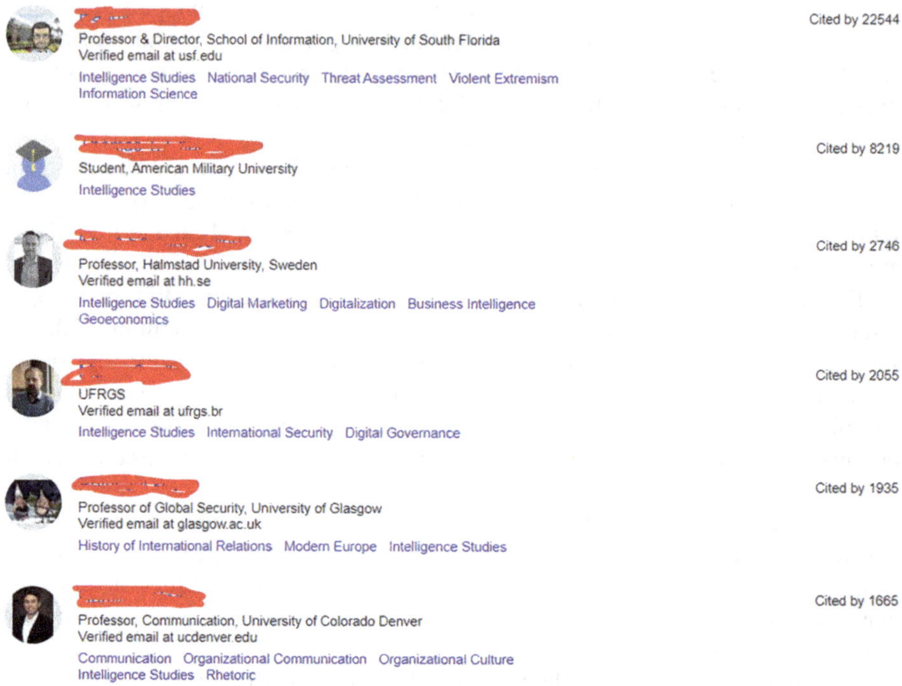

Fig. 7.3 Using Google Scholar to check individuals' relative competence levels

knowledge worldwide based on five keywords that the authors select themselves (Fig. 7.2):

Now, the abovementioned example is not be the best one, but it was chosen to avoid implicating any unsolicited researcher to the readers of this book. By clicking on the keywords, we see how that person ranks worldwide as a researcher in the field "Intelligence Studies", "Digital Marketing" etc. according to Google Scholar (Fig. 7.3).

Now, this is only one indication, and there are many variables to consider. Some academic experts simply do not have a Scholar profile, but their work will still show on Google Search anyway; we just have to do the calculations manually. However, many experts have not published any work in their field of expertise. This is the case for most practitioners whose practical knowledge and experience frequently surpass that of academics in their respective fields. You can be an expert in how to perform

Intelligence without having published anything on the topic. The biggest challenge with Google Scholar is that researchers often use different preferred terms, so to be thorough, we need to check for parallel keywords such as 'competitive intelligence,' 'market intelligence,' 'foreign intelligence,' and 'anticipatory systems.' Google Scholar metrics like the h-index and h10-index measure the breadth and depth of a researcher's work, with the h10-index reflecting the number of times the tenth most cited paper was cited. Comparing the 'all' time and 'since 2019' rankings helps determine if a researcher has been recently active and remains relevant in their field.

Expertise in the non-academic world is primarily evaluated based on practical results, measurable outcomes, and the ability to solve real-world problems effectively. Big consulting firms, for example, value individuals who demonstrate a proven track record of success, adaptability, and innovative thinking, often honed through diverse industry experiences. Unlike academia, where credentials, publications, and peer recognition hold significant weight, non-academic expertise is frequently judged by client satisfaction, the impact of implemented solutions, and the ability to drive profitability. Higher pay in these environments reflects the demand for professionals who can deliver immediate value, navigate complex challenges, and contribute to organizational growth. This results-driven approach often attracts individuals seeking opportunities to apply their skills in dynamic, high-stakes contexts.

7.2 Effective Intelligence Teams (ITs)

Proficient ITs is interdisciplinary because no single analyst can be an expert in multiple areas. It's much like in a game of quiz, each team consist of people with somewhat different specialties. Specialized knowledge in international politics, macroeconomics, technology, international law, and anthropology is essential, especially for extensive reports in large companies. These experts aren't necessarily employees; many are external consultants which may turn out to be a more expensive solution, so depends on the resource available for each assignment.

Besides, AI components will be integrated at all levels today, making machines part of the team. This means it's not only about the individual competencies each analyst brings but also how proficient they are as prompters, since every analyst now essentially operates with two brains. Analysts must be able to effectively utilize both their own knowledge and the capabilities of AI

7.2.1 Interdisciplinary Team Dynamics

Working in interdisciplinary teams requires a unique cooperation style. Differences in background and approach can lead to frustration unless managed with respect, understanding, open-mindedness, and patience. While critical thinking is essential, it must be balanced with social intelligence to foster productive interactions.

Interdisciplinarity does not mean that all members possess a bit of all the knowledge needed; rather, it means that each member brings their own expertise and collaborates with others who have different expertise. Interdisciplinary studies conducted by a single person are problematic, as no one individual can be an expert in many areas simultaneously. Generalists, especially those with experience, are best suited for leading teams, but they are not always the best source of expert advice in any specific area.

Teams must also be flexible and patient. Researchers often like to stick to a hypothesis once empirical work begins, risking inflexibility. In intelligence, it's common for the client to revise their questions throughout the process, requiring the analyst to confirm understanding continuously. Effective communication and clarification of the intelligence aims are critical, ensuring that the analyst not only understands the questions but also internalizes their significance to increase the relevance of their findings.

Anyone providing good intelligence is a vital part of the team and should be allowed to continue. In principle, it does not matter what they know or who they are as long as they contribute. For example, sales representatives are valuable intelligence gatherers, often having the best access to information about customers, competitors, and markets. However, their potential is frequently underutilized due to a lack of incentives, time constraints, and insufficient understanding of their strategic importance.

Customer service representatives interact directly with customers and can gather insights about customer pain points, preferences, and trends, which are valuable for product development and marketing strategies. Maintenance technicians oversee the upkeep of equipment and facilities, often identifying operational inefficiencies and suggesting improvements for productivity and safety. Delivery drivers, by transporting goods to customers, can offer insights into logistics and supply chain efficiencies, customer interactions, and competitive market observations during their routes. Receptionists manage the front desk and initial customer interactions, providing an understanding of first impressions and common queries or complaints about the company. Accounts payable clerks process invoices and manage payments, giving them a detailed view of supplier relationships and the ability to identify trends in spending, cost-saving opportunities, and discrepancies that may indicate larger issues. These roles, while not typically associated with intelligence gathering, provide crucial insights that can benefit the company in various ways.

Organizations employing sales staff for intelligence tasks typically use a Down-Up Intelligence Model, whereas those where top management primarily gathers information use an Up-Down Model. Most companies lean towards an Up-Down approach, which can be inefficient and expensive. Trust issues and inadequate training often hinder the effective use of information gathered by sales representatives.

Organizational approaches to intelligence vary. Many large companies use a Central Intelligence Model, where intelligence functions are consolidated into a single unit, which may be linked directly to top management or function independently. This model facilitates coordination but can depend heavily on the integration of insights from various departments.

Alternatively, the Departmental Intelligence Model is common, where each department manages its own intelligence efforts. This approach often leads to redundancy and missed synergies, such as multiple departments purchasing the same reports or duplicating monitoring efforts.

A more integrated approach involves Multi-Departmental Intelligence Teams (MDITs), which combine expertise from various departments like marketing, finance, and technical departments to address complex intelligence needs. While this promotes a comprehensive approach, initial integration challenges can impede effectiveness.

The advisor model represents a shift towards integrating intelligence more closely with executive decision-making, facilitating direct communication between analysts and top management. This model emerged in response to the inadequacies of previous systems and reflects a trend towards more strategic intelligence deployment.

We shall look more closely at each one of these models in greater detail next.

7.3 Organizational Placements and Models of the Intelligence Function

Organizations that decide to implement some sort of intelligence function need to determine the best placement for this function within their structure.

First, information gathering is conducted in every function of the organization without necessarily calling it intelligence. Part of the reason for this is that it's considered a basic and common-sense activity in all organizations in every department. Information gathering is what everyone does, and it is assumed that all employees know how to do it.

What we will focus on here is the employees whose main function is information or intelligence gathering. Up until recently, companies have handled the information gathering and analysis part of their business processes in many different locations within the organization simultaneously. Business intelligence tasks have been a major concern for the marketing department, determining what customers want and what competitors are doing; in the finance department, finding out what it takes for competitors to enter the market, or finding the financial strength of competitors and suppliers. During the past decade, research on the topic has been conducted, and several models have been described and discussed.[2]

Most companies go without any organizational model for intelligence gathering. Instead, everyone does a bit of everything, depending on what is needed at the moment. This is not an organizational model per se, but more of an ad-hoc structure. Some intelligence tasks may be part of the job description, and it is just assumed that the employee knows how to go about fulfilling that task. As employees, not

[2] See for example Söilen (2010a). Most models presented in this book are based on this article.

only in business, we typically do not like to spend large amounts of time gathering information; even less do we enjoy the task of analyzing it. We are "men of action," who prefer interaction with like-minded individuals to excessive desk work and large analytical exercises. Therefore, we often base reports on what we already know to be the truth, what we think is the truth, our industry experience, and from whatever we have extracted from conversations with people we have talked to and trust. We often name our findings intuition, which also implies that the discussion is ended as arguments and argumentation become more difficult. In some cases, as time runs out before the deadline of a report, we sit down and try to put it all on paper. This approach, or method if we can call it that, is a standard working procedure in many organizational cultures. The problem is that it's not compatible with the aspiration to gain a competitive advantage in the global marketplace, far less so in the future. For that, we need a more organized structure for intelligence work.

7.3.1 The Special Department Model of Intelligence

The main idea behind the special department model is that the intelligence function will be more valuable if it is placed in a separate department where employees will have time to build a strong organizational culture; much like is done in military and state intelligence organizations. E.g. Examples often given are BAE Systems, Accenture, IBM and GE. Shell even used to have a special department for futurology (Fig. 7.4).

The major problem with this model is its potential isolation and its consequences. Special intelligence departments tend to close themselves off and develop projects they think will be useful for the company but do not actually know. Their more or less self-initiated projects will only be useful to the extent that the special department knows exactly what intelligence is needed. If they do not communicate well with top managers, their choice of topics will be based too much on guesswork, and the output will be less relevant. In other cases, the department will have the report and the answers needed, but the results never reach the manager who needs them, at least not in time.

In response to the problems caused by this model, it was thought in some companies that the intelligence functions needed to be closer to the major decision-makers in the organization. Even more importantly, it was concluded that the person delivering the intelligence needed to have the full attention and trust of the managers personally. Otherwise, the person may have been present in the meeting, but never really listened to. In response, companies like Ericsson in Sweden developed

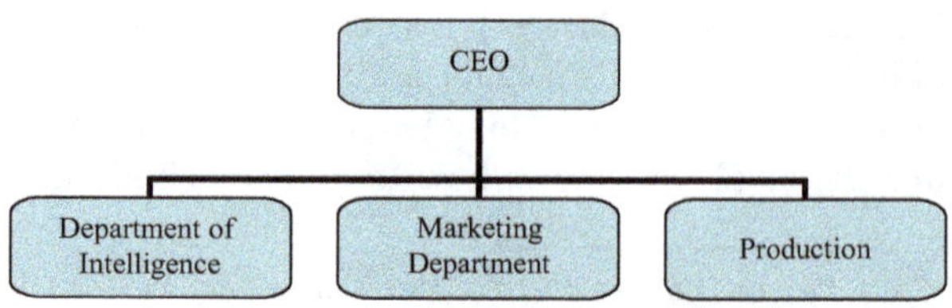

Fig. 7.4 The special department model of intelligence

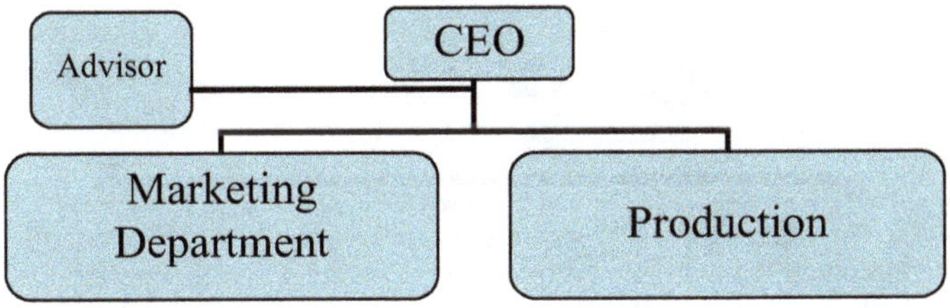

Fig. 7.5 The advisory model of intelligence

"the advisory model" in the 1990s under the guidance of people like Göran Pagel-Fick.

7.3.2 The Advisory Model of Intelligence

The main idea behind the advisory model was to place a senior advisor to the CEO and to top management as responsible for two functions in the intelligence cycle: formulating the questions to be answered and delivering the results. The information gathering and the analysis could be performed elsewhere, whether in a separate department, on the outside, as suggested by Fahey (2007), or in different departments, all according to needs. The senior advisor did not have the time, often not even the skills, to search for information himself, nor did he have the time or the skills to conduct thorough analyses. Even though this is changing today, not the least, with the help of AI, a decade ago, he often did not have the technological competence required, e.g. to run business intelligence projects on software, which have become even more technical since (Fig. 7.5).

In the advisory model, a senior advisor has a certain number of people working for him, or he has the right to allocate the time and resources of specific employees who possess the required intelligence skills.

One problem with not having specific staff dedicated to intelligence work is that the outcomes, namely the intelligence reports, tend to be of lower quality. As the intelligence function is not the employee's main activity, and they very often have inadequate training and understanding of the assignment, intelligence work tends to receive low priority. It is often executed in a hurry, and the reports suffer as a result. There was, in other words, a need for someone who could dedicate more time and resources to intelligence work. This was the starting point for the development of the professional intelligence model.

7.3.3 The Professional Model of Intelligence

The professional model allows specialized personnel to undergo adequate training to make intelligence work their priority. This often includes university studies and practical training. Some intelligence professionals will discover that they prefer

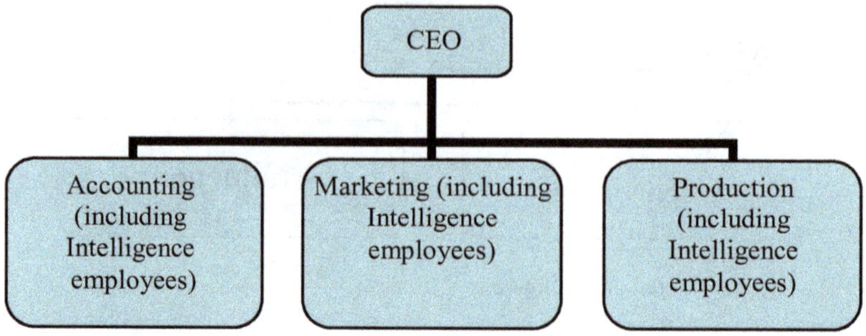

Fig. 7.6 The professional model of intelligence

more field-like activities, including on-the-ground intelligence gathering. Others discover that they are more comfortable with desk jobs, such as intelligence analysis, reporting, and presentation. This may later determine each person's specialty, even though the amount of fieldwork required is more restricted in the private sector, often limited to market surveys. Together, the two types of intelligence work encompass a wide understanding of the intelligence field, including the use of related technologies. An example of the professional model can be found today in ABB's headquarters in Switzerland. In the case of ABB, the intelligence professionals sometimes have backgrounds as controllers, many with experience as auditors (Fig. 7.6).

In the end, whether or not to implement the professional model is often a question of resources. Few mid-sized and smaller companies will find that they have the funds available to invest in specially educated intelligence personnel. Instead, they will focus on what they see as their core activities: production and sales.

Even among those companies that can afford it, there are often a number of misconceptions about the value of intelligence activities. For example, many managers believe that it is enough to rely on secondary sources, like reading trade magazines and special reports. It is thought that some general market research and a course in statistics are enough. It follows that confident managers often think that they themselves can bridge the gap between understanding the industry (secondary sources) and understanding their own company (personal experience). They also think that it is sufficient for them as managers to tell their employees what is important. This is sometimes referred to as the top-down model of intelligence.

7.3.4 The Top-Down Model of Intelligence

The top-down model of intelligence is based on the idea that intelligence is gathered and communicated mostly from the top of the organization, and that this is the best approach. Top management receives or generates intelligence and information, which is then spread throughout the organization on a need-to-know basis. This model is often found in small and mid-sized, production-based, low-tech organizations, where most employees are low-skilled workers, and the CEO feels he needs

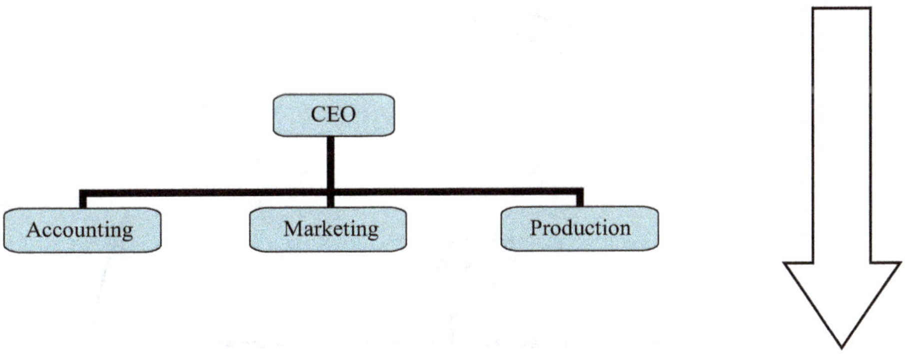

Fig. 7.7 The special department model of intelligence

to control all major processes himself. The CEO and the top managers typically have the best qualifications for identifying what is important for running the firm. After all, that is why they have been selected to run the company. At least, this is the logic (Fig. 7.7).

One of the dangers with this model is that top managers become know-it-alls and stop listening to what others have to say about what really matters in the business. The other employees do not develop enough personally in their jobs and start to find the work repetitious. Thus, the risk is that the company stagnates due to a lack of intellectual stimulation and innovation suffers as a consequence.

The assumption that others cannot contribute intelligence to the organization often builds on a misconception. To find a piece of vital information concerning the running of the company, it is not necessary to be a manager. A regular employee might come across an interesting article or notice something worth our attention, such as a large shipment of raw material on the way to a competitor's plant or a video on YouTube about the discovery of substantial new natural resources relevant for exploring new markets. Finding useful information can be a matter of pure coincidence, being in the right place at the right time. For this reason, everyone can and should be encouraged to take part.

The truly intelligent company is the one that can divide and distribute different areas of knowledge, competencies, and sources among employees according to needs. In this way, some employees could look at local newspapers, others go to a specific trade show, etc. Together, they try to cover as many arenas for potentially useful intelligence as possible. The model that helps everyone play as an orchestra of intelligence is referred to as the Integrated Intelligence Model. This model is often encouraged in Asian countries, seen in Japan during the 70s and 80s, and today in China.

7.3.5 The Integrated Intelligence Model

This model has been typical for the way in which many larger Japanese companies have run their competitive intelligence activities, drawing on the collective experience and efforts of employees across the entire organization. There will also often

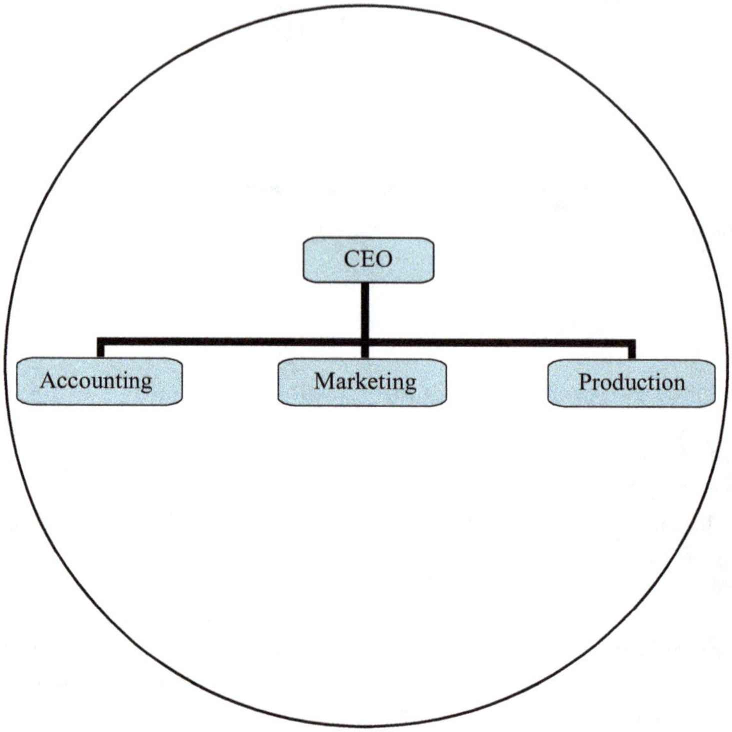

Fig. 7.8 The integrated intelligence model

be a superstructure of support at the Ministry of Industry or some other state department. There are many advantages to this model. An integrated intelligence model makes intelligence work seem less dangerous and less secretive. It is a sign of trust when all employees are told that they can come across pieces of important information which they are encouraged to share. This trust can, in turn, create a better atmosphere within the organization making employees feel they are indeed part of the knowledge economy (Fig. 7.8).

Organizations that make a big fuss about intelligence tend to create extra and unnecessary tension. This is often the risk with the model we call the departmental model. This, in turn, can lead to a reduction in productivity and creativity within the organization.

Companies need a system of information classification, but they also need to downplay the importance of secrets. One way to present this problem is with the allegory of the family: There are certain facts, incidents, and stories that are no one else's business and are therefore best kept within the family. We do not talk about these facts as secrets. Father and mother know things they will not tell their children, as do mother and grandmother, not to mention wife and mother-in-law. That it is so is a natural part of social life and we are fine with it if it is handled respectfully.

It is much the same in companies: all employees do not have to know everything for the organization to work harmoniously. To think that humanity is moving towards a society with no more secrets is an illusion. The competitive advantage of companies builds on secret information. Instead, having and guarding secrets is a part of human nature, and also of organizational life. Many companies that have a more open relationship towards information are also those that are willing to listen to people at all corners of the organization, even at the bottom or at the front line.

7.3.6 The Down-Up Model of Intelligence

The opposite of the top-down model is the bottom-up model of intelligence. This model shows an openness towards information gathering and inclusion. In some companies, employees at the bottom of the organization tend to get access to especially important information. This model is often seen in competitive, sales and marketing-driven organizations. It is primarily the salespeople, who are visiting customers and who are in the field, out of the office, who will potentially bring the most valuable intelligence back to the company. CEOs and top management will often spend their days with each other, inside the office. When they are outside, they will spend much time in airports, on planes, and in hotels—not the kind of environments where one is likely to pick up specific news about the company's immediate surroundings unless you are a supplier of goods and services to airports.

In a bottom-up model, when salespeople return, they can enter what they think is valuable information into a database, which is then sorted, analyzed, and distributed by an intelligence function within the company. Much of this information may not have any value at all and will be disregarded. In other cases, salespeople will come home with information that leads to changes in the KPIs, which will then in return change the dashboard of top managers. To encourage this, it is necessary to have some sort of Intelligence Reward System for employees. The problem in most companies is that the salespeople and those who are out in the field do not bring home intelligence because they lack incentives. Even worse, if they look for valuable information, it takes time away from their paid job and eventually leads to lower sales, or so management often thinks, looking only at the short term. Without an intelligence reward system, sales risk being punished for spending time gathering information (Fig. 7.9).

This is how a reward system for intelligence could look in an organization: An efficient reward system could be a scaled system, categorized into A, B, C, D, and E intelligence, each connected to a particular reward, or in the case of useless information (E), no reward at all. The actual evaluation is performed by intelligence professionals in the company. The financial results are reflected in the next month's paycheck. Each employee can access the company's intranet system to see how their intelligence contributions are being classified. A and B may be secret information distributed only to specific employees on a need-to-know basis, while C is open to anyone inside the company, and D is available to all outside. As soon as a piece of information is valuable to the company, we do not want to share it with other

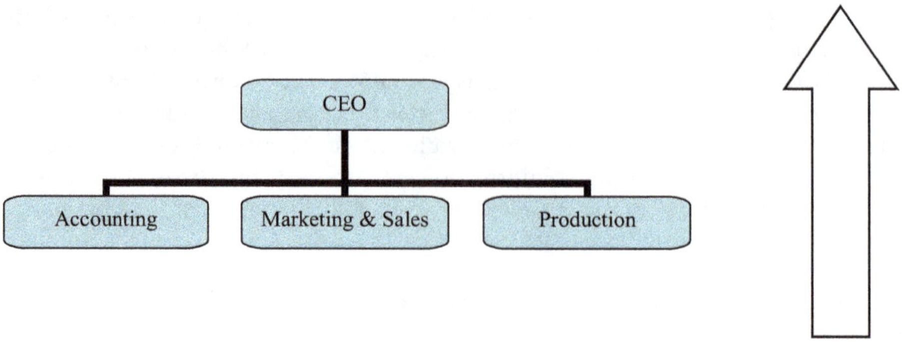

Fig. 7.9 The down-up intelligence model

companies. With handheld devices that can be used in the field and business intelligence software, there are no longer any technical or practical reasons to disregard such systems.

All competitive information is classified information by definition, even if we think our competitors possess the same information. The intranet system, which is password-protected, helps employees know what they can discuss and with whom. Depending on their level in the organization, employees see a different set of information. This is no longer exclusive to military and state intelligence services but is implemented in most larger companies today.

In most companies, the employees who are interested in intelligence and have the knowledge will be in one department, possibly because that is where the competence was developed first or where there are the most intelligence requests. As a consequence, the most common organizational model is the departmental model of intelligence.

7.3.7 The Departmental Model of Intelligence

In this model, the intelligence function is performed within an already existing department, most often the marketing department. When the SEB bank in Stockholm developed its first intelligence capabilities more than a hundred years ago (the bank celebrated its 150th anniversary in 2007), they set up an intelligence function in the "statistical department." In reality, it served as a cover for what was to be an intelligence department, with the objective of gathering information not only about larger customers but also about competitors and the surrounding environment. A cover, not because what was done was illegal or even immoral, but because it was deemed sensitive.

This was an early start—after all, the CIA was established after the Second World War, and the British intelligence apparatus took its form between the two world wars—but the Wallenbergs, the owners of SEB, were continuing a longer tradition among great banker families in Europe. Conducting serious information gathering about customers, competitors, and market conditions had been the practice in the world of banking and trade for centuries, with roots back to Renaissance Italy. The height of this practice may be seen in the writings of Venetian ambassadors of the sixteenth and seventeenth centuries, but even centuries earlier, the Médicis spent much time gathering intelligence from all major European trading cities and families, from places like Bruges, Antwerp, and Augsburg.

The early Médicis knew that they were only as good as their network and the trust they enjoyed in the markets. To build trust and to grow, they needed fast and reliable information. This information had to be documented, creating substantial trade archives. The Médicis also continued the medieval tradition of marrying their children into wealthy and preferably royal families, a practice that has since been abandoned since despite it being hard to beat when it comes to access to valuable information. It was like having your own flies on the wall in the large families that mattered, also internationally.

It is no coincidence that much of the accounting system we use today was invented in Venice, by Luca Pacioli. It was all part of the need to take accurate notes and numbers to avoid having errors or mistakes in your ledgers and ultimately to make the right decisions. This tradition was continued by the Fuggers in Augsburg, who developed their own newsletters, and the Rothschilds, who later also supported the building of the newspaper The Economist much in the same spirit. Anyway, these ideas often evolved from being mere functions to developing their own reports, eventually giving birth to the first specialized departments within existing functions in the organization.

In academia, the study of marketing is probably the discipline that has taken the function of information gathering furthest through the establishment of Marketing Research Departments (MRD), the development of Marketing Information Systems (MIS), and Business Marketing Intelligence (BMI). It is no surprise that early developments in the study of Business Intelligence also came from academics within the study of marketing.[3]

We will notice that the process of marketing research is similar to the methods used in Intelligence Studies. We could also say that market research is the biggest single market for intelligence in most companies. We also notice that competitive intelligence initiatives often come from the marketing department of a company, as that is often where the best competence in systematic information gathering is found. The problem is that the ability to gather information in a marketing department is often very one-sided, with a focus on customers and to a lesser degree competitors. Micro factors, such as information about suppliers for components used in production, or macro factors, such as information about international politics, macroeconomics, or demographics, can be equally important for the competitive intelligence function. However, the marketing function often struggle in front of these tasks simply due to a lack of competence and resources (Fig. 7.10).

[3] Examples in Scandinavia include Frankelius and Jenster. See Frankelius and Rosén (1993) and Hussey and Jenster (1999). See also Lekvall and Wahlin (2001).

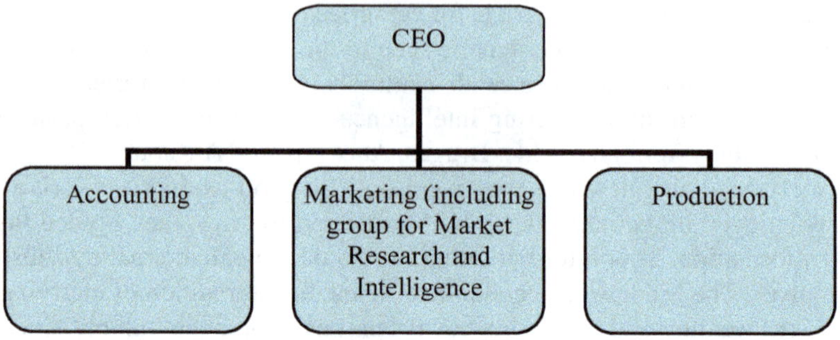

Fig. 7.10 The departmental model of intelligence

Macro factors are studied in Strategy, but that function seldom have their own department in business organizations. Strategy covers a wider area than business intelligence, but the process of gathering information in the field of Strategy is often assumed. The study of Strategy traditionally paid little attention to the business intelligence process, which may again explain why Intelligence has appeared as a separate field of study and not as a part of a Strategy curriculum. In a company, it is almost unthinkable that the same people who are involved in strategic decisions should work with business intelligence simply because they will not have the time to do the work needed. Strategic decisions are made by top management. From an intelligence perspective, strategy is often synonymous with the decision-makers, who are their proper and major customers. It is considered a waste of company resources if decision-makers must go around and collect small pieces of information for a report. However, because the study of Strategy assumes a process of Intelligence, we may say that they are twin studies, part of the same business process. Thus, it is no coincidence that in the US and North America, many of the experts in intelligence came from the field of Strategy.[4]

It is still uncommon to see outright intelligence departments in private companies like we find in state and military intelligence organizations. To the degree that companies have full-time intelligence officers or analysts, these often work in other departments or with other assignments as well, mostly related to market research and competitor intelligence.

Companies still do not want to be perceived as overly secretive and are uncertain about what this might do to the organization internally, potentially increasing the level of distrust among employees, not to mention their reputation. It is for this reason that many companies often prefer to speak about "insights" instead of "intelligence"; it sounds less hostile and more constructive, but it means about the same.

[4] Examples include Michael Porter, John E. Prescott, Jonathan Calof, and Creg S. Fleisher.

Because so many threats now come over the internet, via email, and through hackers, the intelligence function or competence is now often found within the IT department. During the past few years, especially since Putin's invasion of Ukraine and the increased competition from China, it has also become more common for public organizations to hire security personnel. Many of these employees are former intelligence officers so they also bring intelligence know-how to the organization. It is a booming market. The security industry thrives in periods of fear.

In real life, most companies will have or implement a mixture of several different organizational models, depending on the kind of industry they are in. Still, they will tend to adhere more to one model than to another. This will be the intelligence model characteristic of the company.

For a while, at the turn of the millennium, we saw a development from the departmental model to more of a bottom-up advisory model, largely due to increased competition and globalization. Now, with globalization on the decline and isolation and trade barriers becoming part of a new two-world order, we are seeing more defensive organizational structures making a return. Times of increased competition are times of crisis, and new organizational models appear when things go wrong, and sometimes because of it. One such example is the Court Jester model.

7.3.8 The Court Jester Model of Intelligence[5]

What happens to the intelligence function in organizations that work less well? One observation, based on empirical results, is what we can call the court jester intelligence model:

> Companies in difficult situations tend to be a bit like mediaeval rulers, who may decide to execute the messenger. This resembles the role of the CI specialist in Ericsson [under a period of difficulties]. By changing his role from one of being a bringer of facts to one who asks questions instead, the CI specialist managed to save his life, but only to find himself turned into another medieval figure, the court jester. The court jester is focused on pleasing his superiors, not on delivering need to know information and telling the truth. When a company is in a difficult situation the organization tends to becomes more political, and therefore less concerned with facts. Managers become occupied primarily with defending their own positions and existing perks rather than with keeping the company alive. (p. 31)

Another problem that was raised in conversations with Ericsson employees in this study is that managers often have expectations of the CI function that are too high. They expect to be able to "see into the future," which, unfortunately, is even promised in much of the academic literature on the topic of "foresight" and by consultants eager to sell business intelligence solutions. This reduces the intelligence function to a somewhat ridiculous and unproductive function isolated in the organizational chart, like a spoiled opportunity or a misunderstood person (Fig. 7.11).

[5] See Söilen (2017a).

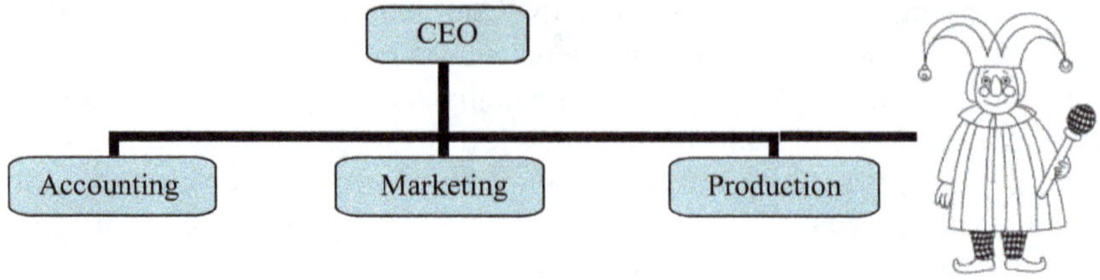

Fig. 7.11 The court jester model of intelligence

If the intelligence function cannot meet the expectations of senior management, it risks falling out of favor, potentially leading to the shutdown of entire departments or individual personnel. This is a common response in companies facing crises, as part of a strategy to "get back to basics." While sometimes this can be disastrous, in other instances it is necessary because the intelligence function, despite being built on lofty ideas, did not significantly impact the company's success. Unlike state sector intelligence organizations, private intelligence functions must continually prove their value to avoid being abolished. Therefore, they must demonstrate their usefulness consistently to remain integral to the organization.

7.4 Integrating Knowledge Management and Intelligence in Organizations

In academia, it's not uncommon for scholars of Knowledge Management (KM) to also venture into the field of intelligence, as the fields share many aspects of knowledge and information. However, there are hardly any departments of knowledge management in organizations, and intelligence studies have left the larger question of how knowledge is created, used, and stored in organizations. Said differently, intelligence studies assume that the intelligence analysts have the knowledge acquired, without going into the details of how they got it and what it consists of, just like the subject of Strategy assumes that intelligence is provided inside the organization. we have earlier referred to both KM and Strategy as twin studies, but they are more than that, namely closely related parts in the same process (Fig. 7.12).

One question that arises from time to time is whether the Knowledge Management (KM) function and Intelligence (I) should be placed in the same department. KM is a concern of top management but is often carried out by the Human Resources Department (HRD). Several authors (e.g., Canongia, 2007) have pointed out the clear synergy between them. However, this integration is not without challenges. HR excels at its core responsibilities: recruiting,[6] managing, and laying off employees. While this may include gathering employees' knowledge and know-how and setting clear KM strategies for the company, specific knowledge demands are often

[6] On Recruiting Intelligence (see Kidder, 2022).

Fig. 7.12 The process of defining the need for knowledge in the organization

known best within the individual departments. For this reason, the KM function struggles with many of the same placement issues as the intelligence function. One solution is to have a person responsible for the entire information and knowledge process, termed a Chief Intelligence Officer (CIO). The CIO would also be responsible for overseeing the organization's AI Strategy, thus have a much larger role than the previous Chief Information Officer with the same acronym.

7.5 The Vulnerability of the Intelligence Function in Organizations

Because the intelligence function has no natural place in the organizational chart and often does not respond to a proper department, there is a risk that the function becomes vulnerable to the loss of knowledge in corporate or organizational intelligence. As we have seen, it is common for organizations that were once excellent in intelligence to suddenly become poor at the same function. A reason for this is that the intelligence function does not have a natural home in the organization, like it does for example in the military, and is instead often associated with specific individuals in the organization who may leave at any moment. In many cases, there are no routines to regenerate that capacity and knowledge within the organization, so it becomes lost, or attempts to regenerate it are done incorrectly or half-heartedly the second time around.

We have mentioned the example of Ericsson earlier. The company Marriott developed a war room in the 90s that became the envy of other companies and formed the model of how HP constructed its intelligence function around the turn of the century. This same model has influenced other companies since, to build a world-class intelligence function today. Looking back now, Marriott is no longer known for having a strong intelligence function, and HP seems to handle the function less well than it did only a decade ago.

Investing a lot of resources in the intelligence function is also no guarantee it will perform well. A good example of this is Motorola. Few US companies spent more resources on the intelligence function than Motorola in the 90s, but the company still split up and faded away, outcompeted by Apple, Nokia, and Samsung, missing opportunities in the smartphone market; meaning they did not see it coming or could not adapt.

Having a well-functioning intelligence system in the past then is no guarantee for future performance. One reason is that people change jobs and take the knowledge with them, or they simply retire without having passed their knowledge and skills on to a new generation in the organization. Training new key intelligence people takes years, not months. Few private companies seem to be able to look that far ahead, except for some family run companies. Another way to say this is that organizations do not have the best memory. Hopefully technology can be a part solution to that problem.

8 The Technology of Intelligence

This chapter aims to provide a comprehensive understanding of the technologies essential for intelligence professionals. It highlights the interconnectedness of practical intelligence work and technical systems by exploring various tools and methods for data collection, analysis, and dissemination.

Even though this is not a book on intelligence technology, it is important to understand the kind of technology required in organizations to assist with information gathering and analysis. This also provides the managers with a realistic idea of the budgets and competencies needed.

From a learning perspective, readers will gain insights into some of the dilemmas associated with intelligence gathering, particularly in the context of global business practices. The chapter encourages critical thinking about the balance between technological advancements and ethical integrity, preparing readers to navigate the complexities of modern intelligence work with a nuanced understanding of both its capabilities and limitations.

8.1 Key Technologies in Intelligence Studies

Intelligence encompasses two aspects: a practical, managerial side, which focuses on how to conduct intelligence work and is the main focus of this book, and a technical side, which involves setting up software and hardware systems to support these activities, often studied under the umbrella of business intelligence and computer science. These two areas are interdependent; one cannot exist without the other, and the technical systems are becoming increasingly comprehensive.

In both private and public/state-run organizations, a variety of technologies are employed to support intelligence functions. These technologies aid in collecting, analysing, disseminating, and storing intelligence, ensuring that decision-makers have timely and accurate information. Here are some key technologies commonly

K. Solberg Söilen, *Intelligence Studies in Business*, Management for Professionals,
https://doi.org/10.1007/978-3-031-76491-2_8

used in the intelligence function of organizations today (likely to change soon, but valuable as examples now) (Table 8.1):

To help make this easier, categories of software analysis may be divided into: (1) Relationship analysis, used to analyze relationships between companies and persons; (2) Analysis of unstructured text, where the software can find important information in the unstructured text (such as a text document); and (3) Comparative analysis, where the software compares information in the system. This kind of software has a wide range of application areas. Some focus on comparing quantitative data, others on qualitative data. Some of this software helps the user apply existing theoretical models such as SWOT and Porter's Five Forces.

How the technology is set up: There are many ways of organizing the Intelligence Function on the Intranet and other corporate IT platforms. Some companies have direct links to their competitors on the first page behind a password. Here, you may find not only the home page of the competitor and their annual reports, but also other key information and internal reports concerning their organization. Other companies have a joint link to the intelligence team in relation to the library function. In many cases, "the team" will simply be a librarian, maybe supported by a data scientist. Exactly how it is done technically depends on the use and preference of the individual organization. What is important is that the system is set up based on clear logical principles and employee requirements, that the people providing the system with intelligence are qualified, and, perhaps most importantly, that someone is responsible for all of its updates and maintenance.

The internet is a vast network accessible to the general public, hosting a wide array of information, from news articles to academic papers, and social media posts, which can be valuable for open-source intelligence (OSINT). The dark web, a part of the deep web, is intentionally hidden and requires specific software to access, often housing illicit activities and confidential information, making it a source for intelligence on criminal activities and underground markets as well. Unlike the internet, where data is generally indexed by search engines, the dark web's content is not indexed and is more challenging to navigate. Intelligence gathered from the internet is typically more abundant and easier to verify, while dark web intelligence is harder to obtain and verify but can provide unique insights into covert activities, illicit markets, crypto accounts, stolen logon passwords, credit cards and access to others' CCTVs. Both platforms complement each other, with the internet offering broad, publicly accessible information and the dark web providing deeper, more secretive and criminal intelligence.

These technologies collectively enhance the capabilities of intelligence functions in organizations, enabling them to gather, process, and analyze vast amounts of data efficiently and securely. All these solutions will soon be AI-enhanced. The next step will be to integrate AI and robots, another technology that has made remarkable progress over the past decade. At that time, when this happens, we will have not only AI factories, or AI data centres, facilities designed to provide the infrastructure and resources necessary to deploy complex AI-powered applications and models, but also Autonomous Intelligence Systems.

Table 8.1 Key technologies used in the intelligence function

#	Function	Tools	Purpose
1	Data Collection and Aggregation Technologies	Web Scraping Tools	These tools automatically extract data from websites and online sources. Examples include BeautifulSoup and Scrapy.
		Social Media Monitoring Tools	Platforms like Hootsuite, Brandwatch, and Mention track social media activity and trends.
		Sensors and IoT Devices	In public/state-run organizations, sensors and Internet of Things (IoT) devices gather real-time data from physical environments.
2	Data Storage and Management	Databases	Relational databases (e.g., MySQL, PostgreSQL) and NoSQL databases (e.g., MongoDB, Cassandra) store structured and unstructured data.
		Data Warehouses	Systems like Amazon Redshift, Google BigQuery, and Snowflake consolidate data from multiple sources for analysis.
		Data Lakes:	Platforms like Apache Hadoop and Amazon S3 store vast amounts of raw data in its native format.
3	Data Analysis and Processing	Big Data Analytics Platforms	Tools such as Apache Spark and Cloudera process and analyze large datasets.
		Machine Learning and AI:	Platforms like TensorFlow, PyTorch, and Azure Machine Learning develop predictive models and identify patterns in data.
		Statistical Analysis Tools	Software like R, SAS, and SPSS conduct statistical analysis and visualize data.
4	Intelligence Analysis and Visualization	Geographic Information Systems (GIS):	Tools like ESRI ArcGIS and QGIS analyze spatial and geographic data.
		Data Visualization Tools	Platforms like Tableau, Power BI, and D3.js create interactive and static visualizations of data
		Natural Language Processing (NLP):	Tools like NLTK and spaCy analyze and interpret human language in text form.
5	Communication and Collaboration	Collaboration Platforms:	Software like Microsoft Teams, Slack, and Asana facilitate communication and project management.
		Secure Communication Tools	Technologies like Signal, PGP encryption, and secure email services ensure confidential communication and risky Dead drops and Brush passes almost obsolete.

(continued)

Table 8.1 (continued)

#	Function	Tools	Purpose
6	Cybersecurity and Data Protection	Encryption Technologies	Tools like AES, RSA, and SSL/TLS protect data in transit and at rest.
		Intrusion Detection Systems (IDS):	Systems like Snort and Suricata monitor network traffic for suspicious activity.
		Firewall and Security Management	Solutions like Palo Alto Networks, Fortinet, and Cisco manage and secure network access.
7	Intelligence-Specific Software	Intelligence Management Systems	Platforms like Palantir, IBM i2 Analyst's Notebook, and ClearStory Data integrate, analyze, and visualize complex data.
		Open Source Intelligence (OSINT) Tools	Tools like Maltego and Shodan gather and analyze publicly available information.
8	Emerging Technologies	Blockchain:	Used for secure and transparent data transactions and record-keeping.
		Quantum Computing	Promises to revolutionize data processing and cryptographic analysis in intelligence functions.

At the end we will note that Business Intelligence does not teach you how to build systems; that knowledge is acquired through fields such as Computer Science, which covers software development, algorithms, data structures, and computer theory; Computer Engineering, which focuses on the hardware aspects of computing; Software Engineering, which involves the design, development, and maintenance of software systems; and Electrical Engineering, which includes the principles and applications of building computers and other electronic devices.

8.2 Artificial Intelligence (AI) and Autonomous Intelligence Systems Scenarios

Artificial Intelligence (AI) is revolutionizing the field of Intelligence as this book is published, being integrated into every part of the processes and practically in everything we do, much like a second brain.[1]

Business Intelligence (BI) is built upon querying, visualization, and workflow as applied to AI. Querying in BI and prompt engineering in the context of AI models like large language models (LLMs) are both methods of extracting information but cater to different systems and processes. Prompt engineering involves crafting inputs (prompts) to an AI system to elicit the most accurate or useful outputs, leveraging the AI's capabilities effectively. In essence, querying in BI is about extracting specific information from structured databases, while prompt engineering is about

[1] For example, on electronic word of mouth or eWOW, Nuortimo (2023), on AI regulation Bisson et al. (2023). Skill sets needed for AI, Freyn and Hoffman (2022). On AI and hiring, Amzile et al. (2022).

optimizing interactions with AI models to generate or refine responses based on a wide array of trained data.

Just like we have regular factories today, with large systems of supply chain management, much of which is controlled and managed by robots, we are going to have AI factories in the future. These AI factories will consist of a collection of CPUs (Central Processing Units), DPUs (Data Processing Units), large amounts of software, and extensive cabling. These AI factories will be a combination of AI processes all working towards the same final output, with companies like Dell and Nvidia supplying much of the hardware. To some extent, these will also be intelligence factories, ensuring the quality of the data that goes into their systems in order to assure the quality of what comes out on the other side.

We can imagine a scenario where an organization employs Autonomous Intelligence Systems, leveraging AI and advanced business intelligence (BI) solutions to streamline data gathering, analysis, and decision-making. Here's how such a system could look (Table 8.2):

To take an example, we'll look at a "Market Expansion Strategy": The AI system detects a growing demand for eco-friendly products in Southeast Asia from social media trends and market reports. It scrapes relevant data, performs sentiment analysis as described in Chaps. 4 and 5, and integrates economic indicators of the region. Using predictive modeling, the system forecasts the success probability of entering the market with a new eco-friendly product line, considering local competitors, the regulatory environment, and consumer preferences. It suggests a phased market entry strategy, highlighting potential risks and mitigation plans, supported by visual data insights. In this scenario, the Autonomous Intelligence System not only automates data collection and analysis but also provides strategic recommendations aligned with the organization's goals, significantly enhancing decision-making processes. It can leave a selection of decision-making to a human or do it itself based on the probability calculations for success. In this scenario, humans are an option.

If we continue down the road of this scenario called here AIS#1, in the first stages of AI integration we are going to be swarmed with an abundance of perfectly written reports that we do not know what to do with because we are unsure if we can trust it, questioning no doubt who wrote it, a human or a machine (percentages please), citation marks and references. But gradually, we are going to see that these reports are far better than what human beings can do and much faster and cheaper. When we reach that point—and I would argue we are already there in year 2 of commercial AI now in 2024—we are going to see increased layoffs. The production of hardware and software is going to go through the roof and demands on more electricity is also going to increase. More people are going to study everything that is related to this AI paradigm shift and those who do not use the technology will soon be considered illiterate for work in organizations with a competitive focus.

Then there is the question of what the others should do as efficiency will increase. Some form of citizen salary will be inevitable, I estimate. We can imagine a scenario where man is instead going to treasure what is truly human, which will turn out to be—no, not our intelligence in the sense of brains and 'homo sapiens'—but our

Table 8.2 Scenario for an Autonomous Intelligence Systems

Steps	IC phase	Tech solution	Description
1	Data Gathering	Automated Web Scraping and API Integration	The system continuously scrapes data from various internet sources, including social media, news websites, industry reports, and market analysis platforms using web scraping tools
			It integrates with APIs of relevant databases, such as financial markets, economic indicators, and industry-specific data providers, to fetch real-time data
		Internet of Things (IoT) Devices	IoT sensors and devices in the field collect data on environmental conditions, machinery performance, and logistics. This data is sent to the central AI system for real-time analysis
2	Data Processing and Analysis	Big Data Analytics	The system processes large volumes of structured and unstructured data using big data platforms like Apache Hadoop and Apache Spark
			Machine learning models and algorithms analyze the data to identify patterns, trends, and anomalies. These models are continually updated and trained using frameworks like TensorFlow and PyTorch
		Natural Language Processing (NLP)	NLP tools like spaCy and NLTK interpret and categorize textual data, extracting relevant information and sentiment from articles, reports, and social media posts
		Data Integration	The system consolidates data from various sources into a unified data warehouse using platforms like Amazon Redshift or Google BigQuery, ensuring that all information is available for comprehensive analysis

(continued)

Table 8.2 (continued)

Steps	IC phase	Tech solution	Description
3	Scenario Analysis and Decision Making	Probability Calculations and Predictive Modeling	AI algorithms run probability calculations for various scenarios based on historical data and current trends. Predictive models forecast potential outcomes and their likelihood, helping to understand possible futures
			Bayesian networks and decision trees are used to assess the probabilities of different scenarios, incorporating the organization's strategy and historical data to refine predictions.
		Strategic Alignment	The system aligns its analysis with the organization's strategic goals. It understands the company's objectives, such as market expansion, cost reduction, or product innovation, and evaluates scenarios in this context.
			It utilizes reinforcement learning to adapt strategies based on real-time feedback and outcomes, improving its recommendations over time.
		Decision Support	The AI system generates suggested actions and decisions, presenting them with a confidence score based on the probability calculations.
			It visualizes the scenarios and their potential impacts using data visualization tools like Tableau or Power BI, making the information accessible and actionable for decision-makers.
		Continuous Learning and Improvement	The system incorporates feedback loops where outcomes of decisions are fed back into the models, enabling continuous learning and improvement.
			It uses techniques like reinforcement learning to adjust strategies and improve decision accuracy over time.

emotions. Maybe with that comes a sense of humility and appreciation for everything living.

There are various scenarios regarding the implementation of Autonomous Intelligence Systems (AIS), but the most likely one at present involves a significant shift in how we handle information. One consequence of AIS and the semi-AIS phase we have already entered is that we will reject much more quality information. In this semi-phase, employees become enthusiastic about the new technology and start sending out large amounts of unsolicited yet high-quality data or push intelligence.

In the past, we have learned that people react negatively to information that does not help them in their work and only takes up their time. Information can be classified based on how well it meets the professional interests of its readers according to several criteria:

- The information may be irrelevant because it does not relate to what the person is working on (intelligence subject error).
- The person already knows the content (intelligence knowledge error).
- The information arrives too late (intelligence time error).
- The information is not interesting enough (intelligence target error).

However, what happens when we face an overload of valuable information? This is the situation we are entering now:

- There is simply too much interesting content (reports, video, audio) to consume, even though we know it's important.

Given the situation where we are overwhelmed by an abundance of high-quality information, leading to difficulties in selecting the most relevant and useful data, we refer to this phenomenon as TMIQ (Too Much Information Quality).

In the past, the principle of Garbage-In Garbage-Out (GIGO) emphasized the importance of input quality for achieving accurate and useful outputs. GIGO remains a problem, especially on the Internet. However, with advanced AI and information systems, the challenge has somewhat shifted. Now, we also face a scenario with an overwhelming amount of high-quality information. This abundance makes it more difficult for individuals and organizations to filter and prioritize the most relevant data effectively (Table 8.3).

Table 8.3 Characteristics of TMIQ and how to find solutions

#	Problem	Explanation	Addressing TMIQ
1	Information Overload	The sheer volume of high-quality information can overwhelm decision-makers, making it challenging to process and utilize the data efficiently.	Advanced Filtering Algorithms: Developing and utilizing more sophisticated algorithms that can better prioritize and filter information based on contextual relevance and specific needs.
2	Difficulty in Prioritization	With so much valuable information, it becomes hard to determine which pieces are most critical for a particular decision or context.	AI-Assisted Decision-Making: Leveraging AI to not only gather and analyze data but also to assist in making decisions by highlighting the most relevant information and providing actionable insights
3	Cognitive Strain	Constantly sifting through high-quality data can lead to cognitive fatigue, reducing the overall efficiency and effectiveness of individuals and teams.	User-Centric Design: Creating interfaces and tools that allow users to customize the information flow according to their specific requirements and preferences, reducing cognitive load.
4	Risk of Missing Key Insights	Important insights may be buried under a mountain of other relevant information, increasing the risk of missing critical data points.	Continuous Learning Systems: Implementing systems that learn and adapt over time, improving their ability to filter and prioritize information based on user interactions and feedback.

By acknowledging and addressing the TMIQ problem, organizations can better manage the flow of high-quality information, ensuring that decision-makers have access to the most relevant and actionable data without being overwhelmed.

Machines will produce reports that are read by machines. We are already there with scientific journals. Researchers use AI to create articles that are peer-reviewed by machines. Instead of reading, we are passing on, running bits of text through the machine.

This automated content creation and consumption cycle creates information overload, making it crucial to develop better filters and relevance metrics to ensure that only the most pertinent information reaches human decision-makers. As AIS continues to evolve, the focus will shift towards optimizing the quality and relevance of information rather than merely increasing its volume. This will lead to the development of Information Quality Control Systems, built around clearinghouses and new controller positions.

8.3 Technological Advancements and Their Applications in Business

All industries have been transformed by faster computers and information technology, but some are particularly significant for intelligence studies, such as digital marketing and financial trading:

- Retail and Inventory Management: Algorithms predict purchasing trends and automate restocking procedures, greatly enhancing supply chain efficiency. Personalization engines in e-commerce analyze customer data to offer personalized shopping experiences.
- Financial Trading: Financial trading systems have evolved significantly with contributions from academics like Edward O. Thorp, Victor Niederhoffer, and Jim Simons. These systems incorporate macro factors from newspapers and other sources to inform trading strategies.

The development of intelligence systems in financial trading has been influenced by Claude Shannon's information theory and probability theory. Quants, who often lack an understanding of the companies or industries they trade in, primarily focus on the short term, making massive bets and drawing small margins that translate into significant amounts due to the large volumes they handle. However, this strategy has not been effective for long-term investments, as evidenced by the 2007–2008 financial collapse. The reason is that they have so far struggled to incorporate the full complexity of social life, especially major risks, but they are also bound to get smarter. The best eample may be BlackRock. BlackRock, Inc., founded in 1988, is an American multinational investment management corporation that has grown to become the world's largest asset manager. The company's success is significantly influenced by its strategic utilization of big data and advanced analytics. Several industries have achieved remarkable success by leveraging big data to transform their business strategy. Spotify uses sophisticated algorithms to analyze listening habits, creating personalized playlists and recommendations that keep users engaged. Amazon has mastered the art of big data in e-commerce, optimizing inventory, pricing, and customer recommendations to dominate the global marketplace. In the same way, Netflix relies on data analytics to predict viewer preferences, fine-tune its content offerings, and decide on new productions, ensuring its leadership in streaming. In transportation, companies like Uber and Lyft utilize real-time data to match drivers with riders efficiently, improving service and reducing costs.

The use of sophisticated technology for information gathering has rapidly developed since the Second World War, particularly during the Cold War, often referred to as an "Intelligence War." Today, technology plays an increasingly important role in the competition between private organizations. This has again triggered a need for defining intelligence risks and taking counterintelligence measures.

8.3.1 Intelligence Risks

Assessing security risks posed by eavesdropping equipment today demands considerable knowledge and training. This knowledge is mostly found through key people in the police and military intelligence services but can also be acquired by private companies through short courses in security.

In today's international organizations, an employee faces three kinds of intelligence risks:

1. Internal Environment:	Competitors, suppliers, etc.
2. External Environment:	Political organizations and national security services.
3. Own Organization:	Known as Employee Surveillance.

Awareness of increasing technology use for intelligence gathering has led to a focus on counterintelligence measures. Companies invest in counterintelligence technology to protect against eavesdropping, which can escalate costs and reduce the profitability of intelligence technology investments.

A common form of counterintelligence is to secure a room or car against bugs before a meeting. Many companies will contact a Technical Surveillance Counter Measures (TSCM) Specialist to have this done unless they are large enough to have such competence on their own security staff.

8.3.2 Eavesdropping Equipment

Eavesdropping equipment has evolved significantly with advancements in technology. The following list reflects more current tools used for surveillance and intelligence gathering:

- Miniature Digital Recorders: Modern devices that can be hidden in pens or other inconspicuous items to record audio discreetly.

- Micro Cameras: Tiny cameras that can be concealed in everyday objects, such as tie pins, buttons, or even eyeglasses, for covert video recording.
- Laser Microphones: Devices that use laser beams to pick up sound vibrations from surfaces like windows, enabling the eavesdropper to listen to conversations from a distance.
- Spy Software: Programs installed on smartphones, tablets, or computers to monitor communications, track locations, and record activities without the user's knowledge.
- Network Interception Tools: Advanced software and hardware tools used to intercept and monitor network traffic, often employed for cyber espionage.
- Radio Frequency (RF) Bugs: Small transmitters that can be hidden in rooms, phones, or other objects to send audio data to a remote receiver.
- Drones: Equipped with high-resolution cameras and microphones, drones can be used for aerial surveillance and eavesdropping.
- Wi-Fi Interception Devices: Tools that intercept and decrypt Wi-Fi communications to access data being transmitted over wireless networks.

These tools reflect the ongoing evolution of eavesdropping technology, making surveillance more discreet and efficient. While it,s true that many of the more affordable versions of this technology lack reliability, advancements have made these technologies accessible even to smaller companies. Organizations need to be aware of the different forms of intelligence risks and implement robust countermeasures to protect sensitive information *without exaggerating the fear*.

8.3.3 Counterintelligence Measures

For every type of attack, there is a corresponding way for an organization to defend itself. Given the advancements in eavesdropping technology, organizations need to enhance their counterintelligence measures to safeguard sensitive information. Common counterintelligence practices include:

- Technical Surveillance Counter Measures (TSCM): Regular sweeps and checks by TSCM specialists to detect and neutralize surveillance devices.
- Encryption: Use of strong encryption protocols for communications and data storage to prevent unauthorized access.
- Secure Meeting Rooms: Designated secure areas for sensitive discussions, often equipped with counter-surveillance technologies.
- Employee Training: Regular training for employees on recognizing and mitigating espionage risks.
- Network Security: Implementing robust cybersecurity measures to protect against hacking and data breaches, known as APTs.

Advanced Persistent Threats (APTs) are sophisticated, long-term cyberattacks often orchestrated by well-funded and skilled groups, typically targeting specific organizations or nations to steal sensitive information or disrupt operations. These attacks are characterized by their stealthy, continuous presence within a network, evading detection while achieving their objectives.

By staying vigilant and adopting comprehensive counterintelligence strategies, organizations can mitigate the risks posed by modern eavesdropping technologies.

Technical Surveillance Counter Measures (TSCM) specialists prevent or detect the interception of sensitive information, performing services such as radio frequency spectrum analysis, physical searches, and identifying security weaknesses.

Eavesdropping equipment can, first of all, be classified by the senses involved in the information-gathering process. Thus, we have ear, eye, and vibration intelligence equipment. It may be a miniature cassette player hidden in a pen, a camera small enough to sit on a tiepin, or a radar detecting voices in a room from the vibrations on the windows. Radars can also be used to eavesdrop on a computer or a cellular phone from a distance. Hackers use computers to tap into other computers, which has opened up a whole new market for Computer Security & Recovery.

Companies increasingly install software to monitor employees' computer usage, raising concerns about privacy and trust within organizations. This is known as Employee Surveillance. On top of all this intelligence and counterintelligence equipment, there exists an entire industry of consultants and security experts of various specialties and expertise too long to list even in this book. It's easy to feel overwhelmed by the sheer volume of technologies and consultants, which is why it's crucial to focus on a few simple principles. Essentially, you need to know what critical information to safeguard, preferably keeping a secure copy, and have a clear plan for who to contact when things go wrong. Following these steps can take you a long way in protecting your organization. For example, consider the case of Sandvik, which allegedly had much of its mining equipment copied in China due to carelessness with blueprints of its production processes when setting up operations in Asia.

The extended use of technology for intelligence gathering also raises many ethical questions, which will be discussed next.

Intelligence Ethics 9

This is the most difficult and most important chapter to write. Ethics refers to philosophical discussions and principles that aim to determine what is right and wrong in a more universal or professional context, while morality deals with personal beliefs about right and wrong. Thus, the focus here will be on ethics rather than what is understood as "moralizing" or taking sides, as much of our daily reflections on moarlity has no place in a constructive textbook or as a university subject.

At the same time—and this is what makes it difficult—we need to understand the ethical components of intelligence work and how we can address them from a principled perspective. However, we also need to be open and blunt. We have to deal with the real world and owe it to the reader not to be surprised when entering a real job in intellgence. Therefore, there can be no sacred issues or incidents when teaching students about the reality of intelligence work in practice. In other words, there can never be a question of hiding facts or truths. The difficulty lies in achieving this without being in any way "moralizing."

9.1 Ethical Intelligence Risk

The concept of "ethical intelligence risk" encompasses the various ethical and moral dilemmas that intelligence analysts or employees might encounter while performing their duties. This includes the risks associated with violating personal or professional ethical standards, and it can cover a wide range of issues from privacy concerns to the manipulation of information.

Intelligence work often involves activities that can be ethically questionable, such as surveillance, infiltration, and the handling of sensitive or classified information. These activities might interfere with civil liberties or result in the exploitation of individuals and groups. To mitigate these risks, it is crucial for intelligence operations to be guided by stringent ethical frameworks and oversight mechanisms.

K. Solberg Söilen, *Intelligence Studies in Business*, Management for Professionals,
https://doi.org/10.1007/978-3-031-76491-2_9

For example, in the intelligence community, there is an ongoing debate about how politics can influence intelligence activities, leading to potential ethical breaches. Ensuring that intelligence officers are well-trained in ethics and that their operations are closely monitored by legal counsel and subject to rigorous oversight can help maintain ethical standards. This ensures that intelligence work supports national security without compromising individual rights or ethical integrity.

Furthermore, the use of artificial intelligence in intelligence work introduces additional ethical risks, such as algorithmic biases and the potential for decisions that may infringe on individuals' rights. These risks highlight the importance of implementing robust ethical frameworks to govern the use of AI and other advanced technologies in intelligence operations.

It can also involve participating in operations where there is a disconnect between what is communicated and what one is asked to do. This dissonance between the orders and the suggested actions renders the words unbelievable. Carrying out these actions can leave us with a sense of distaste, as it often means breaking with our own ethical standards. These dilemmas are significant because ethical risks are a major problem in the field of intelligence. The moral dilemma is inherent to the nature of the work, and there are no easy solutions.

9.2 An Introduction to Double-Dealing

General von Clausewitz, who had learned much from observing Napoleon,[1] said that war was the continuation of politics just with other Means.[2] The final goals of political and business activities are, firsthand, economic in one way or another. This can be said to have been partly true when Napoleon attacked northern Italy, as it was when President George W. Bush led the war against Iraq. To gain public support, it's common to claim you are fighting for the freedom of your opponents or some other unselfish ideal. Revolutionaries like Daniel Ortega say they are fighting for what is best for the people, and maybe at some point in the beginning, that was at least partially true. But then you desire power and money, and the ideals become at the end just another media strategy. In the end, you don't care if you imprison or kill thousands. It's an all too common story, even in our own time.

Napoleon Bonaparte used a combination of methods to persuade the French public to support his wars, including newspapers, official bulletins, posters, and pamphlets. He also strengthened his authority through commissioned artworks and promoted cultural nationalism. These techniques have not changed much since then. Napoleon's main objective, it could be argued, was to enrich himself and his family, but historians seldom draw this conclusion. Just, look at the palaces and infrastructure he built; they will tell you. This does not mean he wasn't a brilliant military strategist.

[1] See e.g. Chandler (1966).

[2] von Clausewitz (1932–34).

While many ambitious individuals in our own time spend considerable time discussing their philanthropy, it's essential to recognize that these motives are not purely altruistic. Part of this effort may stem from a genuine desire to help others, but another part often serves as a form of window dressing, cushioning the impact of their families' more unethical business practices. Pledging fortunes often includes non-binding commitments and garners much-needed goodwill for the wealthy elite. Thus, all such announcements should be taken with a degree of skepticism, especially if they are not legally binding.

This in turn raises questions about the ethical integrity of our leaders, the manipulation of public perception, and the moral implications of using ruthless business practices or even war to achieve political and economic objectives. These are critical issues in the study of ethics and morality, especially in the context of leadership, governance, and international relations of which Intelligence is an integrated part.

An intelligence service or a department in a private organization is inevitably aligned with its employer, but this shouldn't prevent individual analysts from maintaining clear and ethical perspectives. Employees often compromise truth and ethical standards for their employers' interests, especially in state and military services, where they are constantly reminded of higher goals and values. However, most people can only tolerate so much compromise before it becomes uncomfortable, leading many to leave their positions in disbelief. This internal conflict underscores the importance of balancing professional duties with personal integrity.

9.3 All Means Have a Moral Component Attached

Now, there is a major difference in ethics between working in military intelligence and business intelligence. This difference is first of all seen in the use of means to gather information. The question of means is important for the study of intelligence in relation to the larger ethical question: Any organization, whether a business, local government, or state department, has a large number of means available for gathering information.

For example, an employee in a marketing department collecting information for this year's marketing plan may gather information by such diverse methods as:

- Reading or writing a book or a report: It is generally considered morally unproblematic today. However, during the Middle Ages, reading texts that contradicted or questioned the teachings of the Catholic Church, such as works by heretics or early scientific works, was deemed morally problematic and even heretical. Galileo faced the Inquisition for supporting heliocentrism, and Darwin delayed publishing "On the Origin of Species" due to anticipated controversy. Today, there are less dangerous but not unsignificant threats to science, such as DEI (Diversity, Equity, and Inclusion) initiatives, where university and department heads sometimes try to shape research, teaching, or debates to fit with personal values.

- Contacting government agencies for statistical information: This is morally unproblematic and even encouraged as a democratic right, at least in the Western world. However, statistical transparency varies across different countries and contexts.
- Searching online databases: Unproblematic if they are your own or something you pay for.
- Drive-by and on-site observations: Can be sensitive to some employees but acceptable with others if you do not ask them to trespass.
- Competitive benchmarking: A common practice and generally unproblematic if it is done ethically, such as not taking photos in a competitor's booth at a trade show without permission.
- Reverse engineering (analyzing a competitor's product): Generally unproblematic, such as buying your competitor's product and taking it apart. This is done frequently in many industries focused on production.
- Seducing a competitor's employee (honey-potting): Considered unethical in many cultures, but not illegal. Less common in business.
- Industrial espionage: Illegal but still practised, especially if the chances of being caught are low, such as online. Cyber espionage is a major problem for most competitive nations, especially for organizations with weak IT security.

The point is that all methods have an ethical component attached. Unlike military organizations at war, most private and public organizations will not insist on means that directly cause physical harm to others. There are several reasons for this: legal, ethical, political, and economic. Overall, it risks being detrimental to business in the end, although some get away with it, especially in totalitarian states.

Another example is psychological warfare. It refers to the use of psychological tactics to gain an advantage over competitors, influence market behavior, or manipulate the internal dynamics of an organization. These tactics are designed to disrupt the target's decision-making process, create doubt, or elicit certain behaviors. It is a strategic approach that leverages psychological principles to achieve business goals (Table 9.1).

Psychological warfare is more common in highly competitive industries where the stakes are higher. It is often seen in sectors like technology, pharmaceuticals, and finance, where market position and intellectual property are critical. The tactics can vary in their subtlety and legality, and while some are openly acknowledged as part of competitive strategy, others operate in more shadowy, ethical grey areas.

The impact or consequences can be devastating: Psychological warfare can damage a competitor's reputation, lower employee morale, and disrupt operations. It can lead to a loss of customers and revenue. Negative campaigns and rumors can shift market perceptions, influencing stock prices and consumer confidence. Within an organization, these tactics can create a culture of fear, reduce trust among employees, and hinder collaboration.[3]

[3] For more on psychological warfare, see e.g. Michaelson (2001).

Table 9.1 Examples of psychological warfare in business

#	Tactic	Explanation	Solution
1.	Rumor and Disinformation Campaigns	Spreading false information or rumors about a competitor's financial health, product safety, or management can create uncertainty and mistrust among customers and investors. For instance, a company might leak false news about a rival's impending bankruptcy to discourage investment or partnerships.	Implement a robust public relations strategy and crisis management plan. Quickly address and counteract rumors with factual information and transparent communication. Utilize social media and press releases to disseminate accurate information. Building strong relationships with trusted media outlets can help ensure your side of the story is heard.
2.	Predatory Pricing	Setting prices extremely low to drive competitors out of the market. This can create the perception that the competitor is weak or unviable, causing their customers and partners to lose confidence.	Focus on differentiating your products or services by emphasizing unique value propositions, quality, and customer service. Engage in value-based pricing strategies rather than competing solely on price. Explore legal avenues if predatory pricing breaches anti-competitive laws.
3.	Negative Advertising	Running advertisements that highlight the flaws or failures of competitors. These ads are designed to create doubt and fear among customers about the reliability or quality of the competitor's products or services	Highlight your strengths and counter negative campaigns with positive marketing. Address any valid criticisms openly and improve upon them. Legal action can be considered if the negative advertising crosses into defamation or false claims.
4.	Employee Poaching	Aggressively recruiting key employees from competitors to disrupt their operations and gain insider information. This tactic can demoralize the competitor's workforce and create operational challenges.	Foster a positive work environment with competitive compensation, career development opportunities, and strong organizational culture. Implement retention strategies such as employee engagement programs and recognition systems. Non-compete agreements can be used, but they must be legally enforceable and reasonable.
5.	Litigation Tactics (especially in the US)	Using lawsuits to tie up a competitor's resources, distract their management, and create public doubt about their business practices. Even if the lawsuits are unfounded, the legal pressure can be a significant psychological burden.	Maintain rigorous legal compliance and documentation. Establish a legal team to handle disputes efficiently and explore settlement options to avoid protracted litigation. Utilize public relations to manage reputation during legal battles.

(continued)

Table 9.1 (continued)

#	Tactic	Explanation	Solution
6.	Internal Sabotage	Introducing disruptive elements within an organization, such as planting a mole to create internal strife, spread misinformation, or leak sensitive information.	Implement strong internal controls, cybersecurity measures, and regular audits. Foster a culture of transparency and trust where employees feel safe reporting suspicious activities. Swiftly address any incidents of sabotage with thorough investigations and appropriate consequences.

In all cases, the individual is exposing the company or organization to intelligence risks. In a situation of war, causing harm may be considered less grave, as the objective is often the destruction of the adversary. However, in business, this is a significant issue, illustrating that the war metaphor in business should not be taken too far unless one is prepared to accept the associated risks and consequences. State and military intelligence operate in a middle ground—they are not technically at war during peacetime but often engage in offensive actions. These actions have been known to breach moral, ethical, and even legal boundaries.

9.3.1 When Your Adversaries Follow a Different Set of Rules

State and military intelligence services are limited by national laws, although these are frequently breached, more in some countries, less in others. Internationally, these services will try to prevent escalation. The actual methods used depend on the historical practices of each country. Most Western countries have clear laws governing intelligence activities, but other democracies like Israel's Mossad and Shin Bet operate with significant autonomy. In weaker democracies and non-democratic countries, intelligence agencies often operate without legal constraints, limited only by political feasibility, and in some countries they are the government, at least de facto.

Public reactions in the Western world often come from media revelations about intelligence activities like luring, bribery, and extortion. Many citizens feel that these methods are undemocratic and conflict with human values. However, others argue that to maintain an open society, the state must protect its openness by restricting those who oppose it.[4] The challenge lies in identifying threats to freedom and balancing the use of intelligence methods. In democracies, the questions about what methods are acceptable is often adjusted first after there has been a major scandal. For example, the Edward Snowden revelations about NSA surveillance led to public debate and adjustments in acceptable intelligence practices in the West.

[4] E.g. The German philosopher Kant considered the use of any means which may contribute to the destruction of peace to be immoral. Those who oppose this view argue that the state must protect itself.

Media leaks about eavesdropping, kidnappings, and similar incidents act as ventilators in our democratic systems. There is no comprehensive democratic and legal mechanism for handling such mistakes, and the prevailing culture is to "sweep under the carpet" and wait out the storm. Intelligence policy in Western countries often focuses on minimizing the damage caused by their own services, in some cases with departments and institutions blaming each other during scandals.

Currently, these issues are mainly associated with national intelligence services and do not affect private and public intelligence to any major degree. However, as globalization continues, larger companies increasingly adopt the practices of national intelligence services when possible. This trend has been observed in the US, particularly in Southern and Central America, where cooperation between intelligence agencies and businesses has been known to undermine free competition and supported dictatorships. This has once again raised questions in other major economies about whether they are being too passive in their business dealings with other countries. It suggests that it might be in the national interest for their secret services to take a more active role in ensuring their own companies secure more contracts.

9.4 Analysis and Strategies for Information Gathering

To hope to make any progress in these issues we need to approach them from a systematic and analytical perspective. To better understand the methods used in intelligence gathering, we can categorize sources into three broad groups:

1. Information Directly from People: This includes direct communication and interviews with individuals.
2. Traces of Human Actions: Non-intentional information given by a person, such as emails and digital footprints. With the development of new technology, this source has become increasingly significant. We all leave so many digital traces now that it's hard to even move around freely without being noticed. Thus, we sometimes speak of Ubiquitous Technical Surveillance (UTS). This has again made it difficult to use spies under false cover through legend building, making it necessary to move over to spies with "natural cover", like journalists, diplomats and researchers.
3. Traces Made by Nature: Non-human intelligence obtained by studying environmental factors affecting business decisions, such as climate conditions at a textile industry location.

Another way to classify intelligence-gathering methods is by the competencies required. On-site observation demands different skills than searching for information in a library or database. Specialists tend to stick to familiar techniques. For example, an analyst who has spent years understanding specific magazines and newspapers will likely continue using those sources. We refer to this as an "anchoring bias", a bias that occurs when individuals rely too heavily on an initial piece of information (the "anchor") when making decisions.

The different sources or means of information gathering may be classified in several ways, for example according to their ethical and legal attributes (Fig. 9.1):

Information gathering in business and public life is governed by laws and ethical codes. Most companies will avoid methods of information gathering that are illegal. The difficult methods to decide between are those that are legal but unethical. This group of methods belongs to *the grey zone of information gathering.*

The grey zone becomes even more apparent when conducting business abroad in a foreign country (FC). As soon as we move into the international arena, the problem of which means to use becomes more complex as ethical codes, but also laws, are different. This raises the question: whose ethics do we follow? There are now suddenly two gray zone areas, one domestic (D) and one in foreign country number 1 (FC1). What is ethical in both countries is not a problem. What is unethical in both countries likewise is clear (Fig. 9.2).

Many expats will choose to leave their own domestic set of moral rules and adapt to the rules of their new country. Others will stick with their domestic moral rules even though they move. In both cases, the choice of means is less complex. To be clear, there are three sets of morals possible: either you follow the ethics of the country you are born in, the ethics of the country where you operate, or a combination of both. The key is to reflect on this, both personally and as an organization.

Research shows that companies will often adapt to the laws and ethical codes of the country where they are conducting business instead of imposing their own codes.[5] It is a dilemma that a company may be judged ethical in one country and unethical in another based on differing values. Because of these varying standards and practices, companies are careful about what information they disclose about their methods of information gathering and other potentially unethical actions they may have taken.

Based on the classification above, we can define four pure strategies for intelligence in organizations (Fig. 9.3):

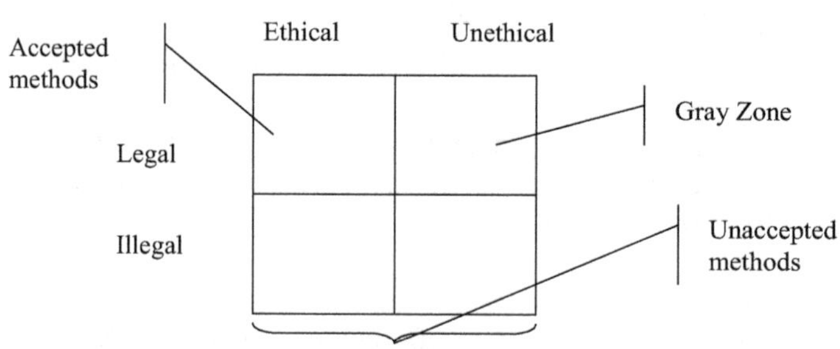

Fig. 9.1 Ethical considerations for means of gathering information

[5] Söilen (2004).

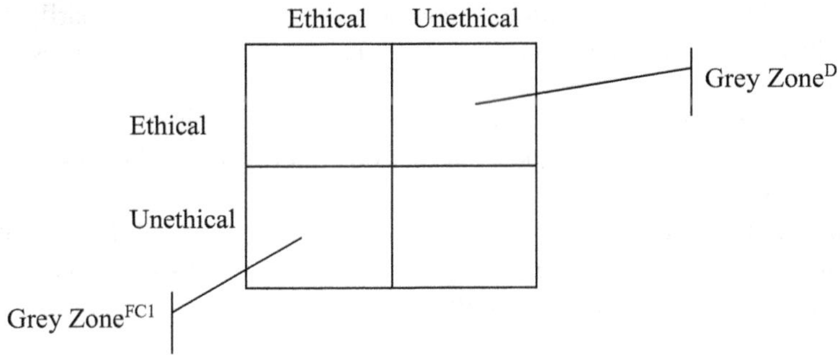

Fig. 9.2 Ethical considerations for means of gathering information in foreign countries

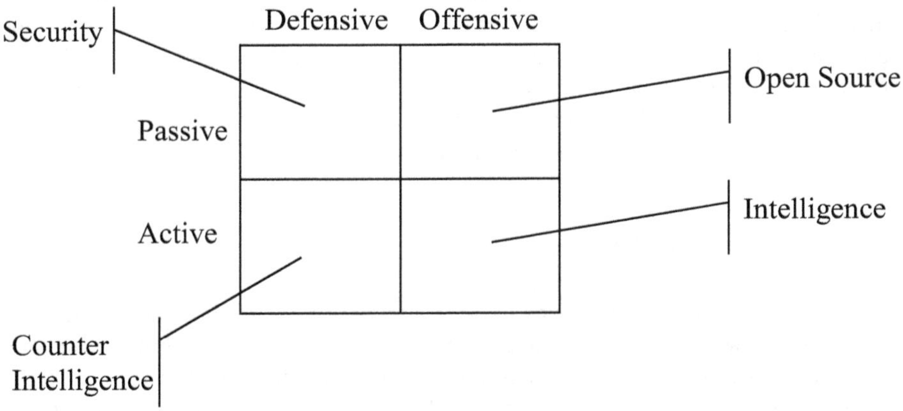

Fig. 9.3 Pure strategies for intelligence work in organizations

1. Passive-Defensive:
   - Description: Focus on security, prioritizing the protection of data and systems.
   - Example: Financial Institutions (e.g., JPMorgan Chase) prioritize securing their data and systems against breaches, focusing on strong cybersecurity measures to protect sensitive financial information.
2. Active-Defensive:
   - Description: Use competitor attacks to gather information or provide false information to attackers.
   - Example: Cybersecurity Firms (e.g., CrowdStrike) actively monitor and respond to cyber threats, engaging with attackers to gather intelligence and sometimes feeding them misleading information.
3. Passive-Offensive:
   - Description: Emphasize open-source intelligence, using publicly available information without engaging in covert activities.

- Example: Research Institutions (e.g., RAND Corporation) primarily use publicly available information and open-source intelligence for their research and analysis.

4. Active-Offensive:
   - Description: Actively gather and analyze intelligence using both open and covert sources.
   - Example: Technology Companies (e.g., Palantir Technologies) gather and analyze intelligence using a variety of methods to provide comprehensive data analytics and security solutions.

The choice of strategy will depend on the industry we are in, the degree of competition, and our willingness to take intelligence risks. The intelligence risk depends on both the personal ethics of the employees and the corporate or organizational ethics where the person works. Organizational ethics is often set by the leaders, top management, and the owners of the company. To become a part of the organizational culture, the organizational ethics needs to be communicated through clear declarations of conduct or similar documents of conduct. These documents set the standard for acceptable behavior in the organization.

9.4.1 Virtue Signaling

It's also possible for organizations to adhere to the rules of other entities, such as employers' or workers' organizations or other professional bodies. For intelligence work, some companies, especially in the US, are members of SCIP, the Strategic and Competitive Intelligence Professionals, formerly known as the Society of Competitive Intelligence Professionals. SCIP has developed ethical guidelines that all members are encouraged to follow. As stated on their webpage:

> The SCIP Code of Ethics is a set of guidelines for ethical behavior for CI companies and practitioners which SCIP expects its members (and third parties hired by its members) to adhere to. The Code is not a corporate policy; rather the Code contains guidelines by which companies and practitioners can set their own standards along the ethical spectrum.

There have been different versions of this code over the years, and an older and simpler one stated (Table 9.2):

A newer version state:

(a) Obtain and use information legally and ethically: To avoid conflicts of interest, avoid actions that would violate the legal rights of others, including the rights of privacy and property.
(b) Disclose all relevant information, including one's identity and organization, prior to all interviews: This ensures transparency and honesty in gathering competitive intelligence.

Table 9.2 SCIP ethical rules (SCIP, 1996)

Ethical rules
(a) To continually strive to increase the recognition and respect of the profession.
(b) To comply with all applicable laws, domestic and international.
(c) To accurately disclose all relevant information, including one's identity and organization, prior to all interviews.
(d) To fully respect all requests for confidentiality of information.
(e) To avoid conflicts of interest in fulfilling one's duties.
(f) To provide honest and realistic recommendations and conclusions in the execution of one's duties.
(g) To promote this code of ethics within one's company, with third-party contractors and within the entire profession.
(h) To faithfully adhere to and abide by one's company policies, objectives, and guidelines.

(c) Provide honest and realistic recommendations and conclusions in the execution of one's duties: Ensuring that all intelligence and insights provided are accurate, truthful, and fair.
(d) Promote honesty and integrity in the profession: Upholding the highest standards of ethical behavior in all professional interactions and activities.
(e) Faithfully adhere to and abide by one's company policies, objectives, and guidelines: Ensuring alignment with organizational goals and ethical standards.
(f) Comply with all applicable laws, domestic and international: Understanding and adhering to the laws that govern the profession in various jurisdictions.
(g) Safeguard confidential and proprietary information obtained in the course of one's duties: Protecting sensitive information from unauthorized disclosure.
(h) Avoid conflicts of interest in fulfilling one's duties: Ensuring that personal interests do not interfere with professional responsibilities.
(i) Adhere to the highest standards of accuracy and truth in all statements made, reports, and communications: Ensuring that all communication is honest, clear, and accurate.
(j) Do not engage in illegal or unethical activities, such as bribery, theft, espionage, or deception: Avoiding any actions that could harm the integrity of the profession or the organization.

The SCIP Code of Ethics provides a robust framework for ethical behavior. However, its implementation in real life can be challenging due to potential conflicts between organizational goals and ethical standards, as well as the inherent complexities of competitive intelligence work.

By being a member of such an interest group, companies aim to show that they adhere to specific ethical rules. Whether they actually do so is another question, and there is always the chance that some companies use similar memberships for window-dressing, meaning they want to present a better image to outsiders than what is accurate. Still, if both parties in a business negotiation clearly state that they are members of such an organization, there are reasons to believe that they will try to adhere to its rules because they automatically raise the consequences of their own ethical failures (a form of virtue signaling).

In the future, we could imagine intelligence certification programs for ethical information gathering, akin to what Veritas does in the shipping industry. However, auditing intelligence methods is more challenging than inspecting ships, even though such certification could foster trust among competitors and possibly benefit the free market system.

9.5 Ethical Challenges in International Business

It is often said that financial interests are the most effective reducer of business ethics.[6] The higher the stakes and more intense the competition, the lower the adherence to ethical standards. This is particularly true in international business, where clear laws are often lacking, and definitions of ethics vary widely across different cultures.

Major international negotiations present significant ethical risks.[7] Companies with substantial stakes may resort to methods to obtain information that the other party might deem unethical. Research shows that companies victimized by eavesdropping attacks may not react if they believe the reaction could harm their financial interests.[8] This can be seen as rational behavior. Often, the response to being targeted is to acknowledge the attacker's cleverness and resolve not to be fooled again. Retaliation usually occurs only when the competitor, supplier, or customer is significantly weaker than the opponent and may take the form of higher prices and less favorable contract terms.[9] Anyway, these were some of the findings of my own PhD on industrial espionage completed some two decades ago.

There appears to be a rule of ethical adaptation in international business. Employees of multinational companies in competitive third-world countries often adapt to the ethical standards of the foreign country, even if those standards conflict with their personal ethics. This suggests that individuals may change their ethical stance depending on the situation and the people involved, complicating decision-making in business ethics.

Business ethics scandals reported in the media are predominantly domestic affairs. International incidents receive less attention, and public protests are generally stronger against cases that affect the community directly. Interest in business ethics often diminishes with geographical distance from the incident, indicating that proximity influences ethical reactions. Said differently, we react most strongly to ethical risks that directly affect us.

[6] Business Ethics, an applied field of study, is simply the application of Moral Philosophy to the problems of private organizations.

[7] For a critique concerning the potential negative effects of spying for negotiations, see e.g. Kober (1998).

[8] Söilen (2004).

[9] Ibid.

Corruption is a specific case of ethical risk and is often the rule rather than the exception in many non-Western countries. It is also prevalent in some Western countries, particularly in the Mediterranean region. From a company's rational perspective, it may make little difference whether money is paid as taxes or bribes, as both are seen as expenses that reduce profits.

Another example is the violation of free competition laws through the formation of business cartels where prices and market conditions are agreed upon among "competitors" to ensure the market's total value does not decline. Under names such as slush funds, rebates, and consulting fees, executives and managers often gain extra income. Larger companies operating abroad set aside funds for these expenses, later hiding them as project costs that are difficult for auditors to detect. These practices are almost standard in international business, more visible in some countries and organizations than others.

There has been considerable discussion in recent decades about whether private companies are becoming less ethical. The emergence of business ethics as a field of study reflects these discussions. The increase in perceived unethical business activities may be due to evolving values, greater insight, and an increased ability to react and be heard. Historical practices such as child labor were once common and accepted but are no longer so and for that we are all glad today.

The state intelligence apparatus is also used for political and economic means. Developing countries often fall prey to debt schemes orchestrated by Western nations, where intelligence services play a critical role, often from the beginning. The services can identify corrupt officials and politicians willing to accept substantial industrial loans in exchange for kickbacks. Once secured, these loans, backed by the IMF and World Bank, predominantly pay Western companies for infrastructure projects. The benefits of these projects are frequently exaggerated by expert economists. When these countries fail to meet their repayment obligations, they fall into a debt trap, making it easier for Western countries to influence their policies. It's what we call debt-trap diplomacy. No doubt, emerging Asian powers have been learning to adopt similar strategies.

This pattern are observed in various instances, such as the IMF's role in Argentina before the 2001 crisis, where substantial loans were provided to support an overvalued currency, leading to economic turmoil and eventual default. Similarly, the Belt and Road Initiative (BRI) by China has also been cited for creating debt dependencies through infrastructure projects funded by opaque loans with stringent conditions. Other examples in the past include US's business dealings in Chile under Pinochet, in Indonesia under Suharto, or in Iran during the Shah's regime. Or we simply go in and remove those in power without further ado. Notable incidents in the past include CIA operations for ITT in Chile and United Fruit Company in Guatemala. Western services have also been known to help remove democratically elected leaders, such as Mossadegh in Iran and Patrice Lumumba, the first Prime Minister of the Democratic Republic of the Congo. When Dag Hammarskjöld, the Secretary-General of the United Nations, went to the Congo to try to resolve the crisis, he was killed in a plane crash. These examples raise serious ethical questions about the use of state intelligence to assist private organizations, either directly or indirectly.

9.5.1 Industrial Espionage

Industrial espionage represents a clear ethical breach but has received relatively little interest from researchers.[10] In our previously discussed matrix, it corresponds to actions that are both illegal and unethical. Industrial espionage may be defined as any action taken by a second party to obtain strategic information about an organization through illegal and unethical means. From one perspective, it's also how developing countries with high ambitions compete in the global marketplace. As such, it can drive economic development and have positive effects on the attacker's entire economy.

The United States gained its industrial position in large part due to industrial espionage against Britain. Japan achieved its position through the efforts of its Chamber of Commerce, the Ministry of International Trade and Industry (MITI), and the Japan External Trade Organization (JETRO), established in 1958. China has taken this further by emphasizing joint ventures in their home country, a fast way of acquiring other countries' know-how. This was facilitated by Western countries' short-sighted focus on short-term profits and the advent and heavy adaptation of the Internet:

> The internet, the ultimate symbol of freedom and knowledge, has become the ultimate surveillance tool. We as citizens have accepted walking around with a mobile phone, which is the spy's dream tool. Can the internet be recreated in its former self, or was it naïve to think that the state would let it be uncontrolled? For companies, this means a more encrypted reality. [11]

The advent of easy-to-use, easy-to-buy technology for information gathering has raised new ethical questions. Legal limits apply to most national territories, but ethical limits vary by country, company culture, and personal ethics. Situational ethics complicate matters further, as people may allow certain practices in one context but not another.

The best way to learn about a competitor is often to hire one of their employees. Headhunting is not classified as industrial espionage as long as the employee changes jobs for reasons other than to spy. The labor market is free, and any company can make an offer to a competitor's employee. However, it is recognized that this method is used to gain access to the strategic information of competitors. An

[10] The first global expert on industrial espionage was Jacques Bergier (1912–1978), a Ukrainian-born chemical engineer whose family immigrated to France in the 1930s. Bergier wrote numerous books and article on industrial espionage, "L'espionage industriel" (1967), "La guerre scientific" (1970), "L'espionage scientific" (1971), "L'espionage strategique" (1973), "L'espionage politique" (1973).

[11] Söilen (2016a, p. 62).

employee may change jobs for a year or two and then return to their original company, or worse, never return but continue to deliver information to the competitor. Alternatively, you could hire an expert after they retire, offering them small consulting jobs with their new employer—a common way to supplement their pension. This approach is something the Chinese have notably mastered. The damage to the affected company can be significant: loss of trade secrets to competitors and eventually loss of market share.

Trade secrets can be anything from a favourite recipe in an Italian restaurant to Coca-Cola's closely guarded formula for its soft drink, which is kept in a high-security vault and known to only a few employees. Another example is the Google search algorithm, which remains a confidential and proprietary system that gives the company a significant competitive edge.

The CIA has addressed this problem for many years. Chinese, Korean, and even French companies have been known to send industrial spies to the U.S., and there are more examples from other attacked countries. Employing a competitor's employee is a delicate situation, even when the new employer has good intentions. It is tempting for the new employer to ask questions about the former employer's company. If the former employer finds out, which is often the case among multinationals, the damage can be severe.

As a result, many companies refrain from interrogating new employees, believing that it will backfire when they lose employees to competitors. Because of this, some companies have an unspoken policy of not interviewing employees who come from competitors, leaving it to the new employees to decide whether to share any information about their previous employer. This behavior is understandable for companies operating in markets dominated by a few large companies. A structured interrogation can lead to unnecessary tension and a spiral of distrust, hurting all companies involved and stigmatizing the industry.

Common ways to obtain information from an organization's employees include:

1. Phantom Interview: When the competitor poses as a potential employer.
2. False Flag Job Seeker: When a competitor's trusted employee, disguised as a potential job seeker, visits your company and asks questions. A false flag operation involves committing an act with the intention of disguising the actual source of responsibility and blaming another party.
3. Infiltration: Secretly penetrating an organization, group, or area to gather intelligence, disrupt operations, or influence actions from within. The infiltrator poses as a member of the target group to gain trust and access. When we blame another party, we call it False Flag.
4. Seduction: When an employee is flattered to encourage the disclosure of important information.

Estimates of financial losses due to industrial espionage vary, and the secret services themselves cannot be said to be neutral when they do their estimates as they stand to get larger budgets by exaggerating threats. Still, those are the figures we have. For example, the CIA and FBI think that these losses run into the hundreds of billions of dollars per year in the U.S. alone. It is certain that losses due to unfriendly attacks are significant in several business sectors that are more sensitive to espionage activities. The CIA's list of identified industries at risk includes:

- Materials
- Manufacturing
- Information and Communications
- Biotechnology and Life Sciences
- Transportation
- Energy and Environment

Strategies to prevent industrial espionage include A. Employee Training; regular training sessions on recognizing and handling espionage tactics can be crucial. B. Security Protocols: Implementing stringent security protocols and regular audits can help in early detection and prevention. C. Legal Action: Pursuing legal action against entities found guilty of industrial espionage to deter future incidents. D. Advanced Technology: Investing in advanced cybersecurity measures to protect against digital espionage. E. Confidentiality Agreements: Ensuring that all employees sign robust confidentiality agreements that are legally enforceable and F. Intelligence Gathering: Conducting counterintelligence activities to stay ahead of potential espionage threats.

In general, any company heavily involved in international business and in an industry where technology, rather than price, is the main competitive advantage should always take security and counterintelligence measures seriously. Companies that succeed best against industrial espionage are those able to maintain a low-security profile and not overplay the tension resulting from intelligence activities while installing an efficient business intelligence system. Unlike in military wars, there is no ceasefire in the competitive war.

9.6 The Role of Intelligence in Economic Warfare: The Evolution of Global Surveillance Systems

It has been suggested that we now live in "the age of surveillance capitalism".[12] Public life is, to a large extent, influenced by hacking, troll factories, fake news/propaganda, and interference in elections. Private life is in the same way much influenced by massive surveillance. The ethical questions related to these issues cannot be ignored in a free and open society.[13] Are we, as citizens, accepting to live in such a system, or is it that we don't fully understand the extent to which we are sacrificing our privacy and the degree to which nothing seems private anymore? On the other side of the table, the same data is the new gold for both private and state actors.

[12] Zuboff (2019).

[13] Söilen (2021b).

The study of modern economics began with questions of national competitive advantage.[14] Today, larger countries that can afford it are funding powerful data mining tools used for much the same purpose, for economic intelligence. The most competitive nations in the world gather information about corporations and private businesspeople to gain or sustain a competitive edge globally.

These systems are getting ever more sophisticated. Future systems of mass surveillance are expected to combine various databases, including driving records, tax filings, phone records, emails, and all websites visited, all in one system. These programs require cooperation between military, state, and private companies and have faced criticism from human rights organizations and civil liberty groups.

The largest of these systems is the ECHELON, a joint effort by Australia, Canada, New Zealand, the UK, and the USA to gather communication intelligence worldwide. The system monitors and intercepts telephone, email, fax, and telex communications, targeting primarily non-military organizations and individuals: foreign governments, businesses, and private citizens.

Numerous eavesdropping stations around the world tap into the international telecommunications network. Each member country can use the facilities of others, monitoring communications satellites, land-based networks, and radio communications. Computers search for preprogrammed keywords, much like a data mining system. The system features capabilities like:

- Global Reach: ECHELON taps into communication satellites, undersea cables, and other telecommunications infrastructure to gather vast amounts of data.
- Keyword Monitoring: The system uses keyword filters to search intercepted communications for terms of interest, which are then flagged for further analysis.
- Collaboration: The system benefits from the combined resources and expertise of the Five Eyes nations sharing intelligence to enhance collective security and surveillance capabilities.

ECHELON is designed to intercept and process electronic communications globally. It's forming the basis of the "Five Eyes" alliance, but at the same time it's also getting more ineffective.

End-to-end encryption has made the job of spy satellites much more difficult. Spy agencies have other ways of getting to your data, such as direct attacks on your devices (endpoints) and direct access to your personal data through requests for handing over your data from large data companies like Google, Facebook, and Microsoft through the CLOUD Act of 2018 and Section 702 of the Foreign Intelligence Surveillance Act (FISA).

Internal leaks, especially from New Zealand's Government Communications Security Bureau (GCSB), have revealed that the system's aim includes economic intelligence, particularly about countries who participated in GATT negotiations, later replaced by the World Trade Organization (WTO) negotiations. This has raised

[14] Smith (1776/1977).

moral questions, particularly in Europe, where it is believed the system has been used against allies, blurring the line between allies and enemies.

SIGINT is only one method states use to help their companies gain a competitive advantage globally. HUMINT is also widely employed in economic intelligence. States often hire senior executives to gather information about foreign companies and markets. These activities are typically legal and conducted by most industrialized countries. There are well-documented cases of Eastern European and Russian companies spying on Western businesses and of course the opposite occurs also. At the turn of the century, there used to be a clear line between corporate and state espionage. However, as nation-states increasingly hire private contracting firms not restricted by the same laws that govern data gathering on nationals, for example on satellite intelligence, this line has become blurred, raising numerous unresolved ethical and legal questions.

A European ECHELON has been in the planning for a long time but have not yet materialized. Instead, several European countries have developed their own significant surveillance capabilities and collaborate through various intelligence-sharing agreements. For example, the European Union Intelligence and Situation Centre (EU INTCEN) is a body that collects and analyzes intelligence from member states, focusing on external threats and security issues. Many European countries, including Germany (through the Bundesnachrichtendienst, BND), the United Kingdom (GCHQ), and others maintain robust SIGINT programs. For example, France operates a similar surveillance system, often referred to as "Frenchelon." Managed by the Directorate-General for External Security (DGSE), it focuses on signals intelligence (SIGINT) within and beyond France.

There are similar surveillance systems outside of Europe and the Five Eyes alliance too. Many countries have developed their own systems to gather and analyze electronic communications for intelligence purposes. Notable examples include Russia's System for Operative Investigative Activities (SORM) SORM (Система оперативно-розыскных мероприятий) is a comprehensive surveillance system that allows the Federal Security Service (FSB) to monitor telephone and internet communications.

In China there is the Golden Shield Project (also known as the Great Firewall) an extensive surveillance and censorship initiative by the Chinese government to monitor and control internet use within the country. The system combines hardware, software, and human resources to filter content, block access to certain websites, and monitor online activities of citizens. China also engages in global cyber-espionage efforts, targeting foreign governments and corporations to gather intelligence and intellectual property.

India has their Central Monitoring System (CMS) designed to intercept and monitor telecommunications and internet communications for national security and law enforcement purposes. The system allows government agencies to monitor phone calls, emails, and online activities. It is managed by the Centre for Development of Telematics (C-DOT). CMS provides direct access to communications data to several intelligence and law enforcement agencies without involving telecom operators.

Israel has Unit 8200 a highly specialized unit within the Israeli Defense Forces (IDF) responsible for SIGINT and cyber operations. The unit engages in electronic surveillance, cyber espionage, and decryption of intercepted communications. It plays a key role in gathering intelligence on regional threats and global cyber activities. Unit 8200 is known for its advanced technological capabilities and has been involved in numerous high-profile intelligence operations.

In Brazil, there is the Sistema Brasileiro de Inteligência (SISBIN), a national intelligence system that coordinates the activities of various intelligence agencies. The system integrates intelligence from multiple sources, including electronic surveillance, to address national security threats and crime. Managed by the Brazilian Intelligence Agency (ABIN), SISBIN aims to enhance the country's ability to gather and analyze intelligence across different sectors.

Many countries collaborate on intelligence gathering through formal alliances and informal agreements, sharing information and technological resources to enhance their surveillance capabilities.

9.7 Theft as a Way to Gain a Competitive Advantage

Countries engage in gathering economic intelligence to help their own companies gain a competitive advantage. This practice involves using various intelligence-gathering techniques to acquire valuable information that can aid domestic businesses in competing on a global scale. A few examples: China employs cyber-espionage, human intelligence (HUMINT), and other means to gather information on foreign companies. Techniques include hacking into corporate networks, infiltrating companies through personnel, and leveraging joint ventures to access proprietary technologies and trade secrets. Several high-profile cases have been reported where Chinese entities have been accused of stealing intellectual property from Western companies. For instance, the indictment of Chinese hackers in connection with the theft of sensitive information from aerospace firms and other technology companies.

From another perspective, corporate espionage can also be seen as a form of economic development. History shows that those who engage in these activities are often the scientifically and industrially weaker party, the party that is learning or trying to catch up. Britain became a superpower largely by copying the Dutch of the seventeenth century, their commercial shipping and trade routes. At the turn of the nineteenth century, the USA stole technology from Britain on how to build a textile industry.

In Putin's Russia, the Federal Security Service (FSB) and other state apparatuses have been involved in various activities that effectively 'steal' entire companies. For instance, in the early 2000s, the Russian oil company Yukos was dismantled by the state under the guise of tax evasion charges. Its assets were then redistributed to state-controlled companies, illustrating a modern example of how state apparatuses can appropriate private enterprises, a practice not uncommon in the history of economic development.

Another historical example is the British East India Company's seizure of Indian industries and resources during the colonial period, systematically dismantling local economies to benefit British interests. This practice, often referred to as "raiding" or "reiderstvo," in Russian involves a combination of legal and extralegal methods to take over businesses, typically targeting profitable or strategically important firms. Common techniques used in these operations include (Table 9.3):

What modern-day Russia has created is a systemic atmosphere of fear and paranoia where citizens even hide what they are looking at on their phones when on the

Table 9.3 Russia's current system of "reiderstvo"

#	Technique	Method	Explanation	Example
1.	Legal Maneuvering	Fabricated Lawsuits and Bankruptcy Proceedings	The FSB, often in collaboration with corrupt judges and officials, initiates bogus lawsuits against targeted companies. These lawsuits can lead to court orders freezing assets, appointing receivers, or declaring the companies bankrupt. Through manipulated bankruptcy proceedings, the ownership of the companies can be transferred to state-friendly entities or individuals.	The Yukos Oil Company case, where legal and financial pressures led to the dismantling and acquisition of the company by state-owned Rosneft.
2.	Intimidation and Coercion	Threats and Arrests	Company owners and executives are frequently subjected to threats, arbitrary arrests, and criminal charges. The FSB leverages its power to intimidate individuals into relinquishing their control over their companies.	The case of William Browder and Hermitage Capital, where Browder's lawyer, Sergei Magnitsky, was arrested and died in custody after uncovering a massive tax fraud scheme involving Russian officials.
3.	Hostile Takeovers Using Force	Hostile Takeovers Using Force	Armed men, sometimes posing as private security, physically take over company offices and facilities. This tactic is often backed by forged documents that claim a change in ownership.	Numerous reports of armed takeovers in various sectors, including agriculture and manufacturing, where businesses are forcibly seized and handed over to new owners with state backing.

(continued)

Table 9.3 (continued)

#	Technique	Method	Explanation	Example
4.	Administrative Pressure	Inspections and Regulatory Pressure	Regulatory bodies are used to conduct frequent and disruptive inspections, impose fines, or revoke licenses, crippling the targeted businesses and forcing them to sell at a low price.	The use of health, safety, tax, and environmental inspectors to harass companies into submission.
5.	Media and Public Opinion	Media Campaigns and Defamation	State-controlled media is used to launch smear campaigns against business owners, accusing them of fraud, corruption, or other crimes. This tarnishes their reputation, making it easier to justify legal and extralegal actions against them.	The vilification of Mikhail Khodorkovsky, former head of Yukos, who was portrayed as a corrupt oligarch in state media before his arrest and the subsequent breakup of his company.
6.	Politically Motivated Seizures	Nationalization Under Pretext of National Security	The state justifies the seizure of companies by claiming national security concerns or strategic importance, effectively nationalizing private assets.	The nationalization of assets in the oil and gas industry, where private firms were taken over to ensure state control over energy resources.

metro system, afraid that someone will take a photo of them and report it. You cannot trust anyone outside of your own circles.

In the United States, there are mechanisms in place where companies can request assistance and coordination with intelligence agencies, including the NSA, for business-related intelligence. Primary channels through which such coordination occurs:

1. National Security Council (NSC) and the Economic Intelligence Support: The NSC plays a role in coordinating intelligence activities related to economic security. It facilitates the sharing of intelligence relevant to U.S. economic interests and national security, often involving input from multiple intelligence agencies, including the NSA.
2. Office of the Director of National Intelligence (ODNI): The ODNI coordinates intelligence efforts across the 18 elements of the U.S. Intelligence Community (IC). The National Intelligence Manager for Economic Security within the ODNI oversees economic intelligence and ensures it supports U.S. business interests.
3. Department of Justice (DOJ): Within the DOJ, the National Security Division (NSD) handles issues related to economic espionage and intellectual property theft. It works closely with companies to address threats and coordinate with intelligence agencies for necessary support.

4. Department of Commerce: The International Trade Administration (ITA) within the Department of Commerce offers support to U.S. companies in international markets. While it does not directly coordinate intelligence requests, it works in conjunction with other agencies to support U.S. businesses.
5. Federal Bureau of Investigation (FBI): The FBI has programs dedicated to protecting U.S. companies from economic espionage. The Counterintelligence Division works to safeguard U.S. intellectual property and critical infrastructure, often collaborating with other intelligence agencies.
6. Defense Industrial Base (DIB) Cybersecurity Program: This program, led by the Department of Defense (DoD), provides threat information to defense contractors to protect against cyber threats, including those involving economic intelligence.

While there seems to be no direct office within the NSA specifically for coordinating business intelligence requests, the NSA's work often intersects with other agencies and departments that liaise with the private sector. For example, the NSA's Cybersecurity Directorate collaborates with businesses to protect against cyber threats.

So Economic intelligence gathering by state actors to support domestic businesses is a widespread practice. Countries like China, Russia, the United States, and France use various intelligence-gathering techniques to acquire valuable information which may give their companies a competitive edge in the global marketplace. Other, mostly smaller countries with limited resources are not unfamiliar with these same practices but have more modest capabilities. This practice, though often controversial and sometimes illegal, highlights the significant role of intelligence services in maintaining economic and industrial competitiveness.

For the very last section of the book, we have saved a theory that attempts to explain how organizations reduce risk by delegating actions and behaviour that may be criticized for being unethical by a counterparty or a domestic or foreign government or government body.

9.8 Diversification of Moral Risk Model (DMRM)

Ethical problems studied within economics are sometimes presented from a bargaining or Principal-Agent Model (PAM) perspective.[15] We can use PAM, which we have presented in much detail earlier in the book, and some basic notions from financial economics to present a model showing how moral risk may be reduced or diversified:

[15] See Söilen (2004, pp. 85–86). Moralisches Risiko durch einen unmoralischen "Principal". The idea of the Diversification of Moral Risk Model (DMRM) was first introduced in an unpublished paper for a course on game theory at the University of Oslo. See Søilen (1993).

Within a company, a manager offers a subordinate or agent a contract to do part of a job that contains a moral dilemma. If the agent wants to keep the task, he can perform the action himself. Alternatively, he can diversify the risk by engaging another agent. In this new situation, the first agent becomes the principal. This new agent, in turn, faces the same choices, and so on. In no way can the new agent trace the decision back to the original principal, as he only knows his immediate principal. The more levels of delegation in the model, the more difficult it becomes to identify the person responsible for the initial order. If an agent refuses, the principal can always ask someone else or sanction the agent.

The model was conceived on the basis of how some oil companies work in developing countries in the 1990s.

Diversification to agents outside of one's own organisation reduces the risk exponentially, as it becomes much more difficult to trace. We may define this as a diversification of the second order.

The major question then becomes: When will the action be performed, i.e., after how many levels of delegation? This will depend on the nature of the moral dilemma. The larger the moral dilemma, the more levels. The problem can be modelled as follows (Fig. 9.4):

Where,

- P = Principal
- A = Agent

P = The point where the Principal decides whether to bear the moral risk himself or to diversify it. If he decides to diversify, he has to decide how much he wants to transfer. The circles are the end nodes. Each end node is equivalent to a specific

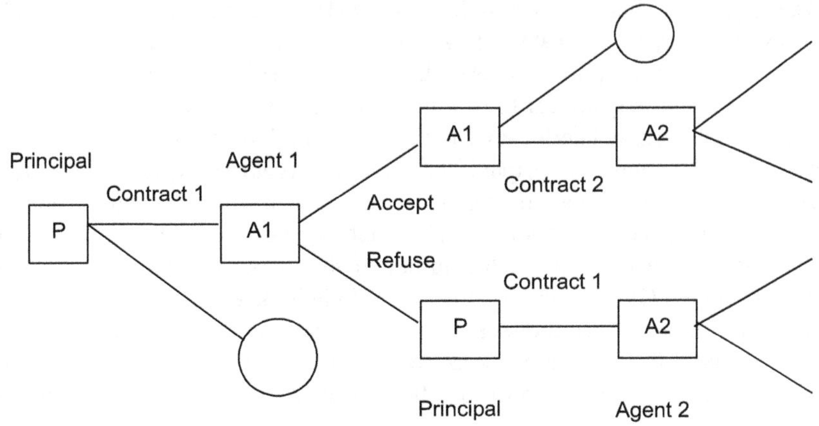

Fig. 9.4 Diversification of moral risk model (DMRM)

quantity of risk, which may even be defined by the expected financial penalty or its expected financial consequences. The more actors involved, the lower the risk.

A1 = The contract goes to the first Agent, who can accept or refuse it. If A1 accepts the contract, he will, in turn, make the same decision as the principal: whether to perform the action, how much risk to take on himself, and how much to diversify.

A2 = If A1 refuses, P can give a contract to another agent, A2, who will then accept or reject, etc.

Equation 9.1 Algebraic representation of the model for the diversification of moral risk.

$$R = \sum_{n}^{i=1} r_{A_i,\text{accept}} + r_P$$

Where:

- R is the total moral risk.
- r_P is the risk retained by the principal.
- $r_{A_i,\text{accept}}$ is the portion of risk accepted by each agent A_i.
- n is the number of agents involved in the diversification process.

The formula shows that the total moral risk R is the sum of the risks accepted by each agent and the principal.

The theory continues to find support empirically in discoveries reported by the media. In 2004, SAAB Aerospace in Sweden used British BAE (A1), who again used a local agent (A2) to bribe politicians in the Czech Republic to persuade their national government to accept the hire of 14 SAAB Jas 39 Gripen air fighters.

From other research we know that an agent will gladly lie about his product's quality (Akerlof, 1970), that the agent will lie about his firm's output (Diamond, 1984), the value of shares (Myers & Majluf, 1984), about his proneness when about to be insured (Rasmusen, 1989), or as someone who "tries to shirk and steal by excessive perk consumption" (Jensen & Meckling, 1976). Dasgupta (1988) suggests that an agent may appear to be ethical because he is investing in a reputation for trust (which he may later destroy for some future, larger gain).

Brennan (1994) emphasizes that if the Principal-Agent Model (PAM) is taught as a theory where the Principal and Agent are primarily trying to outsmart each other without any ethical considerations, it may eventually become a self-fulfilling prophecy. This is not the intention of the author of this book in presenting the above-mentioned model. On the contrary, the aim is to help detect and describe unethical schemes, not to encourage them. Similarly, the purpose of writing this book is to enable companies and organizations to improve their intelligence function to strengthen their competitive position, but not at the expense of the well-being of others.

This approach is consistent with the principles laid out by Stevan Dedijer, who referred to this discipline as "Social Intelligence," meaning that the intelligence function should be taught for the benefit of all mankind and, more broadly, as an integrated part of the social sciences. Only then can it aspire to become a science and gain its rightful place at our universities.

The Intelligence Ecosystem 10

After having read the previous nine chapters, the question remains: how do we make it all work? A short answer is that it involves integrating analytical abilities with the best organizational models, forming a diverse intelligence team, and adhering to ethical considerations. This is part of the challenge of what we understand as the Intelligence Ecosystem.

The Intelligence Ecosystem is a dynamic and interconnected network of various entities, processes, and technologies involved in collecting, analyzing, disseminating, and applying information to support decision-making. It encompasses a wide range of participants, from individual intelligence analysts to large organizations, each contributing to and benefiting from the flow of information. It binds together different kinds of organizations, processes, technologies, information sources, and an all-important ethical and legal framework—what some may understand as the industry or community (Table 10.1).

By its very nature, this discipline is interdisciplinary, built around the concept of competitive advantage among nations, which has been central to the study of economics since its inception.To make the Intelligence Ecosystem work, we need to build interdisciplinary teams where each member is an expert in their field. These fields include sociology, economics, political science, and computer science. This diversity will enable comprehensive analysis and varied perspectives. We must foster a continuous learning culture and adaptation to new technologies and methods. Regular training and professional development will keep the team updated on the latest trends and techniques.

In a business, fostering collaboration between different departments is crucial. Regular meetings, shared databases, and collaborative tools should be used to ensure seamless communication. Additionally, promoting collaboration between different organizations and sectors to share best practices and intelligence is essential. This can be achieved through industry conferences, joint ventures, and strategic alliances.

K. Solberg Söilen, *Intelligence Studies in Business*, Management for Professionals,
https://doi.org/10.1007/978-3-031-76491-2_10

Table 10.1 Key components of the Intelligence Ecosystem

#	Component	Activity	Examples
1.	Entities	Organizations	Intelligence agencies, private companies, NGOs, academic institutions.
		Individuals	Analysts, researchers, decision-makers
2	Processes	Collection	Gathering data from various sources including open-source intelligence (OSINT), human intelligence (HUMINT), signals intelligence (SIGINT), and more.
		Analysis	Employing analytical techniques to make sense of the data, such as trend analysis, sentiment analysis, and predictive modeling.
		Dissemination	Sharing the analyzed information with relevant stakeholders in an understandable and actionable format.
		Application	Using the intelligence to inform decision-making, strategic planning, and operational tactics.
3	Technologies	Data Mining Tools	Software and algorithms to sift through large datasets to find relevant information.
		Analytical Tools	Statistical software, machine learning models, and artificial intelligence to analyze data.
		Communication Tools	Platforms to securely share intelligence reports and findings.
4	Information Sources	Primary Sources	Direct information from interviews, surveys, and field reports
		Secondary Sources	Information from books, articles, and reports
		Tertiary Sources	Aggregated data from databases and encyclopedias
5	Ethical and Legal Framework	Ethics	Adhering to ethical standards such as honesty, integrity, and respect for privacy.
		Legal Compliance	Ensuring all intelligence activities comply with relevant laws and regulations.

Optimal technological integration at each level is necessary. This includes developing and utilizing sophisticated algorithms to prioritize and filter information based on contextual relevance and specific needs. Leveraging AI to assist in making decisions by highlighting the most relevant information and providing actionable insights is also important. All of this needs to be done with user-centric design in mind. We want to create interfaces and tools that allow users to customize the information flow according to their specific requirements and preferences, reducing cognitive load.

To create a sound culture, we need to establish clear ethical guidelines and ensure that all team members are trained to adhere to them. Regularly updating these guidelines to reflect changes in laws and societal expectations is essential. To the degree possible, maintaining transparency in intelligence activities is crucial. Ensuring stakeholders know the methods and sources used will help build trust. We need to ensure that all intelligence activities comply with relevant laws and regulations. Regular audits and legal consultations can help in maintaining compliance. Implementing robust data privacy measures to protect the information of individuals and organizations involved is also necessary.

The Internet has the potential to be a powerful source of knowledge and communication for everyone. However, issues like mass surveillance and data manipulation need to be addressed. First, implementing robust encryption can help ensure data privacy. Second, returning control of personal data to users, rather than private companies, could shift the business model away from "free" services towards more subscription-based products. Lastly, addressing the dominance of large tech companies by properly taxing and potentially breaking up monopolies could foster a more competitive and fair digital landscape.[1] We must address these ethical questions if Intelligence activities are to maintain legitimacy among the public and be taught at our universities.

In conclusion, the Intelligence Ecosystem is a comprehensive framework that integrates various components to support effective decision-making. By understanding and leveraging the interconnected nature of these components, organizations can enhance their intelligence capabilities, making informed decisions while maintaining ethical and legal standards. The discipline of intelligence studies—or any similar label—prioritizes practical application above tribal affiliations, academic prestige, or ivory tower snobbery. Its primary focus remains on what effectively contributes to gaining and maintaining the competitive advantage of nations. In our view, the intelligence approach remains the most convincing strategy for how any organization, regardless of size or level, can achieve this goal. It is in this practicality and effectiveness that its true value lies. Its foundation is firmly rooted in the scientific method and, as I have attempted to demonstrate in this book, can be supported by one of the most robust frameworks in all of science: evolutionary theory.

[1] Söilen (2021b).

References

Agostino, A., Söilen, K. S., & Gerritsen, B. (2013). Cloud solution in Business Intelligence for SMEs–vendor and customer perspectives. *Journal of Intelligence Studies in Business, 3*(3), 5–28.

Agrell, W. (1998). *Konsten att gissa rätt*. Studentlitteratur.

Akerlof, G. A. (1970). The market for "lemons": Quality uncertainty and the market mechanism. *The Quarterly Journal of Economics, 84*(3), 488–500. https://doi.org/10.2307/1879431

Albaum, G. S. (1962). *A new approach to the information function in marketing*. Department of Commerce, University of Wisconsin.

Alden, B. H. (1959). *Competitive intelligence*. C. I. Associates. (Original work published by University of Minnesota; Digitized January 24, 2018, by Harvard University Graduate School of Business Administration).

Amara, Y., Solberg Söilen, K., & Vriens, D. J. (2012). Using the SSAV model to evaluate Business Intelligence Software. *Journal of Intelligence Studies in Business, 2*(3), 29–40.

American Psychological Association. (1994). *American Psychological Association Publication manual*. American Psychological Association.

Amzile, K., Beraich, M., Amouri, I., & Malainine, C. (2022). Towards a digital enterprise: The impact of Artificial Intelligence on the hiring process. *Journal of Intelligence Studies in Business, 12*(3), 18–26.

Anderbjörk, G., & Martell, J. E. (2021). *Gardens of intelligence*. Technics Publications.

Ansoff, H. I. (1984). *Implanting strategic management*. Prentice Hall International.

Ashton, W. B., & Klavans, R. A. (1997). *Keeping abreast of science and technology*. Battelle Press.

Asimov, I. (1980). *Book of facts*. Grosset & Dunlap.

Bensoussan, B. E., & Fleisher, C. S. (2013). *Analysis without paralysis: 12 tools to make better strategic decisions*. Pearson Education, Inc.

Bisson, C., Giron, A., & Verin, G. (2023). A comparative analysis with machine learning of public data governance and AI policies in the European Union, United States, and China. *Journal of Intelligence Studies in Business, 13*(2), 61–74. Open Access: Freely available at http://jisib.com

Björk, U. (1997). *Omvärldsanalys och framtidsstudier hos statliga myndigheter*. Report. Forskningspolitiska institutet.

Borg, L., & Rossander, O. (Eds.). (1996). *Omvärldsbevakning och konkurrenskraft*. FOA and SAF.

Borg, L., Hamrefors, S., Nicander, L., Nilsson, L.-L., & Wormuth, D. W. (Eds.). (1998). *Omvärldsbevakning för en ny tid*. SAF.

Bostrom, N., & Cirkovic, M. M. (Eds.). (2011). *Global catastrophic risks*. Oxford University Press.

Brealey, R. A., & Myers, S. C. (1981/2000). *Principles of corporate finance*. Irwin-McGraw Hill.

Brennan, M. J. (1994). Incentives, rationality, and society. *Journal of Applied Corporate Finance, 7*(2), 31–39. https://doi.org/10.1111/j.1745-6622.1994.tb00403.x

Brown, J. S., & Duguid, P. (2000). *The social life of information*. Harvard Business School Press.

Burwell, H. P. (1999). *Online CI*. Facts on Demand Press.

K. Solberg Söilen, *Intelligence Studies in Business*, Management for Professionals,
https://doi.org/10.1007/978-3-031-76491-2

Calof, J., Söilen, K. S., Klavans, R., Abdulkader, B., & El Moudni, I. (2022). Understanding the structure, characteristics, and future of collective intelligence using local and global bibliometric analyses. *Technological Forecasting and Social Change, 178*, 121561.

Canongia, C. L. (2007). Synergy between competitive intelligence (CI), knowledge management (KM) and technological foresight (TF) as a strategic model of prospecting—The use of biotechnology in the development of drugs against breast cancer. *Biotechnology Advances, 25*(1), 57–74.

Chaliand, G. (Ed.). (1982). *Guerrilla strategies*. University of California Press.

Chandler, A. D. (1962). *Strategy and structure*. MIT Press.

Chandler, D. G. (1966). *The campaigns of Napoleon*. MacMillan Company.

Chopra, S., & Meindl, P. (2016). *Supply chain management: Strategy, planning, and operation*. Pearson.

Comai, A. (2018). Beyond patent analytics: Insights from a scientific and technological data mashup based on a case example. *World Patent Information, 55*, 61–77.

Cook, M., & Cook, C. W. (2000). *Competitive intelligence: Create an intelligent organization and compete to win*. Kogan Page.

Dasgupta, P. (1988). Trust as a commodity. In D. Gambetta (Ed.), *Trust: Making and breaking cooperative relations* (pp. 49–72). Basil Blackwell.

De Ville, B. (2001). *Microsoft data mining: Integrated business intelligence for e-Commerce & knowledge*. Butterworth-Heinemann.

Dedijer, S. (1998). Competitive intelligence in Sweden. *Competitive Intelligence Review, 9*(1), 66–68.

Dedijer, S., & Jéquier, N. (Eds.). (1987). *Intelligence for economic development*. Berg.

Delmar, R., & Hancock, M. (2001). *Data mining explained*. Digital Press.

Diamond, D. W. (1984). Financial intermediation and delegated monitoring. *The Review of Economic Studies, 51*(3), 393–414. https://doi.org/10.2307/2297430

Drucker, P. F. (1956). *Managing the educated* (D. H. Fenn, Ed.).

Drucker, P. F. (1985). *Innovation and entrepreneurship: Practice and principles*. Harper & Row.

Dutka, A. (1999). *Competitive intelligence for the competitive edge*. NTC Business Books.

Dylewski, P. (2023). *Offensive intelligence: 300 techniques, tools and tips to know everything about everyone, in business and elsewhere* (Paperback). ISBN: 979-10-96819-26-3.

Ebbinghaus, H.-D., Flum, J., & Thomas, W. (1978/1996). *Mathematical logic*. Springer.

Eells, R., & Nehemkis, P. (1984). *Corporate intelligence and espionage*. MacMillian Publishers Company.

Fahey, L. (1999). *Competitors*. Wiley.

Fahey, L. (2007). Connecting strategy and competitive intelligence: Refocusing intelligence to produce critical strategy inputs. *Strategy & Leadership, 35*(1), 4–12. https://doi.org/10.1108/10878570710717236

Fialka, J. J. (1997). *War by other means*. W. W. Norton.

Fleisher, C. S., & Bensoussan, B. (2002). *Strategic and competitive analysis: Methods and techniques for analyzing business competition*. Prentice Hall.

Fleisher, C. S., & Blenkhorn, D. L. (2001). *Managing frontiers in competitive intelligence*. Quorum Books.

Förster, A. (1997). *Maulwürfe in Nadelstreifen, Wirtschaftsspionage – der neue Job der Geheimdienste*. Henschel Verlag.

Frankelius, P. (2001). *Omvärldsanalys*. Liber Ekonomi.

Frankelius, P., & Rosén, B. (1993). *Konkurrensanalys och omvärldsanalys: Praktikfall från Sverige*. Liber-Hermods.

Fredriksson, C., Sandberg, M., & Sandén, P. (1999). *Omvärldsanalys för Tierps kommun*. Report. SKB.

Freyn, S., & Hoffman, F. (2022). Competitive intelligence in an AI world: Practitioners' thoughts on technological advances and the educational needs of their successors. *Journal of Intelligence Studies in Business, 12*(3), 6–17.

Fuld, L. M. (1994). *The new competitor intelligence: The complete resource for finding, analyzing, and using information about your competitors*. Wiley.

Furustig, H., & Sjöstedt, G. (2000). *Strategisk omvärldsanalys*. Studentlitteratur.

Gilad, B., & Gilad, T. (1988). *The business intelligence system: A new tool for competitive advantage*. Amacom, American Management Association.

Gilad, B., & Herring, J. (Eds.). (1996). *Advances in applied business strategy: Part A: Business intelligence theory, principles, practices & uses*. JAI Press.

Gordon, I. H. (2001). *Competitor targeting: Winning the battle for market and customer share*. Wiley.

Gray, L. H. (1939). *Foundations of language*. The Macmillian Company.

Grönroos, C. (1990). *Service management and marketing: Managing the moments of truth in service competition*. Lexington Books.

Gummesson, E. (1997). Relationship marketing as a paradigm shift: Some conclusions from the 30R approach. *Management Decision, 35*(4), 267–272.

Gummesson, E. (2011). *Total relationship marketing*. Routledge.

Halliman, C. (2001). *Business intelligence using smart techniques: Environmental scanning using text mining and competitor analysis using scenarios and manual simulation*. Information Uncover.

Hamrefors, S. (1998). Spontaneous environmental scanning. *Competitive Intelligence Review, 9*(3), 68–75.

Hamrefors, S. (2002). *Kommunikativt ledarskap: Hur ledare skapar mening genom dialog*. Liber.

Haynes, A. (2001). *The Elizabethan secret services*. Sutton Publishing.

Hedin, H. (1993). Business intelligence: Systematised intelligence activities in 10 multinational companies. *Journal of AGSI, 2*(4), 126–136.

Hedin, H., & Sadström, B. (2006). *Företagets omvärldsradar*. Studentlitteratur.

Herman, M. (1996). *Intelligence power in peace and war*. Cambridge University Press.

Höhne, H. (1998). *Der Krieg im Dunkeln*. Bechtermünz Verlag.

Hoppe, M. (2015). Intelligence as a discipline, not just a practice. *Journal of Intelligence Studies in Business, 5*(3), 47–54.

Hugos, M. (2018). *Essentials of supply chain management*. Wiley.

Hussey, D., & Jenster, P. (1999). *Competitor intelligence*. Wiley.

Ikeya, N. (2001). The Japanese intelligence culture. *Competitive Intelligence Review, 12*(4), 51–56.

Jensen, M. C., & Meckling, W. H. (1976). Theory of the firm: Managerial behavior, agency costs and ownership structure. *Journal of Financial Economics, 3*(4), 305–360. https://doi.org/10.1016/0304-405X(76)90026-X

Jenster, P. V., & Söilen, K. S. (2009). *Market intelligence: Building strategic insight*. Copenhagen Business School Press DK.

Jevons, W. S. (1919). *The elements of logic*. T. C. & E. C. Jack Ltd. and T. Nelson & Sons.

Jönsson, C., Tagil, S., & Törnquist, G. (2000). *Organizing European space*. Sage.

Kahaner, L. (1996/1997). *Competitive intelligence*. Touchstone.

Kidder, J. (2022). *Talent mapping: A recruiter's guide to competitive talent intelligence* (Paperback). Independently published. ASIN: B0BMT438CK.

Knight, F. H. (1971). *Risk, uncertainty, and profit*. Chicago University Press.

Knütter, H.-H., & Winkler, S. (Eds.). (2000). *Der Verfassungsschutz*. Universitas.

Kober, S. (1998). Why spy? The uses and misuses of intelligence. *USA Today, 126*(2634), 10.

Krieger, W. (Ed.). (2003). *Geheimdienste in der Weltgeschichte. Spionage und verdeckte Aktionen von der Antike bis zur Gegenwart*. C. H. Beck.

Krizan, L. (1999). *Intelligence essentials for everyone*. Government Printing Office.

Lekvall, P., & Wahlin, C. (2001). *Information för marknadsföringsbeslut*. IHM.

Liautaud, B. (2000). *E-Business intelligence: Turning information into knowledge into profit*. McGraw-Hill Education Group.

Liebowitz, J. (2006). *Strategic intelligence: Business intelligence, competitive intelligence, and knowledge management*. Auerbach Publications.

Loury, G., & Le Bihan, J. (1993). *Génèse de l'Europe Unifiée Dans le Nouveau Monde du XXIè Siècle*. Compendium. HEC.

Lundqvist, M. (2010). The intelligence advantage: Organizing for success in business intelligence. *BI Research Journal, 3*(1), 45–60.

Machiavelli, N. (1513/1935). *The prince*. Oxford University Press.

Machlup, F. (1962). *The production and distribution of knowledge*. Princeton University Press.

Machlup, F. (1981). *Knowledge and knowledge production*. Princeton University Press.

Madureira, L., Popovič, A., & Castelli, M. (2023). Competitive intelligence maturity models: Systematic review, unified model and implementation frameworks. *Journal of Intelligence Studies in Business, 13*(1), 6–29.

Malik, F. (1984). *Strategie des Managements komplexer Systeme*. Verlag Paul Haupt.

Matheny, J. G. (2007). Reducing the risk of human extinction. *Risk Analysis, 27*(5), 1335–1344. https://doi.org/10.1111/j.1539-6924.2007.00960.x

McGonagle, J. J., & Vella, C. M. (1999). *The Internet age of competitive intelligence*. Quorum.

Michaelson, G. A. (2001). *The art of war for managers: 50 strategic rules*. Adams Media Corporation.

Miller, J. P. (2000). *Millennium intelligence: Understanding & conducting competitive intelligence in the digital age*. Information Today, Incorporated.

Munoz, J. M. (Ed.). (2018). *Global business intelligence* (Vol. 711). Routledge.

Myers, S. C., & Majluf, N. S. (1984). Corporate financing and investment decisions when firms have information that investors do not have. *Journal of Financial Economics, 13*(2), 187–221. https://doi.org/10.1016/0304-405X(84)90023-0

Naylor, E. (2016). *Win/loss analysis: How to capture and keep the business you want*. Park Hill Press.

Neef, D., Siesfeld, A. G., & Cefola, J. (Eds.). (1998). *The economic impact of knowledge*. Butterworth-Heinemann.

Nolan, J. A. (1995). Counterintelligence, on the other hand. *Competitive Intelligence Review, 6*(1), 49–56.

Nuortimo, K. (2023). Bigdata-based university reputation measurement. Towards conceptualizing AI-based university reputation score (URS). *Journal of Intelligence Studies in Business, 13*(3), 6–23.

Nyblom, A., Söilen, K. S., & Hasslinger, A. (2012). Competitive intelligence: The case of Swedish bioenergy companies. *Journal of Intelligence Studies in Business, 2*(1), 5–20.

Ó Tuathail, G. (1999). Understanding critical geopolitics: Geopolitics and risk society. In C. S. Gray & G. Sloan (Eds.), *Geopolitics, geography and strategy* (pp. 166–178). Frank Cass.

Oubrich, M., Hakmaoui, A., Benhayoun, L., Söilen, K. S., & Abdulkader, B. (2021). Impacts of leadership style, organizational design and HRM practices on knowledge hiding: The indirect roles of organizational justice and competitive work environment. *Journal of Business Research, 137*, 488–499.

Oxelheim, L. (1998). *Business intelligence for increased competitiveness: The economic side* (Working paper). Lund.

Pagels-Fick, G. (1999). *Business intelligence: om organisation, metod och tillämpning*. Industrilitteratur and BUSAD.

Pincher, C. (1991). *The truth about dirty tricks*. Sidgwick & Jackson.

Platt, W. (1957). *Strategic intelligence production*. F. A. Praeger.

Pollard, A. (1999). *Competitor intelligence*. Financial Times/Pitman Publishing.

Porat, M. U., & Rubin, M. R. (1977). *The information economy* (No. 77). Department of Commerce, Office of Telecommunications.

Porter, M. E. (1980). *Competitive strategy: Techniques for analyzing industries and competitors*. The Free Press.

Prescott, J. E. (1989). *Advances in competitive intelligence*. SCIP.

Prescott, J. E. (1993). *Global perspectives on competitive intelligence*. Society of Competitive Intelligence Professionals.

Prescott, J. E., & Miller, S. H. (Eds.). (2001). *Proven strategies in competitive intelligence*. Wiley.

Rasmusen, E. (1989). *Games and information*. Blackwell.
Rasmussen, N., et al. (2002). *Financial business intelligence*. Wiley.
Richelson, J. T. (1995). *A century of spies*. Oxford University Press.
Richelson, J. T. (1999). *The U.S. intelligence community*. Westview Press.
Ripa, K. J. (2004). In T. A. Brown (Ed.), *Business security* (pp. 36–50). Crary Publications.
Roberts, D. P. (2004). In T. A. Brown (Ed.), *Business security* (pp. 11–25). Crary Publications.
Rosen, R. (1985). Anticipatory systems. In *Anticipatory systems: Philosophical, mathematical, and methodological foundations* (pp. 313–370). Springer.
Ross, J. B., & McLaughlin, M. M. (Eds.). (1977). *The portable Renaissance reader* (pp. 218–224). Penguin.
Rossander, O., & Borg, L. (Eds.). (1996). *Omvärldsbevakning och konkurrenskraft*. FOA and SAF.
Russell, B. (1903). *The principles of mathematics*. Cambridge University Press.
Rustmann, F. W. (2002). *CIA, Inc.: Espionage & the craft of business intelligence*. Brassey's, Incorporated.
Sabanovic, A., & Söilen, K. S. (2012a). Customers' expectations and needs in the Business Intelligence Software market. *Journal of Intelligence Studies in Business, 2*(1), 5–20.
Sabanovic, A., & Söilen, K. S. (2012b). Factors shaping vendor differentiation in the Business Intelligence Software industry. *Journal of Intelligence Studies in Business, 2*(3), 48–54.
Sandström, B. (1988). *Business intelligence*. Liber.
Sanger, D. E., & Weiner, T. (1995, October 15). Emerging role for the CIA: Economic spy. *New York Times*, 12.
Schauenberg, B. (2000). Korruption als Ordnungs- und als Organisationsproblem. In B. Külp & V. Vanberg (Eds.), *Freiheit und wettbewerbliche Ordnung*. Haufe Verlagsgruppe.
Schmid, G. (2001). *Commission final report on ECHELON*. Report by the Temporary Committee on the ECHELON. The European Parliament. 2001/2098 (INI).
Schmitt, C. (1932/1998). *Legalität und Legitimität*. Duncker & Humblot.
Schmitt, C. (1950/1997). *Der Nomos Der Erde*. Duncker & Humblot.
Schweitzer, J. A. (1996). *Protecting business information—A manager's guide*. Butterworth-Heinemann.
SCIP. (1996). Code of ethics. *Competitive Intelligence Review, 7*(3), Fall.
Shapiro, C., & Varian, H. (1998). *Information rules – A strategic guide to the network economy*. Harvard Business School Press.
Sharda, R., Delen, D., & Turban, E. (2018). *Business intelligence, analytics, and data science: A managerial perspective*. Pearson.
Simon, N. (1999). Managing the CI department – The learning organization. *Competitive Intelligence Review, 2*(2), 40–42.
Smith, A. (1776/1977). *The wealth of nations*. Penguin Books.
Søilen, K. S. (1993). *An introductory analysis of the theory of probability option pricing*. Blekinge Institute of Technology. Retrieved from https://urn.kb.se/resolve?urn=urn:nbn:se:bth-9322
Söilen, K. S. (2004). *Wirtschaftsspionage in Verhandlungen aus Informationsökonomischer und Wirtschaftsetischer Perspektive: Eine Interdisziplinäre Analyse* (Doctoral dissertation). Blekinge Tekniska Högskola.
Söilen, K. S. (2010a). Management implementation of business intelligence systems/Gestion de la implementacion de sistemas de intelligencia de negocios. *Inteligencia y Seguridad, 9*, 46–67.
Söilen, K. S. (2010b). *The shift from Geopolitics to Geoeconomics and the failure of our modern Social Sciences*. The Telos Institute.
Söilen, K. S. (2012). *Geoeconomics*. Bookboon.
Söilen, K. S. (2013). *Exhibit marketing and trade show intelligence: Successful boothmanship and booth design*. Springer Science & Business Media.
Söilen, K. S. (2015). A place for intelligence studies as a scientific discipline. *Journal of Intelligence Studies in Business, 5*(3), 35–46.
Söilen, K. S. (2016a). Economic and industrial espionage at the start of the 21st century – Status quaestionis. *Journal of Intelligence Studies in Business, 6*(3), 51–64.

Söilen, K. S. (2016b). A research agenda for intelligence studies in business. *Journal of Intelligence Studies in Business, 6*(1), 21–36.

Söilen, K. S. (2017a). Why care about competitive intelligence and market intelligence? The case of Ericsson and the Swedish Cellulose Company. *Journal of Intelligence Studies in Business, 7*(2), 27–39.

Söilen, K. S. (2017b). Why the social sciences should be based in evolutionary theory: The example of geoeconomics and intelligence studies. *Journal of Intelligence Studies in Business, 7*(1), 5–37.

Söilen, K. S. (2018). Why you should be interested in intelligence studies. *Journal of Intelligence Studies in Business, 8*(3).

Söilen, K. S. (2019). A deeper look at the collective intelligence phenomenon. *Journal of Intelligence Studies in Business, 9*(2), 4–5.

Söilen, K. S. (2021a). The golden age of cyberpiracy: Industrial espionage against the biggest Swedish companies today. *IMCI Magazine*, 59–62. Retrieved from https://img1.wsimg.com/blobby/go/437ab14c-24c9-4fac-a05b-0fb8eae281e4/downloads/IMCI%20July%20Aug%202021.pdf

Söilen, K. S. (2021b). The internet is leading the world towards forms of totalitarianism: How to fix the problem. *Journal of Intelligence Studies in Business, 11*(1), 4–5.

Söilen, K. S. (2021c). Intelligence studies as an alternative approach to the study of economics. *Journal of Intelligence Studies in Business, 11*(2), 4–5.

Söilen, K. S. (2024). A review of the knowledge worker as prompt engineer: How good is AI at societal analysis and future predictions? *Foresight and STI Governance, 18*(2), 6–20. https://doi.org/10.17323/2500-2597.2024.2.6.20

Söilen, K. S., & Alipour, P. B. (2011). Semantics, classifications and evidence in a model for global catastrophic risks. *Knowledge Organization, 38*(5), 438–454.

Söilen, K. S., & Hasslinger, A. (2012). The business intelligence challenge: A study of key success factors in Swedish organizations. *Journal of Intelligence Studies in Business, 2*(2), 39–50.

Söilen, K. S., Kovacevic, M. A., & Jallouli, R. (2012). Key success factors for Ericsson mobile platforms using the value grid model. *Journal of Business Research, 65*(9), 1335–1345.

Steele, R. D. (2000). *On intelligence*. AFCEA International Press.

Sun Tzu. (6th Century B.C./1963). *The art of war*. Oxford University Press.

Svensson Kling, K. (1999). *Credit intelligence in banks: Managing credit relationships with small firms* (Doctoral dissertation). Lund Business Press.

Svensson Kling, K., Driver, M. J., Hedin, H., & Larsson, R. (1996). *Intelligence professionals and business managers: Synergetic or toxic relationships?* Paper, Department of Business Administration, Lund University.

Thunberger, J. (1998). Strategisk underrättelsetjänst – Några synpunkter. *Kungliga Krigsvetenskapsakademiens Handlingar och Tidskrift, 202*(3), 55–78.

Toffler, A. (1970). *Future shock*. The Bodley Head.

Tontini, G., Söilen, K. S., & Silveira, A. (2013). How do interactions of Kano model attributes affect customer satisfaction? An analysis based on psychological foundations. *Total Quality Management & Business Excellence, 24*(11–12), 1253–1271.

Tontini, G., Söilen, K. S., & Zanchett, R. (2017). Nonlinear antecedents of customer satisfaction and loyalty in third-party logistics services (3PL). *Asia Pacific Journal of Marketing and Logistics, 29*(5), 1116–1135.

Trieu, V. H. (2017). Getting value from Business Intelligence systems: A review and research agenda. *Decision Support Systems, 93*, 111–124.

Tyson, K. W. M. (2002). *The complete guide to competitive intelligence*. Kirk W. M. Tyson.

Ulfkotte, U. (1999). *Marktplatz der Diebe, Wie die Wirtschaftsspionage deutsche Unternehmen ausplündert und ruiniert*. Bertelsmann.

Underwood, J. (2002). *Competitor intelligence*. Capstone Ltd.

Utredningen om en ny myndighet för analyser, omvärldsbevakning och utvärdering. (2000). *Förslag till ny myndighet för omvärldsanalys, utvärdering och statistik: betänkande*. Fritzes offentliga publikationer.

van Dalen, D. (1980/1997). *Logic and structure*. Springer.

Vernon, R. (1966). International investment and international trade in the product cycle. *The Quarterly Journal of Economics, 80*(2), 190–207. https://doi.org/10.2307/1880689

von Clausewitz, K. (1932–34). *Vom Kriege, Hinterlassene Werk des Generals Karl von Clausewitz*. Ferdinand Dümmler.

Vriens, D., & Søilen, K. S. (2014). Disruptive intelligence – How to gather Information to deal with disruptive innovations. *Journal of Intelligence Studies in Business, 4*(3), 63–78.

Ward, J., & Peppard, J. (1996/2009). *Strategic planning for information systems*. Wiley.

Warren, N. P., Neto, M. T., Misner, S., Sanders, I., & Helmers, S. A. (2013). *Business intelligence in Microsoft SharePoint 2013*. Pearson Education.

Wilensky, H. L. (1967). *Organizational intelligence*. Quid Pro Quo.

Williams, S. (1919). *Principles of logic*. T.C. & E. C. Jack Ltd.

Winkler, I. (1997). *Corporate espionage*. Prima Publishing.

Zanden, J. L. (2003). Economic and business intelligence: The link to organizational growth. *International Business Review, 12*(3), 87–98.

Zekos, G. I. (2023). *Artificial intelligence and competition. Contributions to economics*. Springer.

Zuboff, S. (2019). *The age of surveillance capitalism: The fight for a human future at the new frontier of power: Barack Obama's books of 2019*. Profile Books.

Zwingmann, T. (2022). *AI-powered business intelligence*. O'Reilly Media, Inc.

Index

K. Solberg Söilen, *Intelligence Studies in Business*, Management for Professionals,
https://doi.org/10.1007/978-3-031-76491-2

www.ingramcontent.com/pod-product-compliance
Lightning Source LLC
Chambersburg PA
CBHW070108240225
22440CB00003B/95
* 9 7 8 3 0 3 1 7 6 4 9 0 5 *